Millennium and Charisma among Pathans

A critical essay in social anthropology

Akbar S. Ahmed

Routledge & Kegan Paul
London, Henley and Boston

to my mother and father

First published in 1976
by Routledge & Kegan Paul Ltd
39 Store Street,
London WC1E 7DD,
Broadway House,
Newtown Road,
Henley-on-Thames,
Oxon RG9 1EN and
9 Park Street,
Boston, Mass. 02108, USA
Manuscript typed by Reba Lawless
Printed in Great Britain
by Redwood Burn Limited,
Trowbridge and Esher

ISBN 0 7100 8348 3

International Library of Anthropology

Editor: Adam Kuper, University College London

Arbor Scientiae
Arbor Vitae

A catalogue of other Social Science books published by Routledge & Kegan Paul will be found at the end of this volume.

Millennium and Charisma among Pathans

Contents

Millennium and Charisma
among Pathans

Foreword

Certain styles of political legitimation emerged promi-
nently at the very inception of the Muslim community. The
consensus of 'the' Community, the authority of 'the' Book,
kinship with 'the' Prophet: these were the ideas which
were invoked when leadership, authority or succession were
in dispute. The crystallization of the great Muslim sects
and their distinctive characteristics hinges to a large
extent in terms of the relative stress given to each of
these ideas. But the conflicts did not cease after the
early, classical period of Islam; and as men seldom fight
or engage in political struggle without the invocation of
some ideas, these principles continued to live a rich and
complex life in the long and often turbulent history of
Muslim societies.

The vigour of these principles has deep roots in the
life of Muslim communities. Ideas do grip men, but in
order to do so, they generally need a firm anchorage in
the forms of human association, in the needs and sugges-
tiveness of men's groupings. The ideas which have per-
vaded Muslim history do indeed have such concrete social
underpinning. Nomadic, mountain and even sedentary peasant communities have all tended to display, in the Muslim
world, a ferocious independence. They defended the local
group against all others and also against the central
state. Such local communities needed an organization,
both for defence and for internal self-administration.
This organization was generally expressed in terms of kinship. No wonder that the idiom of kinship was also extended to the crucial sphere of religion, that sacred
leadership should also be thought of as passing in the
genealogical line. The autonomous local groups also
generally needed holy personages, both for arbitration
amongst themselves, and for mediation with the outside
world, the central state, and to provide that moral and

economic continuum which 'was' the Muslim world even when
political power within it was fragmented.

At the same time, the idea of the authority of the
Book, and of the importance of communal consensus in interpreting it, was powerfully represented by the corps of
scholars/theologians/jurists, the ulama. The scholars and
the holy men were sometimes opposed and sometimes acted in
unison. Learning, piety, moral goodness, proximity to God
manifested by therapeutic or magical powers, sacred ancestry, capacity to inspire, lead or arbitrate - this was a
kind of spectrum of traits which entitled men to positions
of authority or respect in the community, and these
traits or clusters of them could appear both in combination and in competition. Mr Ahmed tells us

The Akhund gained such an ascendancy over the minds of
his co-religionists that they believed all kinds of
stories about him; that he was supplied by supernatural means with the necessities of life, and that
every morning a sum of money, sufficient for his own
needs and for the entertainment of the pilgrims who
flocked to consult him, was found under his praying
carpet.

Religion is often held to be a conservative force, a
confirmation and ratification of the status quo. A striking feature of Islam is that it can very often also be a
charter of criticism, renovation, purification, which far
from accepting the existing political authorities, subjects them to severe moral scrutiny. The authority of
ancestry and that of learned consensus no doubt fortify
the holy lineage and of the corps of scholars; but the
authority of the Book is transcendent, a permanent remin-
der that the norms of the social order are based outside
and above it, that no society is its own vindication.

The manner in which later political struggles become
conceptualized in terms borrowed from the very beginnings
of Islam is strikingly illustrated in this remarkable
study, when Mr Ahmed quotes from the Wali of Swat and his
invocation of the Age of Ignorance in Arabia:

It would not be wrong to compare the Swat of a few
years before and after 1915, to Arabia prior to the
advent of Islam - both were as ignorant and licentious.
The powerful and the rich were cruel and immoral; the
poor and the down-trodden were weak and uninformed.
The moral laxity of the great, the religious ignorance of
the poor - these themes characteristically reappear as
justifications of new possessors of authority, who will
restrain the indulgent and instruct the ignorant.

State-formation in Swat provides an interesting illustration of the major topics of Muslim political and

religious sociology. The balancing mechanisms of tribal
society make it more easy to choose an outsider as ruler;
and authority, when established, combines political and
religious aspects: '... when called upon by the united
confederation of tribes to become King of Swat, the Akhund
selected Sayyed Akbar Shah as his nominee rather than a
Yusufzai Khan.' In other words, an outsider was preferred
to one of the local nobility.

As Mr Ahmed underscores, both the colonial period and
post-colonial Independence profoundly modified the context
in which the political and religious drama was enacted:
'An expanding non-Muslim (Sikh and later British) presence
is partly the cause of the Akhund's emergence and his religious revivalist preachings an effect of it.'

Unfortunately, the Saint and his nominee did not remain
in harmony. In the period of anarchic conflicts which
followed, 'the legend of the Akhund provided a general
source of religious inspiration which his agnatic descendants sought to mobilize in their claims to Swat political
authority.' A man who was in the end to succeed in imposing his religious authority on the Swatis, comments on
them as follows: 'Swat was a tribal territory in which
power alone could command respect; self-interestedness
and oppression were the law of the land; it had never
been under any firm authority before.' There is perhaps
no contradiction between these two things: reverence and
violence do often come intertwined.

Swat has of course already acquired great fame in
social anthropological literature through the celebrated
work of Professor Fredrik Barth. Mr Ahmed feels that
Barth's study does not do full justice to the processes
through which partially centralized authority, with religious roots, emerged in Swat at all. Certainly, Barth's
now classic account concentrates on the 'acephalous', decentralized political relations, in which leaders drawn
from the dominant stratum compete with each other. The
emergence of the State is only treated at the end of his
study, rather briefly. Even the 'Saints' were seen more
as complementary poles of the secular chiefs, rather than
as exemplars or local expressions of a much wider Muslim
phenomenon.

Mr Ahmed endeavours to complement and complete this
work. No Hamlet without the Prince of Denmark, and no
Swat political structure without the 'State' of Swat, and
no State of Swat without its distinctively Muslim foundations. But he does much more than merely extend the dimensions of our understanding of Swat. The broadening of
the framework is accompanied by a wealth of data, and we
can follow the transformations of Swat from nearly

acephalous society via holy leadership to a locally centralized state, and finally to its full incorporation in
the larger Pakistani State. This study must be welcomed
by all of us interested in these topics. It was carried
out when Mr Ahmed was attached to the Anthropology and
Sociology Department of the School of Oriental and
African Studies in London, with whose members he had detailed discussions whilst writing, and where he prepared
the theoretical framework for the field research in the
North-West Frontier Province in which he is now engaged.
It does indeed constitute a most important contribution to
our understanding of Muslim societies in transition, and
of Pakistan in particular, and will be of very great interest to anthropologists, Islamicists and scholars
everywhere.

Ernest Gellner
Professor of Sociology, London School of Economics
    and Political Science
Fellow of the British Academy

Acknowledgments

This study is an unintended result, though almost an inevitable one, of an academic year (1974-5) in the Department of Anthropology and Sociology, School of Oriental and
African Studies, University of London, preparing the
theoretical framework for a research project called
'social organization of economic life among the Mohmand
with special reference to credit', in the Tribal Areas of
the North-West Frontier Province of Pakistan. Though the
research project itself will be an exercise in practical
or applied anthropology based on field research this present work has a theoretical slant and is an argument in a
dialogue in academic anthropology.

I would like to thank the various agencies and individuals who made this project possible; of the former, the
Central Government of Pakistan and the North-West Frontier
Province Government arranged the funds and permitted me to
proceed on the course; the Ford Foundation provided a
Fellowship for the research project which enabled this
book to be written; the International Students House,
London, provided me with facilities and an atmosphere con-
ducive to work in spite of its central location. These
agencies are not faceless; there were individuals in each
who took considerable personal interest in the research
project.

The list of individuals to be thanked is headed by the
late Hayat Mohammed Khan Sherpao, Senior Minister, Home
and Planning and Development Departments, Government of
NWFP, whose life was so tragically cut short; he was
typically enthusiastic and sympathetic to the research
project. It is a personal tragedy that he is not alive to
see what he so fully helped into existence. I wish to
thank the numerous Swatis who answered my questions
patiently, and particularly Miangul Jahan Zeb, the last
Wali of Swat.

xiii

I acknowledge my gratitude to Dr Hamza Alavi, Dr Talal
Asad, Dr Michael Gilsenan, and to Professors Aziz Ahmad,
Abner Cohen, Christoph von Fürer-Haimendorf, John
Middleton and Sir Olaf Caroe for critical comments at
various stages of the draft. Dr David Parkin and Dr
Richard Tapper provided constant intellectual stimulation
both in and out of class and never hesitated to give of
their time and attention. The book took shape in Dr
Parkin's office and without his unfailing confidence and
support may never have grown. Professor Adrian C. Mayer,
my Supervisor, has repeatedly proved a friend and mentor;
his example helps to remind students that teaching will
always remain a special art in understanding complex problems involving different generations, disciplines and
socio-cultural backgrounds and its finest achievement will
remain the task of building bridges. This book has had
the fortune of having that most generous of academic
patrons, Professor Ernest Gellner. I would like to thank
Professor Gellner especially for the Foreword which is of
academic and personal significance to me but is not necessarily to be read as a commitment to the arguments contained in the following pages.
    I am grateful to Dr Adam Kuper and Mr Peter Hopkins of
Routledge & Kegan Paul for consistently exhibiting a combination of patience and efficiency. I am also grateful
to Mr Khalid S. Ahmed for his help in scrutinizing various
drafts. Finally, my wife is to be thanked for her uncom-
plaining secretarial assistance, mental stimulation and
unbounded enthusiasm; without her presence the logistics
of writing up would have become unmanageable. I would
like to dedicate this book to my parents: my mother, who
embodies for me the finest virtues of her Pathan ancestors
and their code of life; and my father, who through his
personal example has shown me the way of the Sufis.
    It may be emphasized that the faults, whether in the
logic of the debate or the construction of the arguments,
contained below are entirely mine and do not reflect on my
friends and teachers, particularly at the School of
Oriental and African Studies.

The author and publishers are grateful to the Athlone
Press for permission to quote from 'Political Leadership
among Swat Pathans' by Fredrik Barth (1959).

Swat chronology

327 BC Alexander invades Swat on his way to the Punjab.

c.100 AD Swat, where Buddhism flourishes, is part of the kingdom of Gandhara ruled by Kanishka from Peshawar.

403 Fa Hien, the Chinese traveller, passes through Swat.

630 Hieun Tsang, another famous Chinese, observes Buddhist monasteries unattended and the religion in a state of decay in Swat.

1001 The victory of Mahmud, King of Ghazni, over King Jaipal, near Peshawar, marks the beginning of the Muslim invasions of India. Swat is conquered by Mahmud and Pathan tribes, settling in Swat, accelerate the proselytization of the autochthones to Islam.

c.1485 Sheikh Ahmed and Sheikh Malli are among those who escape a massacre of Yusufzai leaders organized by Ulugh Beg, the Chaghatai Turk ruler of Kabul (and uncle of Babar, later to become the first Mughal Emperor of India), and lead sections of their tribe to the Peshawar valley. In a series of conquests the Yusufzai acquire the areas of Peshawar, Mardan and Swat.

c.1515 Sultan Awais, ruler of Swat, is finally deposed and this is followed by mass Swati migrations to Mansehra (across the Indus).

c.1530 Sheikh Malli devises the system of 'wesh', periodic redistribution of land,

	to determine shares in land corresponding to filiation in the Yusufzai segmentary lineage groups.
1586	An abortive attempt by the army of Akbar, the Great Mughal, to invade Swat.
1835	Abdul Gaffur, known as the Akhund and born in Swat some forty years before, returns after years of wandering and Sufic contemplation.
1845	The Akhund selects Saidu as his centre, henceforth the capital and focal point of Swat politics.
1849	British conquer Punjab (and the trans-Indus Districts) from the Sikhs and occupy Peshawar.
1850	The Akhund selects Sayyed Akbar Shah of Sitana as King of Swat. Standing army raised. The foundation, however ill-defined, weak and temporary, is laid for statehood.
1857	King of Swat dies. No successor appointed or elected either from the agnatic descendants of Sayyed Akbar or the Akhund.
1863	An abortive British attempt to lift the 'purdah' or veil of Swat at the Ambela campaign. The Akhund's presence symbolizes tribal resistance and enhances his reputation.
1877	The Akhund dies. The agnatic descendants of the Akhund and the Sayyed begin the long struggle for leadership in Swat, complicated by involvement with the political struggles in Dir and Bajaur.
1881	Miangul A. Wadud, later to be the Wali of Swat, born to Miangul A. Khaliq, the younger son of the Akhund.
1887	Miangul A. Hannan, elder son of the Akhund, dies at the age of thirty-five after failing to establish a state.
1892	Miangul A. Khaliq, the remaining son of the Akhund, also dies at the age of thirty-five, after leading a life of ascetic piety.
1895	Creation of a Political Agency at Malakand to watch British interests in Dir, Chitral and Swat.
1897-8	Popular uprisings in the Tribal Areas.

	Temporary ascendancy of religious leaders like the Ada Mullah among the Mohmand tribe and the Mastan Mullah in Swat and Malakand.
1901	Creation of the North-West Frontier Province (from former Settled Districts and Tribal Areas attached to the Punjab Government).
1903 and 1907	Miangul A. Razzaq and Miangul A. Wahid, sons of the elder son of the Akhund, killed by their agnatic cousin, Miangul Wadud, the son of Miangul Khaliq, who emerges as the eldest male heir to the spiritual and material inheritance of the Akhund. This ends an intense dynastic struggle for political authority.
1908	Miangul Wadud challenges and checks another attempt by Mastan Mullah to foment trouble in Swat.
1915-17	Sayyed Jabbar Shah elected King of Swat by Yusufzai Khans. Miangul Wadud exiled from Swat.
1917	Miangul Wadud returns to be elected 'Badshah' (King) of Swat by the confederation of Yusufzai tribes. The Sayyed returns to Sitana permanently.
1917-26	Internally: intense State building activity and consolidation of authority: roads, telephone lines, forts etc. Externally: border wars that expand and define the new boundaries of Swat.
1926	Formal British recognition of the State and installation of Miangul Wadud as the Wali of Swat.
1947	Accession to the Government of Pakistan.
1949	Miangul Wadud abdicates in favour of the 'Waliahad' (heir apparent), Miangul Jahan Zeb.
1969	The State of Swat is finally and fully absorbed into the administrative structure of Pakistan as Swat District and a Deputy Commissioner posted at Saidu.
1971	Miangul Wadud dies.

1 Introduction

CURRENT QUESTIONS IN THEORY AND METHOD

The relationship of the individual to his society has been as central to thought in the history of mankind as it has been polychromic in its complexity. It has been considered extensively by a number of disciplines - philosophy, history, theology etc. - which include the social sciences. One of the contributions that anthropology can make is the broadness of its comparative material which is combined with fine-grained ethnographic data about diverse and often remote societies. Hence anthropology, far from being peripheral or an irrelevance, can make substantial and heuristic contributions to knowledge about man and his society. Man in anthropology need not be exotic or isolated and the subject need not only concern itself with algebraic genealogical formulae about them. On the contrary, anthropology can define and underline the socio-economic problems that relate the individual to his social situation within the context of development problems and therefore help to arrive at some of the pressing answers to the questions of today as a growing body of literature testifies (Dalton, 1967, 1971; Epstein, 1967, 1973; Firth, 1967; Hunter and Bottrall, 1974; LeClair and Schneider, 1968; Mair, 1972; Myrdal, 1967, 1970; Srinivas, 1974).

Two major interconnected problems for anthropologists, with theoretical and methodological ramifications, emerged after the Second World War and partly as a result of its political consequences: internally, a crisis both of identity and confidence (but more of the former) reflected in such alarmist themes (1) as 'The end of anthropology?' (Worsley, 1966) and, externally, methodological and field-work problems in the face of rapidly disappearing 'primitive' communities.

This related and inherent problem for both theory and method arises from the nature of the location of traditional anthropological laboratories:

Equally symptomatic, though for different reasons, are the increasing difficulties which anthropologists encounter now in getting access to their 'traditional subject-matter'. The new states of the Third World have accumulated a dislike of anthropologists whom they often associate with reaction and imperialism. Although many of these states can and do benefit a great deal from the work of anthropologists, they are more interested in the study of the problems of the day: economic development, political modernization, urbanization, migration and employment. It has recently become difficult - in some cases indeed impossible - for anthropologists to get entrance permits to many of the developing countries (Cohen, 1974a, p.11).

Anthropologists are often and unnecessarily viewed unkindly: 'Anthropologists are regarded as reactionaries by the majority of the African intellectuals' (Ahmed, 1973, p.260).

A two-way effect in anthropology is consequently visible: the growth of native 'national' (and by definition 'committed') anthropologists and the perceptible shift in Western anthropology from 'primitive' towards 'complex societies' (2) (Cohen, 1974b). Professor Leach in a Presidential address to the Royal Anthropological Institute expressed the aims of modern anthropology: 'The ultimate social utility of anthropology, in all its forms is that by learning about "other cultures" we gain better insight into our own' (Leach, 1974, p.9).

In spite of this type of controversy around anthropology, and even inside it, important new theoretical ground has been constantly broken, as with the work of Professors Leach and Barth. The post-war iconoclasts (3) challenged the static structuralist and functionalist equilibrium theories of social systems which held the field in pre-war anthropology and represented the collective tradition of the old giants such as Malinowski and Radcliffe-Brown. The structuralist-functionalist looked at the social totality and explained its parts as organic components functioning to integrate the other parts (kinship, economics etc.) and thereby keeping the whole within a state of equilibrium. This framework was seriously challenged: 'My own feeling at the time was that British Social Anthropology had rested too long on a crudely oversimplified set of equilibrium assumptions derived from the use of organic analogies for the structure of social systems' (Leach, 1954, p.ix). Whereas the previous

generation had explained 'primitive' societies in intrinsic opposition to 'developed' (or 'complex') ones anthropologists like Leach and Barth used the ethnography of
primitive societies to illustrate the universality of
their analytical framework.

For the theoretical and methodological questions raised
in this essay two relevant frames of analytical reference
will be consulted and the positions taken within them
examined: (4) 'methodological individualism' (deriving
its sociological inspiration in the main from Max Weber)
and 'methodological holism' (for which Karl Marx may be
claimed as a foster-father and Durkheim a father). The
former views man as externalized to, and confronting,
society. Man is seen as determined to 'better his
chances' or 'maximize' them by consciously or unconsciously, 'manipulating' or 're-ordering' society and its symbols such as ethnicity and language. He is the archetype
'economic man', forever weighing costs and benefits in an
effort to achieve the 'optimum point'. He is bent on
maximizing, be it pleasure (5) or political power: 'it is
a model which sees the individuals of a society busily engaged in maximizing their own satisfactions - desire for
power, sex, food, independence' (Burling, 1962, pp.817-
18). Man is therefore a free agent faced with the problem
of 'choices', how he 'values' them, and the alternative
'strategies' open to him to mobilize them. Maximization
finds its ultimate expression in the pursuit and attain-
ment of political power: 'I consider it necessary and
justifiable to assume that a conscious or unconscious wish
to gain power is a very general motive in human affairs'
(Leach, 1954, p.10). Social action and analysis is consequently actor-centred:

> This school of thought tends to sweep the theoretical
> pendulum towards the orientation emanating from the
> Weberian 'action theory' (see P.S. Cohen, 1968). This
> theoretical approach (see, for example, Barth, 1966,
> 1967; Boissevain, 1968; Mayer, 1966; Nicholas, 1965)
> distrusts analysis in terms of groups and of group sym-
> bols, and concentrates on the activities of 'political
> man' who is ever impelled to the pursuit of power....
> Anthropologists of this school of thought present a
> picture of political life in terms of a continuing
> 'game', in which every man is seeking to maximize his
> power by perpetually scheming, struggling, and making
> decisions. Every action he contemplates is the outcome
> of a transaction in which the returns are expected to
> be at least equal to, if not in excess of, the outlay
> (Cohen, 1974a, p.40).

The 'holists', on the other hand, would maintain that

man is born into a matrix of interacting and largely fixed
social patterns (what Marxists would call the 'super-
structure'). Accordingly his capacity to manipulate the
symbols of society around him is limited to the extent determined by the needs of society for change:

> The other extreme trend in social anthropology at pre-
> sent concentrates on the study of symbols, or of col-
> lective representations, often quite out of the context
> of power relationships. Its orientation is neatly de-
> scribed by Douglas (1968, p.361): 'Anthropology has
> moved from the simple analysis of social structure cur-
> rent in the 1940's to the structural analysis of
> thought systems.'
>
> Anthropologists of this school are influenced in
> varying degrees by the 'structuralism' of Lévi-Strauss
> who takes in his stride, among many other variables,
> both symbolism and power relationships in his analysis
> (Cohen, 1974a, p.43).

The emphasis shifts from the individual as the focus of
analysis to groups and social structures.

The final expression of the 'individualist's' man is
found in Weber's 'charismatic leader' who is both a concept and a category of authority. The man of charisma
combines inherent qualities of leadership with an external
ambience of authority which is almost 'divine'. The
holists dismiss the man of charisma as sociological fiction and the concept of charisma as sociologically
sterile: 'It is the structural situation of the group
that determines what type of symbols are more effective
than others and hence what type of leader is needed.
Charisma is largely a group function, not an individual
trait' (ibid., p.80).

Somewhere between the holists and the individualists,
though leaning more towards the latter, are social scientists who examine individuals at the centre of 'the social
network' (Barnes, 1954; Bott, 1957). Mayer is concerned
with clarifying the different kinds of networks and
action-sets and measuring their forms and ramifications:
'groups', 'associations', 'quasi-groups' or 'non-groups'
(Barnes, 1969; Boissevain, 1968; Mayer, 1966) and lately
'coalitions' (Boissevain, 1971, 1974). The 'quasi-group'
which may subsequently become a formal group is 'ego-
centred' and manipulated by individuals for their own interest (Mayer, 1966). Patron-client relationships illustrate the formation and operation of such relationships
(Boissevain, 1966).

Recent developments in the holist-individualist debate
within the social sciences argue against the need to compartmentalize:

A conceptual problem underlies both approaches. Both
in structural-functionalist holism as well as in methodological individualism, 'individual' and 'society'
are, each, conceptualised as independent entities, set
apart from, though influencing, each other. The methodological individualist proceeds with analysis of a
pragmatic manipulating, individual who pursues goals
vis-à-vis society. The individual's actions are orien-
ted towards society. The implications of such a proce-
dure is an abstract conception of 'individual' man; or
one which is, at best, limited to that of a biological
and psychic entity endowed with certain intrinsic
needs, capabilities and drives - although it is ques-
tionable whether even such a limited definition of individual man can be sustained without reference to his
social situation. The individual must be defined as a
social being (Alavi, 1973, p.50).
The desirability of dialectical interaction between the
two frames of reference is advocated:
These aspects of man in society are lost from view in
both the approaches which we have considered; each of
them objectifies society and externalises it from the
individual. Our problem is, therefore, to search for a
framework of analysis which might transcend that dicho-
tomy and the associated mechanistic conceptions of relationship between man and society, so that we might
conceptualise man in society as a dialectical unity,
neither being prior to the other (ibid., pp.50-1).
A growing body of anthropological literature uses a
Marxist framework to attack the colonial spirit of anthropology and therefore its methodology and traditional
theories. However, the voices speak mainly on behalf of
the Third World and not from it (Asad, 1973; Oxaal,
Barnett and Booth, 1975). A Marxist framework of analysis
will be sociologically sterile if applied universally to
any and all social situations just as the dogmatic application of the holistic and individualistic frameworks.
For instance, whereas the Swat Pathans may be successfully
analysed in a Marxist framework (Asad, 1972), a satisfactory application of this framework to segmentary, acephalous and stateless tribal societies is still to be made.
The understanding of 'alienation' and 'exploitation' in
'kin' and 'junior-senior' terms (Godelier, 1968;
Meillasoux, 1964, 1972; Rey, 1975; Terray, 1972, 1975)
is not entirely satisfactory as Marxist analysis of segmentary tribal societies is at an early stage of development and still neglected. Such tribal societies are in-
correctly seen in the process of 'sedentarization' and
'detribalization' and hence on the evolutionary path to

becoming agricultural-peasant societies. Although 'marginal' and 'peripheral', segmentary societies such as the Nuer, the Berbers, the Kurds and the Pathans require to be analysed in terms of distinct social categories.

   This brief survey does not pretend to be either complete or sophisticated: it merely constructs a general framework within which to work out the arguments contained in the following pages.

THE PATHAN FRAMEWORK

When typologizing or relating Pathan (6) tribes with African (Fortes and Evans-Pritchards, 1940; Middleton and Tait, 1958) or Indian (Bailey, 1960, 1961; Haimendorf, 1939, 1962; Srinivas, 1952) tribal categories certain features are noted. These features are not exclusive to Pathan tribes and may well be common to other tribes, particularly like the Kurd (Barth, 1953; Leach, 1940) or the Berber (Gellner, 1969a):

I Pathan tribal society is part of the 'larger' or 'greater' tradition of the Islamic world. To the Pathan there is no conflict between his tribal code, 'Pukhtunwali', (7) and religious principles and he boasts no pre-Islamic period. Islamic principles, cultural mores and jural tradition explain part of Pathan normative behaviour.

II The vast tribal population involved: Pathan society, with over fifteen million people in Pakistan alone, is probably one of the largest tribal groupings in the world.

III Pathan tribal society is not 'pre-literate' or oral society (Bailey, 1960; Gluckman, 1971; Sahlins, 1968). The most famous Pashto poets were contemporaries of John Milton. Nor is Pathan society in a state of perpetual anarchy and war. (8)

IV Pathan dynasties have ruled non-Pathan kingdoms far from their original ethnic homelands (in Bengal, from Delhi and nearer home, at Kabul). They have thus extended their political boundaries and carried forward their ethnic identity. The historical role of warrior-king is part of Pathan consciousness. (9)

V While pushing out their political boundaries the Pathan areas, and particularly the Tribal Areas, were jealously isolated from any form of permanent invasion or non-Pathan administration. Imperial generals, leading great armies, have been humbled and destroyed in these mountains (10) (the Mughal, the Durrani and the British tried to 'incorporate' the Tribal Areas).

VI Mountain ecology thus partly shaped Pathan social

identity, political strategy and economic structure: it
also defined 'Pukhtunwali' which approximates to its
'ideal-type' in a segmentary tribal system organized
within an acephalous political framework: 'The system has
been most successful, and self-maintaining, under anarchic
conditions in low production areas' (Barth, 1969, p.134).

Tribal segmentation provides territorial and ethnic
identity and also guarantees a form of pastoral democracy.
'The notion of "segmentation" seems more useful than that
of "democracy" for laying bare the actual mechanics of the
society' (Gellner, 1969a, p.28). However, 'this is a
structural, rather than an ideological democracy. It is
not based on a theory, on a set of principles or norms'
(ibid.). On either side and outside the Tribal Areas the
Afghan and British Governments, over the last century,
attempted a process of assimilating Pathan society within
regular administrative, revenue and criminal laws which
the British called the 'Settled Areas'. (11)

A few words about Pathan genealogies may be useful at
this stage. Pathans claim descent from their putative ancestor, Qais bin Rashid, who went to Arabia from Kohistan,
Ghor, in Afghanistan and was converted to Islam by the
Prophet himself in the seventh century. He is said to
have married the daughter of the renowned Islamic general,
Khalid bin Walid, from whom he had three sons, Sarbarn,
the eldest, Bitan and Ghurghust. All Pathan tribes trace
their origin to the offspring of Qais.

The focus of Professor Barth's study is the Yusufzai
tribe which claims descent from the apical ancestor Yusuf.
The Yusufzai are eastern Sarbarni Pathans and like their
distant cousins the Khalils and Mohmands descended from
Kand. Other Sarbarnis are Hashtnagar Muhamadzais, descen-
ded from Samand, and the Shinwaris descended from Kasi.
Western Sarbarn tribes include the Tarin, the Abdalis
(Durrani) and their cousins, the Popalzai, Achakzai and
Barakzai. The other Pathan divisions are called the
Bitanis, from Bitan, second son of Qais, and include
Ghilzais, Niazis, Lodhis and Suris (the last two ruled
Delhi) and the Ghurghust, including the Kakars, Gaduns and
Safis. The hill tribes, Afridi, Khattak, Orakzai, Mahsud
and Wazir, descend from Karlanri, who is said to have been
adopted into the family of the third son, Ghurghust
(Caroe, 1965; Spain, 1963).

POLITICAL LEADERSHIP AMONG SWAT PATHANS

Professor Fredrik Barth's analysis of Swat society and the
brilliant models he created for it (and from it) are by

now a deservedly classic exposition of the individualist
frame of reference (Barth, 1959a, 1959b, 1966). Apart
from the rich analysis of Swat the study is a major
theoretical contribution to the development of anthropological thought away from structuralist-functionalism and
illustrative of generative 'models of process' (Barth,
1966). Professor Barth begins his thesis by categorically
questioning the traditional functionalist tribal accounts:
   In many anthropological accounts of tribal peoples, one
   has the impression that political allegiance is not a
   matter of individual choice. Each individual is born
   into a particular structural position, and will accordingly give his political allegiance to a particular
   group or office-holder. In Swat, persons find their
   place in the political order through a series of
   choices, many of which are temporary or revocable
   (Barth, 1959a, pp.1-2).
Relationships are dyadic, contractual and voluntary
(ibid., p.3). The two main groups in Swat, 'Pakhtun landowners and persons of holy descent are active as political
pretenders; thus two different types of primary political
group emerge, namely the Pakhtun chief with his following,
and the Saint with his following' (ibid., p.4). Together
these 'primary groups combine to form the wider political
system, which has the form of two large, dispersed, internally co-ordinated alliances or blocs' (ibid.).
   He arrives at this conclusion:
   Where, on the other hand, group commitments may be
   assumed and shed at will, self-interest may dictate
   action which does not bring advantage to the group;
   and individuals are able to plan and make choices in
   terms of private advantage and a personal political
   career. In this respect the political life of Swat resembles that of Western societies (ibid., p.2).
   Professor Barth has argued that his Swat ethnography
supports the main thesis contained in 'Models of social organization' (1966). Social, as indeed all other action, is
channelled into political activity which is seen as 'the
art of manipulating these various dyadic relations so as
to create effective and viable bodies of supporters - in
other words, so as to create corporate political followings' (Barth, 1959a, p.4). This has laid 'Models of social
organization', and by implication, the Swat study, open to
a valid criticism (from a 'friendly' critic): 'The obtru-
sive place given to "self-interest", "profit", and associated symbols imparts to many readers an ambience of
aggressive and ethnocentric market philosophy; on this
account alone, some would wish to brush aside Models as
anthropologically limited and limiting' (Paine, 1974, p.
29).

The Swat analysis leaves itself exposed to three main
and interconnected criticisms:
I It suffers from a degree of ethnocentricity: the Swat
Pathan living within a framework of tribal society based
on primitive modes of production and a highly developed
and defined code of social behaviour in a remote valley of
the North-West Frontier Province of Pakistan, is analysed
in the same terms as the Norwegian 'entrepreneur' (Barth,
1963). This 'entrepreneur', who is not a person, status
or role but an aspect of a role, 'embodies initiative' and
'expansive economic policy'. As his social action is symbolized by 'transactional' maximizing strategy based on
market behaviour his social identity lies in 'laissez-
faire' market philosophy. Life becomes a continuing process or game of strategy in which profits must always
exceed costs:

Put this way, one may see that transactions have a
structure which permits analysis by means of a strategic model, as a game of strategy. They consist of a
sequence of reciprocal prestations, which represent
successive moves in the game. There must be a ledger
kept of value gained and lost; and each successive
action or move affects that ledger, changes the strategic situation, and thus canalizes subsequent choices.
Many possible courses of action are ruled out because
they are patently unsatisfactory, i.e. an actor must
expect that value lost be greater than value gained....
The structure depicted in this model is a successional
one over time - in other words, it is a model of process (Barth, 1966, p.4).

This essay maintains that Kachin religious behaviour or
Pathan social organization cannot be entirely and simply
understood in terms of political 'manipulations', 'strategies' and 'profits' alone. The origin and understanding
of these concepts is embedded in the development of
Western political thought (Hobbes, Locke, Rousseau) and
Western market and trading history. Mauss's 'prestations'
and 'reciprocity' (1954) or Barth's 'transactional' analysis are easily recognizable from the template of the
'social contract'. The idea of the social contract,
covenant or agreement and its concomitant concepts are
central to the understanding of Western, market, industrial and democratic societies and are at the root of
modern social theory. Their applicability to a pre-
industrial, tribal and Asian society can at best be par-
tial and at worst misleading. The holistic socio-cultural
constraints of 'Pukhtunwali' and socio-religious Islamic
values are largely absent or explained in entrepreneurial
terms of the need to 'manipulate' and 'maximize'. The

Swat Pathan mirrors a recognizable image of West European
'market-man':   chapter 9 (Alliances and political blocs)
of 'Political Leadership among Swat Pathans' concludes on
p.126 with a remarkably dense employment of transactionalist terms with which the Swat Pathan operates: he 'wreaks
vengeance', 'kills', 'seizes', 'ousts' and 'attacks' with
almost insatiable compulsion.   He does these things to
gain political power which finds expression through ownership of land: 'he must therefore seize land' (Barth,
1959a, p.126).

Malinowski had warned that 'nothing is so misleading in
ethnographic accounts as the description of facts of
native civilization in terms of our own' (Malinowski,
1922, p.176).   Academic and intellectual ethnocentricity
can be more complex and involuted than the cultural ethnocentricity of the straightforward chauvinist, who contents
himself by categorizing extra-ethnic leaders (12) as
either comical, lunatic, or megalomaniac and their people
as wogs, frogs etc.   It is important to underline that
Professor Barth's own cultural and intellectual background
are impeccable from this point of view: Norway was
neither part of the colonial encounter nor participated
directly in religious wars with Islamic people.   However,
Professor Barth's academic neutrality is somewhat compromised on the question of Pathan character and social behaviour by references which are mainly Victorian and often
written with little understanding or sympathy.   It would
be too much, and perhaps unfair, to expect neutrality from
soldiers' accounts based on Frontier campaigns bent on re-
forming and civilizing missions.   For example, an argument
opens: 'Many observers have noticed how precious is political status among Pathans and Afghans' (Barth, 1959a, p.
12) and is supported by a quotation from Ferrier written a
century ago (1858, p.304).   Other authors who appear in
Barth's text and contribute to his arguments in undisguised and largely ethnocentric positions are: Baden-
Powell (1896), Dr Bellew (1864), General Bruce (1900) and
Colonel Wylly (1912).

The study of 'primitive' men by 'developed' ones implies an element of superior knowledge and civilization
which would mean an extent of compassion or understanding
for 'developing' societies.   Unfortunately the severity
with which academic ethnocentricism may be applied can
lead unthinkingly into cultural ethnocentricity: the comparison of Pathan tribal social organization with American
criminal organizations is one such example (Bailey, 1970).
A major quarrel with 'Political Leadership among Swat
Pathans' is that its theoretical models provide the basis
for the growth of an ethnographic stereo-type and its

subsequent misunderstanding in the social sciences. The
creation of 'the wild Pathan' image is neither fair to the
Pathan nor to Professor Barth, and yet the Swat Pathan's
image appears to worsen proportionately to the popularity
of Barth's analysis. This raises general methodological
problems, for both anthropological field-investigation and
the nature of theoretical models, around the question of
inadvertent 'bias' entering anthropological monographs.
In comparison to the work of anthropologists, sociological
studies usually (a) examine a larger universe (and therefore assume greater dependence on relatively 'value-
neutral' statistics); (b) conduct social investigation in
the form of a 'team' (and therefore provide the possibility of cross-references); (c) exhibit the data gathered
either in tables as appendices or in the main text. Anthropologists, on the other hand, usually prefer to (a)
work alone; (b) with the assistance of a paid and largely
anonymous native 'helper'; (c) and are reputed to be
somewhat secretive about their field-work notes and material (until they appear in a finalized or published form);
(d) vague charges and rumours of spying often crop up
during and after field-work - for instance, anthropologists have been accused of simultaneously spying for as
many as three nations (Barnes, 1966). Charges of ethnocentric bias are therefore not uncommon.

This bias is not necessarily a simplistic phenomenon
confined to large opposing divisions such as an 'Eastern
versus Western' view of the world or an 'Industrial versus
pre-Industrial' one. On the contrary, it may be exhibited
in various degrees in spite of an 'emic' or local stance.
Within a country regional, and within a religion, sectarian, bias may often be as prejudiced and tendentious as
any 'etic' or outside judgment. Awareness of a certain
inescapable bias only underlines the fact that apart from
the personal psycho-sociological make-up and experiences
of the investigator and his politico-cultural background
other factors play a certain part in the eventual formula-
tion of the study. In some studies obvious consideration
is given to the prejudices of (a) the finance-giving
agency; (b) the audience that the study is addressed to,
whether the university department, or a 'general' reader-
ship; (c) the people being studied (depending on the
extent of involvement with them and their causes); (d)
the government of the people studied.
II The Swat analysis is inclined to be reductionist:
this is evident both ethnographically and theoretically.
Pathan society in its numerous socio-economic forms is reduced to the Yusufzai tribe and its social organization in
Swat. However, the Yusufzai Swat Pathan is conscious of

being at the centre of three concentric circles: the
first is comprised of the other Yusufzai areas, the second
of general Pathan areas, and the last of the larger Islamic world and its Muslim societies. Simultaneous to,
and often confirming, his segmentary lineage charter the
Pathan carries this blue-print in his head. The importance of this awareness and the response to it, will be
evident in the chapter on millenarian movements. Barth
has largely left the larger religio-cultural concentric
patterns untouched.

Professor Barth is less guilty of this charge than
those social scientists who have misread his work and
equated general Pathan society to the (Barthian) Swat
Pathan: that is, post-1926 Swat. The unique morphological deviance in Pathan society is taken as the general and
average Pathan model. This will be discussed later.
Theoretically, the Swat Pathan is reduced to an entrepreneur in the methodological individualist mould; holistic
analysis of religio-cultural symbolism does not feature.

III The Swat analysis is synecdochic: a social stratum
of a particular society, the Yusufzai Khans (one-fifth of
the population), has been taken to represent the whole of
Swat society. The activities of this minority are assumed
as representative of those of the majority without supporting field evidence that this is empirically true.
Whereas highly politicized Khans (backed by vast irrigated
estates with annual incomes of 50,000 rupees) manipulating
and maximizing political power may be a plausible thesis
it hardly reflects the social aspirations or behaviour of
the majority with annual incomes of about 300 rupees
(Barth, 1959a, p.79). The Khans themselves might organize
their social behaviour differently over different periods
of time or in a different spatial context, as in 'pre-
wesh' or 'post-wesh' historical periods and in different
geographical locations as in the Tribal or Settled Areas.
The synecdochic nature of the Swat analysis is further
underlined as it rests on socio-demographic data which,
though not 'soft' or imprecise are, none the less, often
meagre and limited. Swat man is thus seen through the
eyes of the Khan as will be examined later in this essay.
Indianists (for example, Dumont, 1972) are often open to
criticism on this score for imposing a Brahmin's eye-view
of the world on entire Hindu society.

The Swat study also bring into relief a potential and
wider crisis in the theoretical and methodological problems of anthropology: is field-work to take its own
pace, often running into years (as with the work of the
older generation of anthropologists) or, in this age of
computers and jumbo-jets, is it to be restricted to short

intensive spells?   Professor Barth himself is a believer
in the latter: he spent seven months conducting field-
work among the Kurds (Barth, 1953), ten months with the
Swat Pathans (Barth, 1959a, Preface), three months with
the Basseri tribe in Iran (Barth, 1961, Foreword), three
months in Sudan (Barth, 1967, p.173), five weeks in the
Marri area (Pehrson, 1966, Preface, p.X), and eleven
months in New Guinea (Barth, 1975) before writing about
them. This raises certain questions related to ethnography and theory: will anthropological output tend to
concentrate on deductive 'theories' and 'models' that rest
on thin ethnographic data? Is the day of the solid and
traditional ethnographic 'village-study' then over? Is
ethnography to be subordinated to theory? For instance
'Political Leadership among Swat Pathans' divides easily
into chapters 2 to 5 containing Swat ethnography and chapters 6 to 9 into model-building exercises.

This essay is worked out on two levels: on one level
it is a straight sociological reinterpretation of socio-
historical developments and their impact on the political
organization of Swat which challenges some of the theoretical and ethnographic assumptions of Barth's models while
attempting to offer alternative ones. In parts this is
complementary to Barth's material which it may help to
view in better relief.

On another level the essay sets out to show that air-
tight divisions between methodological individualism and
holism in social analysis cannot be empirically sustained
and that, on the contrary, a certain dialectic relationship appears to exist between them. In chapter 7 a diachronic analysis of the Swat ethnography will attempt to
illustrate how a particular analytical framework may be
more heuristically relevant at a certain socio-historical
period than another framework within the same spatial universe. The essential irreducibility of cultures or the
phenomenon of charisma is not compromised in a holistic
argument. The millenarian movements are examined within a
larger structural framework and not analysed in terms of
individual action. Similarly, the emergence of the Akhund
of Swat and the skeletal foundations he laid for a state
and, eventually, a dynasty, will be examined methodologically within a holistic framework that includes nineteenth
century Muslim marginal tribal communities feeling the
shock-waves of the colonial presence.

The Akhund's elder son, Miangul Hannan, attempted to
activate the symbols in Swat society that attached to his
famous father in order to gain temporal power, but failed.
On the other hand his nephew and grandson of the Akhund,
Miangul Abdul Wadud, as near the definition of the

Weberian charismatic leader as possible, successfully
overcame a series of challenges and succeeded in being recognized by the British in 1926 as the Wali of Swat.

Charisma remains largely a function of success; its
qualities are both inherent in the person and in the
social situation. The charismatic leader is convinced of
his 'mission' or 'destiny' but he must also convince those
around him of his capacity for leadership. Though his
uncle failed, Miangul Wadud successfully mobilized the
symbols of authority and power and driven by a relentless
belief in his mission to rule and reform, emerged as the
ruler of Swat. The answers are not so simple. They lead
to other theoretical and methodological questions:
accepting for the moment a Barthian Yusufzai situation
(1959b) until the nineteenth century, could an Akhund have
emerged earlier in Yusufzai Swat without the stimulus provided by an expanding Christian imperial presence? If so,
what factors prevented him?

A weakness in Barth's analysis of pre-Wali Swat is the
failure to examine the politico-religious factors that
caused (a) the self-perpetuating circuit that maintained
the politically acephalous Khan-based structure to break
and which (b) allowed for the emergence of the Miangul as
the sole leader of Swat. Related and vital questions to
Barth's analysis remain unasked: (a) could a Khan have
led the millenarian movements against the British? (b)
could a Khan have rallied Swat against the Dir forces and
consolidated power to become Wali in the first decades of
this century? If so, why did this not happen? Similarly,
would Miangul Wadud have been equally successful a generation earlier and before the millenarian movements in the
Frontier areas?

In Miangul Wadud's case personal and inherent qualities
of charismatic 'grace' or 'power' enabled him to succeed
where his agnatic ascendants and cousins failed: the
framework of sociological analysis is methodologically individualist. However, without the understanding of analysis within a holistic framework that accounted for the
emergence of the Akhund and allowed for a continuing
latent familial charisma in Swat society he may never have
succeeded.

Although the diachronic analysis of the Swat Pathans
contains an intrinsic dynamic equilibrium the treatment of
the model is synchronic and reduced within a static framework. Barth's 'generative models' (Barth, 1966) had set
out to offer an important theoretical break from the traditional structuralist-functionalist models. Part of
Barth's thesis is to illustrate that segmentary, acephalous tribal societies need not follow 'fusion/fission'

segmentation in the process of change brought about by external or internal agencies (Fortes and Evans-Pritchard,
1940). He offers the Swat material as 'a deviant case'
(Barth, 1959b) and thus breaks from traditional 'models of
form' which are 'static' to advocate 'models of process'
which are 'dynamic'. These models

> are not designed to be homologous with observed social
> regularities; instead they are designed so that they,
> by specified operations, can generate such regularities
> or forms.... Thus by a series of logical operations,
> forms can be generated; these forms may be compared to
> empirical forms of social systems, and where there is
> correspondence in formal features between the two, the
> empirical form may then be characterized as a particu-
> lar constellation of the variables in the model (Barth,
> 1966, p.v).

Part of the quarrel with the application of 'generative
models' to the Swat situation is based on the underlying
conceptual ambiguity arising from the failure to delimit
time and space boundaries. Had Barth taken a defined pre-
1926 (pre-State) Swat Yusufzai model and, assuming all
other variables constant, introduced the Wali of Swat (and
his State) he would have had the results of a 'controlled
experiment' and an example of a 'generative model' in
action satisfying both (a) 'the means to describe and
study change in social forms as changes in the basic variables that generate the forms' (Barth, 1966, p.v) and (b)
a 'comparative analysis as a methodological equivalent of
experiment' (ibid.).

The major requirements of the 'generative models', and
indeed theoretical contribution to scientific analysis,
would have been satisfied: 'The adequacy of a generative
model, on the other hand, is tested by its success or failure in generating the observed forms; it contains implicit hypotheses about "possible" and "impossible" systems which may be falsified by comparative data' (ibid.,
pp.v-vi). Alternatively, the dimension of space could
have been successfully employed for a similar 'controlled
experiment' by adopting the Malakand Yusufzai socio-
political organization as the basic model and then intro-
ducing defined variables to examine the changes occurring
across the State border and in Swat Yusufzai. In either
case, minimizing the impact of the Wali on Swat socio-
political organization as an epiphenomenon is a more
serious misreading than that which functionalists are
accused of in leaving out Political Agents and District
Commissioners as permanent and fixed agents of change
(Asad, 1973). The Wali, in any case, is not representative of a foreign or imperial power. He is an autarchic

but local ruler. The insignia he selected for the State
are highly symbolic of Swat political reality and its power
base: a religious shibboleth ('Ya-Haddi' - an exclamation
to the Almighty for Divine assistance) emblazoned over a
military fort. The mainsprings of his power are clearly
both religious sanctity and the presence of coercive
authority. This important element is therefore overlooked
when understanding 'generative models' as applicable to
the Swat situation, i.e. 'to explain form one needs to
discover and describe the processes that generate the
form' (Barth, 1966, p.v). The Wali, as will be seen in
later chapters, is explained by the socio-historical 'processes that generate the form' and, in turn, helps to explain them.

Chapter 2 of this essay discusses the Theory of Games
as applied to Swat and will put the ethnographic argument,
subsequently developed, within a theoretical frame.

Chapters 3 and 4 are based on those elements of 'Political Leadership among Swat Pathans' (chapters 2 to 9)
which require ethnographic comment. Chapter 3 is thus 'The
Swat Pathan understood', in which the main elements of
Barth's Swat society and analysis are delineated; the
next chapter argues against the usage and understanding of
some Barthian concepts and terms. Chapter 5 attempts to
build a general economic theory for Pathan social organization. Economic-ecological factors are correlated to
both social and political structures and two types of
Pathan social organization are analysed and categorized.
It is argued that the centralized State of Swat may be explained and understood as a result of, or falling within,
a category of Pathan socio-economic organization.

Sufic orders and Islamic revivalism in the nineteenth
century form the content of chapter 6. Through the examination of certain homologous developments in Islamic
societies a holistic theoretical frame is constructed
within which to explain the emergence of the Akhund of
Swat and the base he provided for the eventual establishment of the Wali and the State. The chapter may be somewhat digressive to those anxious to restrict the arguments
to Swat. Those who wish specifically to avoid it will
find the main points recorded at the end of the chapter.

Between the emergence of the Akhund and the rise of the
Wali of Swat lies the most turbulent period of North-West
Frontier history. This turbulence closes the last century
and marks the final incorporation of the Tribal Areas into
the British Indian Empire. An attempt has been made to
see these related series of tribal revolts in millenarian
terms, led by visionary leaders promising a better order,
couched in apocalyptic language and assuring divine

assistance. Such popular uprisings have been widely
studied. Notable among these are the New Guinea 'cargo
cults'. Worsley, for instance, analyses the New Guinea
movements largely within a Marxist framework and as a reaction to a white, Christian and colonial presence (1970).
Burridge, on the other hand, adds 'ethnographic' 'psycho-
physiological' and 'Hegelian' explanations to the Marxist
one (1969). The Pathan millenarian movements contained
elements familiar in the above theses but were basically
an Islamic tribal response to an expanding and non-Islamic
imperial power.

Chapter 7 forms a triad: the arguments contained are
dialectical and intercausatory. Section one presents the
thesis: it looks at the interconnected outbreaks of millenarian movements in the Malakand (13) in the late 1890s
within a holist frame of sociological analysis. These
religio-populist movements throw up various leaders of
temporary charisma. The Malakand ground is 'predisposed'
to receive the charismatic leader and he appears in the
person of Miangul Wadud. The argument in section two is
seen as antithesis and forms around the concept of charismatic leadership and the processes of institutionalization
of charisma which are seen as antithetical to the millenarian promise and political expectancy of the movements.
The analytic frameworks of the foregoing sections join to
achieve synthesis in section three, which examines the
origin, establishment and nature of a State among the Swat
Yusufzai. The cycle has made a full revolution: from the
Sufic asceticism of the Akhund to the formal Statehood of
his agnatic descendants. A certain linear development in
Weberian types of authority is observed: from the patriarchal traditional authority of the Yusufzai Khans to the
emergence of charismatic leadership in the Wali of Swat
and the institutionalization of charisma in the State.

The last chapter draws in the various strands running
through the book and attempts to sum up. It also contains
a section which clarifies why so much has been made of
Barth's usage of concepts, like Saints, in chapter 4 of
this essay, and gives examples of the misunderstanding of
Pathan society that this has inadvertently caused.

Wherever possible, a deliberate attempt has been made
to confine references to Swat from 'Political Leadership
among Swat Pathans' (Barth, 1959a). A certain amount of
model-building has followed the attempt to challenge
Barth's models in this essay, perhaps with only limited
success. These models are open to charges of oversimpli-
fication especially as they stand in opposition to more
sophisticated ones. None the less, their construction has
been a useful exercise to house the methodological and
theoretical arguments contained in the following pages.

Part one

2 The Swat Pathans and the theory of games

چرک خویو مارغه دے چه چا او نیُوو د هغه دے

The hen is a bird belonging to him who seizes it (1)

MODEL

Professor Barth applies 'some of the elementary concepts
and procedures of the Theory of Games (cf. Neumann and
Morgenstern, 1947; Stone, 1948), as well as the relevant
anthropological theory relating to descent groups and corporate groups' (Barth, 1959b, p.5) to the analysis of the
Swat data which explains the interplay, manoeuvre and
equilibrium that is involved in Swat politics. Political
alliances and configurations in Swat are formed by leaders
attempting to maximize political advantage and power,
which 'define both the necessary and sufficient conditions
for the emergence of a two-bloc system (2) like that observed among Yusufzai Pathans' (ibid., p.15). It is
essentially a 'power' game.
    The rules of the 'game' derive from the prominent fea-
tures of Yusufzai Pathan political organization:
I 'persisting opposition of interests between wards
occupied by collaterals in the agnatic descent system'
based on 'competition for control of the one basic good-
land' (ibid.).
II patron-client type relationships based on 'contractual political alliance between two or several equals'.
It is not altogether clear whether the patron-client relationship refers to landlords and their tenants only or to
big landlords and their smaller client landowners as well.
In the former case, as will be discussed later, reciprocal
and symmetrical relationships between patron and clients
are difficult to conceive as they are perceptibly tilted

in favour of the stronger patron.

III 'the recognition and positive value given to the
status of chief of a ward' i.e. 'a net of indivisible
"bonuses"' (ibid.). Clearly quantity alone is not a valid
referent; quality is weighted too.

The rules of the game allocate a uniform weight to each
player and a free choice in joining alliances to maximize
advantage.   A five-person majority game - Neumann and
Morgenstern, 1947, p.332 ff - where each player 1, 2, 3,
4, 5 for simplicity is vested with an equal value 1.
Though each player is restricted to one unit only 'positive value' accrues to, for instance, the status of chief
of a ward. As the objective of the game is to win, or
maximize one's political advantage, this can be done by
manipulating a 'majority' grouping against a 'minority'
one. A simple majority is a win for the majority group
'where the final sanction is majority in terms of power'
(Barth, 1959b, p.15). It is a 'zero-sum' or 'constant-
sum' game: one man's loss is another's gain. An important inherent assumption is that the arena or field of the
game has fixed boundaries preventing new or foreign elements from participation on one or the other side. This
is intrinsic to the model as it not only defines and
limits the arena and fruits of victory (land) but also the
number of participants. The boundaries are either around
the ward, the village or the State at whatever level the
game is played.

Shifting boundaries or an uncertain number of participants would mean imbalanced opposition and make for uncertain rules, which would make nonsense of the 'zero-sum'
model based on assumptions of equality between the participants. The game is played to win, not destroy; maximize, not create permanent imbalance. This, simply
stated, is the Theory of Games which Barth borrowed from
outside anthropology and so brilliantly applied to it.

APPLICATION

The Game-Theory analyses the activities of Swat leadership, i.e. the Yusufzai Khans, who balance each other in
power to ensure some form of rough equilibrium, while all
the time manoeuvering to join an alliance or bloc
('dalla') that would lead to an advantageous position, and
therefore maximizing of power, over the rival bloc of
Khans. This effectively checks the abrupt ascendancy of
any one Khan and the game proceeds, shifting and balancing, now favouring one bloc and now another. In an ad-
verse situation, loss might be minimized ('minimizing

loss'), or in an advantageous one gain might be maximized
to the full ('maximizing gain'). Internal to the bloc
system, though not directly apparent in the game analysis,
is another factor demanding its own equation and as
delicate as the balance that maintains the Khans in a semblance of equality. This is the presence, at all levels
of social competition, of 'religious leaders', called
'Saints', who counterpoise to an extent, the temporal
power of the local Khans. It is important for the Swat
analysis that both the Saint and the Khan 'are active as
political pretenders' (Barth, 1959a, p.4).

COMMENT

The analytic approach in this essay to the Swat material
would be from the same position as that of Professor
Barth, i.e. examining a tribal society, apparently in conflict and yet maintaining a structural continuity and co-
herence by the paradoxical action of political leaders,
backed by alliances and corporate groups, fighting to
maximize political power. As an abstract construct the
model is both attractive and heuristic in helping to explain the structural equilibrium in Yusufzai society, and
in Swat up to the emergence of the Wali and the State.
However, the points of difference arise at the conceptual
interpretation of the historical and ethnographic facts of
the Swat situation which will be examined later. This
chapter will look at the contradictions in the Game
Theory as applied to the Swat situation.
 I The primary rule limiting units allocated to each
player as 'equal value 1', and therefore of equal value to
those possessed by the other players, is immediately vio-
lated if the Wali of Swat enters the game. It is never
quite clear to what extent he does. The diachronic treatment of Swat creates a certain ambiguity in this regard.
Is the Swat analysis one of pre-1926 tribal society or the
post-1926 State. (3) This, as has been mentioned earlier,
is a crucial question with ramifying results for the subsequent argument.
    If the situation before the establishment of the State
in 1926 is examined then it would be assumed that Barth is
including the presence of Miangul Wadud in the power game
and allocating one unit of value to him. This is an obvious historical error as it underplays the role of
Miangul Wadud who was active since the turbulent days at
the turn of the century, both as a prominent leader in
competition with other religious rivals for a voice in the
millenarian movements and, as the grandson of the Akhund,

inheritor of vast reserves of spiritual authority and
familial charisma against his temporal rivals. He would
surely merit more than one unit. From the 1897-8 movements onwards, and partly as a result of them, his star
was steadily on the rise and by 1907 he was the eldest
male among the Akhund's descendants. Except for a brief
setback in 1915, when he had to leave Swat, he was always
one of its major leaders. By 1917 he was powerful enough
to unite the tribes under him and to be declared their
'Badshah' (king) (Miangul, 1962, p.47). (4) However, with
the above caution in view, the pre-1917 Swat situation
provides valid material for purposes of Game-Theory
analysis. Khans, it could be safely presumed, balanced
each other at all levels of social interaction to maximize
and maintain power. This analysis is partly confirmed by
the Miangul's own vision of Swat political organization
before 1917 which he refers to as the 'Pakhtoon Period'
(or the rule of the Yusufzai Khans).

If, on the other hand, Swat is being examined after the
establishment of the State in 1917 or 1926 (to use the
official date as this essay will do) then the basic pre-
mises of the game are thoroughly and completely upset.
The Wali as head of the State is no 'primus inter pares',
a senior chief among other tribal chieftans. He emerges
as an autarchic and absolute ruler as will be seen later.
The Wali with his police, army, communication system, re-
venues and personal networks, becomes more than a match
for any combination or permutation of Khans. The Wali
pre-empts power by control and distribution of its base,
i.e. land. Through this control he extends his patronage
over the Khans of Swat many of whom are absorbed into the
'administrative' structure of the State where they are
aware of client status to the Wali as 'naukaran' (literally servants) (Barth, 1959a, p.48). Recalcitrant Khans,
bent on maintaining some semblance of independence in the
face of the new and highly centralized authority of the
State, are simply expelled from Swat (5) or their property
and forts razed to the ground (Stein, 1929, p.5). This is
not to say that politics vanishes from Swat in 1926. On
the contrary, the Wali consciously keeps some form of
political activity alive right down to the ward level but
it is now a function of his strategy and plans:

> his policy is explicitly described by the politically
> sophisticated as one of joining the weaker bloc, there-
> by gaining victories over the richest chiefs, and also,
> by 'tipping the scales', gaining a disproportionate in-
> fluence in the bloc. His great success is attributed
> in part to his unique freedom to effect such changes of
> alliance (Barth, 1959b, p.19).

So, as the Wali removes himself from participation in the
'zero-sum' game he none the less allows it to continue
along its traditional patterns at all levels, but as a
valorized function of the State's political strategy.
Politics, if it is meaningfully defined as pursuit of the
ultimate or maximum power in the land, is no longer valid
although 'game-type' configurations of Khans, form and
break alliances. The Wali does not play the traditional
'zero-sum' game of the Yusufzai Khans whereby a check is
kept on any one participant gaining excessive units by
shifting permutations; he creates a new game. He aligns
the teams and orders the rules. The objectives are still
'maximizing'; but the Wali defines the limits, content
and direction of the goals. By creating a 'game-type'
situation he keeps potential opposition involved in its
own localized group conflicts that fall into the mould of
'State politics' revolving around royal families and court
intrigues, and reflect the problematic of encapsulation of
local isolated communities. Partly with this end in view
he is highly mobile and informed: 'The Wali is illiterate
but decides every matter of importance himself verbally
over the telephone' (Hay, 1934, p.245).

The institutionalization of State power does not rule
out the formation of factions at the local level. What is
altered is the mode of factional conflict and the prize
that they contend for. In the Barth model followers would
rally behind a powerful Khan because that would secure for
them the resources for their livelihood - land and peace
and security. Now land ownership is regulated by State
law and security is provided by the State. Why should
anyone need to go to the Khan? In the new situation the
role of the State becomes crucial, and presents a new problem for the peasant. He needs access to the State machinery. The State, likewise, consolidates its local
power base by establishing links with the local level
powerholders. The faction leader now sets himself up in
business to mediate with the State.

The institutional interest of the Wali in the making
and breaking of blocs and alliances at all levels of Swat
politics is intrinsic to the State encapsulating, as it
does, tribal systems:

When I visited Swat last time I came across a curious
confirmation of this when a man whose father had been
killed by his faction leader but who had ambitions to
set himself up in business on his own as a leader of a
faction, said to me that when it was suggested to him
that he might therefore join the rival faction he said:
'That would be a matter of shame' and he went to the
Wali and got his 'permission' to set up a rival

faction. In the old system as conceptualized by Barth, the question of getting the 'permission' of the Wali to set up a faction would not arise. But in the new situation it makes good sense for he can be a successful faction leader only if the Wali can assure him that he will be in a position to mediate with the state machinery effectively - and the Wali's 'permission' is a signal to his potential followers that he will be able to deliver the goods. This is an aspect of the institutionalization of state power (Alavi, personal communication, 1975).

The failure to delineate some time-boundary invites an inherent and continuing contradiction in conceptual terms between the model of an acephalous, segmentary and stateless society (pre-1926 Swat) playing 'zero-sum' games and a highly centralized state (post-1926 Swat) that can only permit play on its own terms. In Swat State the two conditions co-exist, although one condition presupposes and even predicts the other. Centralized authority in Swat is not a compromise with acephalous tribal forms but a surrogate for it with all its social and structural ramifications.

The ambiguity remains unresolved: Professor Barth sees the State's 'centralized system as merely superimposed on this (the acephalous system), presupposing rather than attempting to replace it' (Barth, 1959a, p.132). However, it is earlier maintained that the Swat model is based on tribes living outside the State: 'Chapter 9 described the acephalous political organization of Swat as it actually exists today in the part of the valley included in the protected tribal areas of Malakand' (ibid., p.127). The ambiguity arising from the failure to fix time-boundaries and spatial universe or ethnographic boundaries in the Swat analysis continues to detract from its conceptualization. The study is apparently based on the acephalous tribal system 'relating particularly to the Lower Swat Valley (Malakand Agency, North-West Frontier Province, Pakistan)' (Barth, 1959b, p.7). However, the data are almost entirely gathered from Swat State. The important point revolves around the diacritical political (not ethnic) boundary between the Malakand - Lower Swat - and Swat State: six of the seven villages that provide fieldwork material are in Swat State (Barth, 1959a, map 2, p. 15) and the seventh, 'the giant village of Thana (pop. 10,000)' (Barth, 1959a, p.108) lies just outside the State and because of its urban character is not entirely representative of a tribal village in Malakand. If Barth's ethnographic data are valid then they do not fit easily into his theoretical model; alternatively if his model is

to be applicable to Swat it must fix a time-boundary
before the consolidation of power by Miangul Wadud and the
establishment of his centralized rule.

II   The second point follows from the first though it relates to the main objectives of the Game-Theory which is
to maximize political power. Although played on various
social levels the major thrust of the game appears to be
for political power in Swat and is played by the big
Khans. Some conflicts of this nature 'involved armies of
the order of ten thousand soldiers, and scores of very
prominent chiefs' (ibid., p.71). Now if the Khans do not
stand the slightest chance of winning the game which by
definition, and certainly by a Pathan one, (6) must approximate, within the boundaries of the game, to ultimate,
maximum or the highest possible form of power, as it already stands appropriated by the Wali, then the game
itself loses a vital dimension and even significance. It
is definitionally altered from a power game to perhaps a
social game reduced to a local or ward variant. The shift
is from sitting in the seat of power to the gaining of
permission to sit near the seat of power; from central
actor in the power game to an epiphenomenon. This is
doubly difficult to understand both ethnically in terms of
Pathan politico-historical observed behaviour and in the
theoretical framework of the maximizing transactionalist
man that Barth imposes on him.

Unfortunately the causes why no corporate group or
alliance of Khans could challenge the Wali are not examined. By definition the Pathan Khan has been categorized
as maximizing or political man and could he do so he would
have challenged and toppled the ruler. The fight was
simply too uneven. The peasantry viewed the Khan as an
alien class and an imposition (ibid., p.68) and therefore
the Khans's strength, based on the dubious loyalty of his
tenants, was partly illusory and created constant paranoia
in his mind:

> The fear is prominent in the mind of every Pathan
> chief, that his nominally subject lineage mates, and
> persons of holy status, are intriguing behind his back
> with outsiders, just as he himself is intriguing with
> the nominal followers of other chiefs (ibid., p.11).

The explanation lies mainly in the nature of the Swat
State and the fact that it was a unique morphological deviance in Pathan society.

III   The final point concerns the fixed-boundaries of the
game. All other things are presumed to be equal, 'ceteris
paribus'. This is an essential and elemental tool for
synchronic analysis of pure theoretical models but one
which does not always correlate to empirical data. But

things were never fixed or equal in the Swat situation,
and in the context of the North-West Frontier Province
this is an incredible assumption. (7) The Swat analysis
ought to have taken into account the Yusufzai tribes
living in Dir, Bajaur, Malakand and Mardan for bonds of
endogamy, kinship ties, political alliances etc. regulate
frequent interaction between them which crosses territorial divisions. Fixed boundaries cannot therefore be
assumed unless some local village-level boundaries are determined and it is important here to recall the distinction between 'tribal' village and 'peasant' village politics. The former involves the segmentary group within
which it is nested through filiation reckoned through unilineal descent while the latter is virtually a separate,
independent and multi-group unit.

Even an academic and retrospective pre-State Game-Model
construct would be compromised as larger Khans, endeavour-
ing to absorb neighbouring territory through armed conquest, restructure existing socio-political alliances.
The Swat Game-Theory, however, notes 'the empirical un-
willingness of the stronger bloc to make the most of its
advantage and literally run the opposition out of the
village' (Barth, 1959b, p.17). This is not the case empirically for 'the stronger bloc' invariably and 'literally' ran the opposition out of the village, and often the
Swat valley, as has been seen earlier. Numerous examples
of participants in the 'power game' being expelled from
their localities with their followers can be cited:
Mohammed Sharif, the Khan of Dir, upon occupying the west
bank of the Swat river, exiled local Khans and replaced
them with his own Akhundzadas (Parliamentary Papers, (8)
Enclosure 2, dated 21 July 1897). The Khan himself es-
caped with his followers at one stage to take refuge in
Swat from Umra Khan until the latter was finally expelled
from Dir. Miangul Wadud was forced to quit the Swat
valley with his family and supporters (Miangul, 1962, p.
35) by Sayyed Jabbar Shah, the short-lived leader of Swat,
who, in turn, was removed from Swat when the Miangul was
elected 'Badshah' in 1917. By excluding the larger socio-
political context of the Yusufzai areas, and the constant
political interaction between them, the Swat Game-Model
is given a static quality in spite of the fact that it
functions in dynamic equilibrium. The model is thus
partly guilty of the charges brought against fusion/fis-
sion structural analysis of African lineage (and political) organization: that of creating an isolated and
static model of social analysis.

From the date of Barth's inquiry (which would really
begin at the turn of the century although it has

implications that take the analysis back by another fifty
years to the Akhund's time) the British presence had begun
to make itself felt. By the time Miangul Wadud was a
young man it was clear that internal forces were combining
with external influences in pushing him to a position of
political supremacy in Swat. The British administrators,
now at the Malakand Pass (some thirty-five miles from
Swat's capital), threw their considerable weight behind
the Miangul. Their reasons were complex. The obvious one
was to create a sphere of stability in a turbulent region
and leave it to administer itself through a known or trusted ally: 'Colonial Administrators have a notorious preference for autocratic chiefs' (Leach, 1954, p.198). British recognition in 1926 of Miangul Wadud as the Wali of
Swat ended the hopes of the Khans for power except as a
function of the Wali's political organization and dispen-
sation and confirmed the realities of the political situation delineated by the events of 1917. Henceforth, the
State alone provided the sources of, and avenues for,
power.

Swat socio-political history may be examined in terms
of Game-Theory analysis but the rules, boundaries and
prizes vary considerably and make for differentiated types
of games corresponding to Swat historical stages. Three
distinct stages are seen: (a) pre-Akhund (until c.1850);
(b) post-Akhund (after 1877) but pre-State (1926, with a
qualitative change in 1917); and (c) the final post-1926
stage.

To help visualize the complex and shifting balance between the Khans (representing an acephalous segmentary
system) and the Akhund (and much more his grandson) representing various degrees of centralized authority, a
'power chart' for Swat over the last hundred years is
attempted in Figure 1. This should demonstrate the correlation between increasing central authority and diminish-
ing game possibility.

A marked correlation exists between chaotic conditions
during the millenarian movements in 1897-8, allowing a
degree of local autonomy and a low ebb in the fortunes of
the Miangul family; the two power lines are at their
maximum and greatest conceptual distance. As the Miangul
consolidates his position by a series of victorious moves
his power-line rises in direct relation to the collapse of
the Khan's power-line and cuts the latter in 1917 with the
establishment of the State. By 1926 when the State is
given official recognition the Wali's power-line is seen
rising sharply and irreversibly.

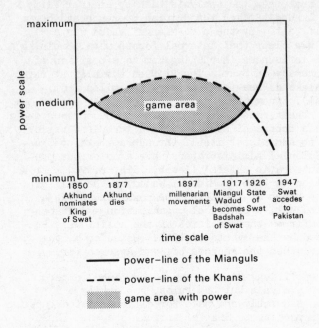

FIGURE 1   The Swat 'power chart' and game possibilities

   The Wali after 1926 was thus creating a new kind of
game situation but no longer participating in it. His
emergence is the causal explanation for the type of game
peculiar to post-State Swat and not a result of it. It is
not quite clear whether or not Professor Barth would exclude the Wali altogether from the game. Would he then
argue for a post-Akhund and pre-State situation in which
the big Yusufzai Khans participate in 'zero-sum' games.
This is a tenable hypothesis but needless to say would
alter the focus and scope of Barth's analysis almost
beyond recognition and rest more on severely limited historical data than ethnographic ones.
   The very real historical, religious, sectarian (inter -
as distinct from extra - religious) conflicts have been
smoothed out from the Game-Theory Model of the Swat situation characterized by rapidly changing conflict situations, structural shifts and constant political upheaval.
It will be seen how the historical religious revivalism of
the pre-Wali period was in fact a graver threat to the
Wali's emergence than even the maximizing machinations of
the local Khans. The 'hows' and 'whys' of Swat State, its
foundation and political organization remain confined to

one-line and fleeting explanations. For example, the critical British interaction with the Wali and the State are
baldly explained thus: 'In 1926 Swat State was recognized
by the British, and Badshah given the title of Wali and an
annual subsidy' (Barth, 1959a, p.128). This only furthers
the ambiguity regarding boundaries in space and time in
the Swat analysis. Neither traditional-functionalist
schemata nor the Game-Model, however dynamic its internal
structural equilibrium, can be therefore fully meaningful
in the dynamic and subjective apperception and interpretation of recent Swat religious and political history.

3 The Swat Pathan understood

خدا ٹے خبر چہ ترہ کافر دے

God knows that the father's brother is an infidel

YUSUFZAI SOCIAL ORGANIZATION: LESSONS IN MYSTIFICATION

(Swat) village organization, and political life in
general, are profoundly influenced by two complexes of
myths and values common to the whole Swat area. One of
these relates to land tenure and the status of the
'landed gentry', and the other to religious ascendancy
and its relevance to daily life. According to the
first, the Yusufzai tribes entered the valley as conquerors; their descendants claim ownership and juris-
diction over all land, with exceptions to be noted
later (Barth, 1959a, p.9).
Land was the basis of power and status: 'The land tenure
system thus emphasized the division between landowning
Yusufzai conquerors and their subjects, the former being a
dominant, cosmopolitan "gentry", the latter a parochial,
subordinate population, serving a succession of different
lords' (ibid., p.10).
    This relationship between a minority Yusufzai élite and
a majority tenant autochthonous population of 'tenant
farmers, labourers, blacksmiths, carpenters and other
craftsmen, muleteers, shopkeepers, barbers, and shepherds'
(ibid.) grew into a symbiotic one but the former remained
largely endogamous (ibid., Figure 1, p.20). From the
1520s when they invaded Swat, as a result of a reversal in
their political fortune in Kabul, (1) under their chief
Sheikh Ahmed, to the middle of the last century when the
Akhund emerged and nominated a non-Yusufzai King of Swat,
the Yusufzai have had over three hundred years of

unchallenged and undisturbed political ascendancy. No imperial army representing centralized authority has ever
penetrated the Swat valley. Akbar the Great tried with
disastrous results in 1586 and the Yusufzai of Swat were
left alone until the British fought Pathan tribesmen at
the Ambela Pass in 1863. This contact with the newly
arrived imperial power was to deepen and by 1895 the Malakand Agency was created to look after affairs in Swat, Dir
and Chitral. The marginal nature of the Swat valley to
the main channels of communication from and to Delhi, the
imperial locus of subcontinental power, and its geographical remoteness reinforced this isolation. Inaccessible
and difficult mountains cut off and surround Swat from all
sides except the southern where there are passes that open
into other Yusufzai territory. The mountains act as a
barrier and the Yusufzai areas below them as a cushion
against invasion and a ready reference of larger and immediate Yusufzai consciousness.

Two related myths for Yusufzai apperception were consequently created and preserved:
I the collective role of an aristocratic military élite
embodying the finest and most chivalric virtues of
'Pukhtunwali' and
II the mystification of this role to mean a sort of
'divine right' charter to land in Swat. All political
configurations work around this mystification and loss of
land is tantamount to loss of Pukhtun status (ibid., p.
112).

The Yusufzai were cast in the role of the blue-blooded
Pathans according to this mystification (2):
The chronicles of the Yusufzai are ancient, going back
well beyond the days when the Pathan genealogies were
created by the Mogul historians. So pure have the
Yusufzai kept their blood-lines and so rigorously have
they obeyed the Pathan code that they are universally
acknowledged by the other tribes as being the most
blue-blooded Pathans of all. This is a rare compli-
ment, since most Pathans spend a great deal of time im-
pugning the Pathan-ness of other Pathans (Spain, 1962,
p.73).
Those who administered them were susceptible to this
mystique:
To know and respect, and be known and liked by, the
leaders of Yusufzai society means that a man has entered into a sort of Pathan freemasonry, and has reached a
position in which the very quintessence of the Pathan
spirit begins to be revealed to him (Caroe, 1965, p.
421).
The Yusufzai developed a marked feudal-chivalric social

organization around their vast estates and followings
which was similar in certain respects to European feudalism. It was a post-slavery and pre-bureaucracy stage in
social history:

>A subject peasantry; widespread use of the service
>tenement (i.e. the fief) instead of a salary, which was
>out of the question; the supremacy of a class of
>specialized warriors; ties of obedience and protection
>which bind man to man and, within the warrior class,
>assume the distinctive form called vassalage; fragmen-
>tation of authority (Bloch, 1961, p.446).

Characteristic of feudal society lord-vassal dyadic and
contractual relationships tended to dominate kin ones.
Even Pathan tribal battle, characterized by its individualistic, temporary and guerilla nature, was transformed
into a stylized and feudal 'set-piece' form (Miangul,
1962, p.29).

Life in Swat for the Yusufzai as seen early last century was that of a leisured country class:

>Most of the labour being done by the Fakeers (3) none
>but the poorest Eusofzyes are obliged to work; the
>others sometimes take a share in the labours of their
>own fields, but it is rather for exercise, and to set
>an example, than to work in earnest (Elphinstone, 1972,
>II, p.32).

Though Yusufzai Swat was organized as an acephelous,
stateless society based on segmentary groups, local Yusufzai social organization was autocephalous in that it re-
volved around the Khan and his estate forming semi-
independent islands of authority: 'It is impossible to
enumerate all the little republics of the Eusofzyes'
(ibid., p.27). The apical and hierarchical organization
based on vast estates is recognizable today:

>However, the clan is to be seen at its most formidable
>in Mardan District, a deceptively peaceful-looking land
>of lush fields of wheat, corn, sugarcane and tobacco....
>Traditionally most of them owe allegiance to one or
>other of the great Yusufzai Khans whose seats are at
>Mardan, Hoti, Zaida, Toru, Topi, and at half a dozen
>other ancient villages. These Khans have in the past
>been the largest land-owners on the Frontier, some of
>them holding more than 20,000 acres (Spain, 1962, p.
>74).

Clearly this feature enabled the Khans to play a form of
'zero-sum' game in keeping themselves in and their rivals
out of power.

Over time, due to their isolation in being cut off from
mainstream Pathan tribal society and mainly due to their
economy based on large irrigated holdings, the Yusufzai

developed marked contrasting characteristics to their
cousins living in the mountains and organized into acephalous stateless and segmentary groups. The two types of
Pathan societies acquired almost polar characteristics.
The Yusufzai based sub- and super-ordinate relationships
around the concept of 'qalang' (lit. rent) and land ownership and developed into a hierarchical order. The other
type was characterized by its emphasis on the primary
'Pukhtunwali' concept of 'nang' (lit. honour) and its
apperception of itself as part of progressively larger
nesting segmentary groups and a social identity based on
membership of the tribe. These categories of Pathan
social organization will be discussed in chapter 5.

What is of interest with regard to the Swat analysis is
the distinct growth of a feudal class based on possession
of land and the inherent right to that land by virtue of
conquest, sanctified, as it were, by the authorship of the
land distribution system attributed to Sheikh Malli, the
Saint who had accompanied Sheikh Ahmed.

TERRITORIAL DIVISIONS AND SEGMENTARY DESCENT GROUPS

The three remaining sections in this chapter are interconnected and attempt to portray the dominant themes of
Yusufzai socio-political organization and Barth's analysis
of it: firstly, 'wesh', (4) the distribution of territory
based on filiation in segmentary groups which determines
both right to land and Pathan identity; secondly, alliances, networks and groups at all levels which form part of
the larger 'two-bloc' political system in Swat and are as
often the result of agnatic rivalry, the third theme, as
the cause of it. Land remains the basis for political
power and conflict.

The concept and practice of 'wesh' provide important
ramifying diacritica for Swat. Historically, 'wesh' marks
the beginning of Yusufzai rule and is symbolic of their
rights in lands through conquest; politically, it confers
superior and superordinate status to members of the
Yusufzai tribe; and, in an ethno-geographic sense, it divides the Yusufzai from the other Pathan tribes who do not
practice 'wesh'.

Sheikh Malli devised the 'wesh' system of periodic distribution (or re-distribution) of land circa 1530 (Caroe,
1965, p.183), which conceptualizes the individual's place
in the Yusufzai descent charter by shares, 'brakha', in
the land based on membership in the lineage segment, 'in
other words, he delimited a hierarchy of territorial segments corresponding to the particular pattern of

segmentation within the major Yusufzai lineages' (Barth,
1959a, p.9). Permanent democracy and equality were ensured by a regular redistribution or rotation of ownership
over every, say, ten years:

> But no two pieces of land are really equal. So rather
> than vest property rights to specific fields permanent-
> ly in any one lineage segment, Sheikh Malli decreed
> that the land should be periodically re-allotted....
> In this way, a completely equitable division of the
> fruits of conquest was assured (ibid.).

Alienation, for example, through sale, involves a
change in the status of land. 'In Pathan terminology the
land has been converted from "daftar" (inherited estate)
to "siri" (the private property of a non-Pakhtun)' (ibid.,
p.67). The significance of this system is not restricted
to mere economic ownership of land alone for 'only the men
who hold "daftar" may speak in this assembly ("jirga");
they are the only full citizens of the community and act
as the political patrons of their followers and those who
reside on their land' (ibid.).

Another implication of periodical re-allotment of land
was that

> to the sedentary villagers, whether tenants, craftsmen,
> or others, the Pakhtun represents an unnecessary im-
> position. They have their own web of kinship ties,
> their local associations for life crises; between them
> they have all the skills and man-power necessary to
> maintain the economic system; they have built and must
> keep up their own houses, they know the fields and the
> irrigation system better than the Pakhtuns (ibid., pp.
> 68-9).

Consequently, to non-Yusufzai apperception 'wesh' had a
'flavour of insecurity, military occupation and temporary
exploitation'(ibid., p.68). So as it asserted the fact of
Yusufzai ownership of land 'wesh' simultaneously established the exclusion of the non-Yusufzai to rights in land.
At a stroke subordinate and superordinate social positions
were created and maintained; economic status was thus
confirmed through genealogical charters.

It is noteworthy that one of the first official acts of
the Wali of Swat was to freeze 'wesh' allotments as they
stood. Apart from the political purpose this served in
consolidating the position of his supporters and exposing
those of his enemies, the Wali was dubious about the
socio-economic rationale behind 'wesh'. To him the results of 'wesh' were unhappy:

> Consequently, for five hundred years the Yusufzai
> Pathans of Swat led nomadic lives. They did not remain
> at one place long enough to found new towns or extend

and beautify the existing ones. This unsettled mode of
life was a great set-back to the development of agriculture, trade and crafts (Miangul, 1962, p.89).

Though 1920-30 (Barth, 1959a, p.66) is fixed as the
period when 'wesh' finally ceased to function (which again
raises ramifying problems of a time boundary for the Swat
study: is it 'pre-wesh' or 'post-wesh'?) it is not quite
clear how widespread and recent this phenonemon was. It
appears on closer scrutiny more as approximating to an
'ideal' rather than 'actual' form of Pukhtun socio-
economic behaviour and part of the template that established Yusufzai consciousness and distinguished it from
the conquered people. Satisfactory data are not forthcoming on how recently the system was practised. It is
known why it was practised and who it benefited. But it
is not clear

I   how long the cycle of allotment took to revolve. For
example, Khan A upon acquiring better land from Khan B
might wish to extend the re-allotment cycle to twenty
rather than ten years.

II   whether there was a revenue and administration secre-
tariate that recorded allotments according to shares and
the time spent at each cycle on particular fields.

III   who, in the absence of an overall centralized authority, supervised and implemented the blue-print of re-
allotments?

IV   what institution dealt with errant or defaulting
Khans? If Khan A was strong enough to refuse to move out
after his time had expired could he stay on? If the
larger segmentary group mobilized to oust Khan A, then who
co-ordinated its movements? For instance, on a much
larger scale, it is historically known that the Mandanr
(reckoning descent from Mandanr, son of Umar and grandson
of Mandai) and their agnatic cousins the Yusufzai (reckoning descent from Yusuf, the apical ancestor of the Yusufzai and son of Mandai), conceptualized regular 'wesh' redistribution between the 'hills' (Swat) and 'plains'
(Mardan) but that almost at the outset the re-allotment
broke down. The Mandanrs have remained in Mardan until
today and the Yusufzai in Swat. The latter had migrated
from the Mardan plains in the first 'wesh' cycle and
Mardan is still mnemonically called after them.

The historical reality and frequency of 'wesh' in Swat
is presumed and supported with somewhat scanty ethnographic material: a single example, with no dates, from the
Nikbi Khel section of the tribe (ibid., p.65; Barth,
1959b, p.10). Elphinstone also selected the Nikbi Khel
('Naikpeekhail') to illustrate the 'wesh' division and re-
allotment of land. (5) Although Barth does not go back

over 150 years to Elphinstone, he does go to the last century to cite Baden-Powell (Barth, 1959a, p.65; 1959b, p.
10). Neither Elphinstone nor Baden-Powell visited the
Swat valley and therefore their information is 'second-
hand'; it merely confirms the existence at some historical stage of 'wesh' but does not convincingly argue its
current practice personally observed or encountered
'first-hand'.

This section is arguing that in the absence of fine
evidence to the contrary, 'wesh' is to be viewed more as a
mechanism to preserve the mythology of territorial rights
based on tribal conquests that underlines Yusufzai
brotherhood and equality than a recent and recorded land
tenure system. It is the conceptualization of a pastoral-
nomadic egalitarian social philosophy which asserts the
rights of every member of the tribe to equal shares in the
joint possessions by defining positions within homologous
segmentary groups. In Swat, however, it served to create
both economic and ethnic divisiveness.

Although its origin and conceptualization are duly
underlined, the 'redistributional' aspect of 'wesh' is
given secondary importance usually with no statistical
evidence of its frequency or existence in creditable
accounts of Swat (Ahmad, 1962, p.12) and the Frontier
(Baha, 1968, pp.245-6; Caroe, 1965, pp.180-4; Spain,
1963, p.84). Some writers speak of 'wesh' ceasing to be
practised by the last century. For example, 'it is
noticeable that the "vaish" the periodical redistribution
of tribal lands, has entirely ceased throughout the Mohmand tribe' (Merk, 1898, p.8). In the Settled Districts,
like Mardan, it ended as a result of the first regular
land settlements between 1868-80. And among the Yusufzai
generally 'these exchanges persisted among certain sections of the Yusufzai into the middle of the last century'
(Spain, 1963, p.84). Dir, the neighbouring Yusufzai area
of Swat, did not practise 'wesh': 'Panjkora and Bajaur
valleys which are similar to Swat in economy but do not
have the land re-allotment system' (Barth, 1959a, p.68).
It is clear from the above that the Swat valley, largely
because of its geographical isolation, was probably the
last Yusufzai area to practise 'wesh' on any scale and
frequency.

This point has been laboured as it has important ramifications for the Swat analysis in showing a linear tribal
development from a stateless, acephalous and segmentary
system to centralized, formal Statehood. It is postulated
that
I the 'wesh' system ceased to function as a viable land
tenure system universally sometime early last century,

although it could have survived in pockets in the Swat valley up to the time the Wali of Swat officially ended it.

II   as a result shifting and ephemeral land ownership became permanent and a feudal, hierarchical stratification began to emerge, symbolized by the presence of the Khan's 'hujra' (men's-house) and its socio-political functions. This is a crucial development in understanding the growth of powerful feudal warlords surrounded by hierarchically ranked and supporting occupational groups and vassals, theoretically equal in the ideological belief in an egalitarian religious system but exhibiting many caste-like qualities of social hierarchy. In turn, the stratification of Swat society helps to understand the base for the emergence of the Akhund, his grandson, the Wali, and the State of Swat and partly explains why Barth fails to see the conflict model developing in Swat by the time of his field-work (Asad, 1972, and Part three of this book).

III   permanent settlement implies the beginning of the end of the socio-political utility of the descent segment. Land as a common tribal property was a vital diacritical boundary that kept the individual within his segmentary descent group and one which Sheikh Malli attempted to maintain through his land system. Once land becomes a personal possession it can, through sale or gift, be alienated. One owns land individually and not jointly by virtue of belonging to a descent group.

IV   consequent to the breakdown of 'wesh' the individual no longer neighbours, and therefore confronts, his collaterals and agnates across the boundary of his land. 'Wesh', ordering en bloc segmentary shifts, carried the seeds of agnatic rivalry within its system as cousins invariably cultivated neighbouring fields and fought for better land, access to irrigation channels etc. (Barth, 1959a, p.108). The implications for agnatic rivalry are examined in the last section of this chapter.

V   permanent settlement also removed a certain mystifying of Yusufzai descent groups and their inviolable claims to the land. The growth of class distinctiveness or awareness may be dated from this event. The Yusufzai Pukhtun is no longer a mythical military figure inherently superior and ordained by descent to rule the land. He becomes a landlord going about the business of increasing agricultural produce and has to come to terms with the tillers of the soil and resolve the problem of 'how to make himself indispensable to the villagers' (ibid., p. 69).

VI   most important of all, a permanent settlement over time meant a growing density of segmentary sub-divisions

as population pressure increased on fixed areas of land
and created problems of inheritance and fragmentation of
plots. Alternative choices were limited: migration, conflict (agnatic rivalry) or further and increased subdivi-
sion of land and falling of the standard of living. The
latter explains the numerous epigonic Yusufzai who own
bits and pieces of land: 'the majority of Pakhtuns are a
sort of yeomanry with only small holdings' (ibid., p.44).
The very existence of this 'yeomanry' in turn suggests
that 'wesh' ceased some considerable time ago. These
crofters form a separate category from the big Khans who
own vast estates, with client tenants cultivating them,
and are in a position to contract tenants in numbers and
convert these into political following. The Pathan yeomanry play a significant role in the growth of class consciousness and class conflict (Asad, 1972).

ALLIANCES, NETWORKS AND GROUPS

The Wali of Swat has described a two-bloc system of alliances in pre-State Swat which is easily recognized in
Barth's analysis:
   In Swat each of the several regions like Babozai
   Shamozai, etc, has two parties, invariably at variance
   with each other. They are headed by two prominent
   Khans of the area. Both these Khans guard the material
   and political interests of their respective parties.
   Whenever a grave situation arises, a meeting of the
   party-members is held in which a decision is arrived at
   by unanimous consent. Members assemble in the 'hujra'
   of the Khans both for consultation and discussion. But
   conditions have undergone considerable change lately.
   Since the establishment of 'Tehsils' and courts of justice parties seldom engage in bloody affrays and all
   controversies are adjudged in courts peacefully
   (Miangul, 1962, p.15).
The Swat bloc alliances and rivalry have been analysed
as 'a divergent case' in anthropology as 'a political
system in which ramifying patrilineal descent is of prominent importance in politics, yet where larger lineage
groups do not emerge as corporate units' (Barth, 1959b, p.
5). What is of interest as a deviant case in the traditional anthropological fusion/fission lineage models is
that
   in a meeting of a council of a wide area, there is not
   the fusion of interests of smaller, related segments of
   a minor council vis-à-vis larger segments which one
   would expect in a lineage system, and which is

exemplified in the above citations from Evans-Pritchard
(Fortes and Evans-Pritchard, 1940, p.4). On the contrary, the opposition between small, closely related
segments persists in the wider context, and these segments unite with similar small segments in a pattern of
two-party opposition, not in a merging series of descent segments (Barth, 1959b, p.9).

This explains 'how the blocs are formed, their political functions, and the way in which certain structural
features of the territorial and descent frameworks are reflected in their composition' (Barth, 1959a, pp.104-5).
The political alliances and networks which crystallize in
Swat into 'two-blocs' are not seen as

a unique situation. A two-bloc alliance system of
named alliances, 'Gar' and 'Samil', is characteristic
of southern Pathans as well (Wylly, 1912), though in
this case the lineage segments which form the units of
the blocs are slightly larger. A corresponding division into two factions, the 'Hinawi' and 'Ghafari',
runs all through Southern Arabia (e.g. Thomas, 1929, p.
98) (Barth, 1959b, p.19).

This dual bloc system is also found in Mansehra Tehsil,
which adjoins Swat, and is largely inhabited by tribes
claiming Swati descent as a result of mass migration following the Yusufzai conquests in the sixteenth century.
These tribes maintain their ethnicity and memory of Swat
by calling themselves Swatis (Ahmed, 1974). Segmentary
groups confront each other in an opposition that divide
alliances on all levels in Mansehra and finds expression
in the two major blocs: the Swatis and the Khan Khels.
But these alliances are neither permanent nor completely
transitive and they do not form any fixed pattern along
pre-determined segmentary lineages. Alliances and links
are established in addition to the segmentary alignment
and may cut across the segmentary structure. This is
paramount in understanding the Swat structure and for
Barth's analysis of it.

What is of key importance to the 'transactionalist'
framework is that

political solidarity between equals is not an implicit
aspect of any other relationship, such as common descent or kinship, common membership in a congregation,
territorial propinquity, etc. It is a separate subject
of contractual agreement and thus of free individual
choice (Barth, 1959a, p.105).

Political choice is therefore free and based on a calcula-
tion to enhance or maximize chances in life, as 'all relationships implying dominance are dyadic relationships of a
contractual or voluntary nature' (ibid., p.3). Swat man

is therefore able to order his life in accordance with the
strategy of maximizing 'profit'. He is 'maximizing'
'manipulating' or 'strategizing' man.

The emphasis on the dyadic, contractual nature of relationships between the Khan and his followers brings out,
paradoxically, the element maintaining stability (and a
semblance of the concept of equality) in Pukhtun social
life. Assuming for the moment that the Khan-peasant or
patron-client relationship is symmetrical and of equal and
mutual reciprocal interest, then neither the patron Khan
nor his tenant client can afford to shift loyalties too
frequently. In a closed 'face to face' society reputa-
tions travel and the value of a fickle client would not be
high in the new patron's eyes or, conversely, the value of
an unreliable patron. Therefore this factor operates as a
built-in mechanism in the social system to maintain stability and balance.

Unlike patrons elsewhere, for instance in Sicily, where
patron-client relationships are disguised in the local
cultural idiom of godfather and godson, (6) the Khan's
patronage is a visible manifestation of the inescapable
facts of economic bondage backed by 'coercive authority'.
This carries a potential conflict situation which may even
exist underneath the facade of 'hujra' solidarity and stability. The 'hujra' merely acts as a social 'integrative
mechanism' and provides a safety-valve to release patron-
client tensions and establish a focal point of social
communication.

The Khan's links in the network connecting him with the
bigger landlords reinforce his reputation as having access
to the higher reaches of the alliance or bloc while his
links with the numerous clients who assemble at the
'hujra' display his political strength and their loyalty.
The blocs and alliances of the Khans are to be seen not as
permanent corporate groups based on unilineal descent operating within a territorial boundary but as 'networks' or
'enduring quasi-groups' mobilized for immediate political
ends(Boissevain, 1968, 1974; Mayer, 1966). Such networks
are therefore temporary and take direction from available
political strategy and choices and may cut across segment
and tribal boundaries or class and 'caste' loyalties. As
a result 'these very prominent leaders, by spreading their
net of alliances very wide, thus create some degree of
consistency in the alignment of local blocs in opposition'
(Barth, 1959a, p.124).

However, what is not satisfactorily illuminated is that
patron-client relationships implying dominance in Swat are
not entirely of a symmetrical order: they involve superordinate and subordinate positions. A client, in theory,

may have choices and strategies open to him but in practice, depending as he does for his land tenancy, 'hujra'
membership and a measure of protection on the Khan, would
find it difficult to break the contract unilaterally.   In
a 'post-wesh' and stratified feudal society the client,
tenant or peasant could have little room for maximizing
manoeuvres and 'choices in terms of private advantage and
a personal political career' (ibid., p.2).   Reciprocity in
this situation assumes an asymmetrical nature and the
power to determine the value of the transaction and the
choices of strategy open to the client partly depend on
the patron Khan.   The aid of a criticism relevant to this
very point is sought:

> the startling conclusion is that Barth neglects power
> as a variable of exchange. A.P. Cohen (personal com-
> munication) makes a succinct summary of this issue.
> Power is critical, he says, because it is manifest in
> the status relationships in which the posited transac-
> tion is made, and because it determines the value for
> the items exchanged. It is true, continues Cohen, that
> power may be mediated by a transaction, but this pos-
> sible function limits the range of transactions that
> can be made and the powerful can better use transaction
> as a resource (Paine, 1974, p.7).

'TARBOORWALI': AGNATIC RIVALRY

A vital aspect of Pathan social organization and political
behaviour is based on the determinate role, markedly peculiar to Pathan society, played by the male agnate ascendants and descendants in the life of ego. This is brought
out by a lucid Barthian analysis that relates agnatic
rivalry to 'wesh' and in turn to political alliances. Opposition of male siblings and cousins is a common Islamic
phenomenon based on agnatic jealousy and rivalry for inheritance (Coulson, 1971; Peters, 1960, p.45). This is
not a unique Islamic feature and is found in other societies as well, for example, it is the equivalent of the
Rajput (7) 'bhai shatru' 'your brother is your enemy'.
    Islamic tribal societies dramatize agnatic rivalry due
to problems of leadership and inheritance of land. Pathan
tribal society has codified 'cousin rivalry' and numerous
acts of normative behaviour may be understood in this
light. 'Tarboor' or cousin (i.e. father's brother's son),
commonly carries a meaning of enmity, as the popular proverb quoted above avers and male agnatic rivalry is embodied in 'tarboorwali', or the code of the cousin.
    'Tarboorwali' is an important characteristic of Pathan

social organization and is succinctly summed up by Barth:

> Such particular cultural factors combine to place close
> agnatic collaterals in a perpetual relation of opposi-
> tion and rivalry. This negative charge on their struc-
> tural relationship is clearly recognized in Yusufzai
> Pathan kinship terminology. Sibling terms are extended
> to the children of all these persons, except to the
> children of Father's Brother, own or classificatory
> (tre), for whom there is a special term ('tarbur').
> Patrilateral parallel cousin is uniquely separated from
> all other cousins and siblings by a separate term.
> Furthermore, this term carries the subsidiary connota-
> tion of 'enemy' (cf. Morgenstierne, 1927). Only those
> collaterals with whom one has unfriendly relations are
> freely referred to as 'tarburan', father's brother's
> sons (Barth, 1959b, p.11).

Marriage and affinal ties would hope to defuse agnatic
tension but marriage patterns do not give preference to
cousins:

> In contrast to what is found in some other lineage-
> based societies in the Middle East (e.g. Barth, 1953),
> marriages are rarely sought with close agnatic collate-
> rals. Several Pathan chiefs volunteered reasons for
> this: - Fa Br Da marriage, they said, is known as a
> device for preventing conflict between agnatic cousins,
> but it is never very successful. It is better to use
> the marriage of daughters and sisters to establish con-
> tacts or reaffirm alliances with persons of similar
> political interests to one's own; then one will be
> strong in the inevitable conflicts with close agnates
> (Barth, 1959a, p.40).

'Wesh' exacerbates the tension between agnates for 'a
re-examination of the land tenure system shows that owners
of neighbouring fields and collateral agnates tend to be
the same individuals. The traditional re-allotments followed the segmentary scheme of unilineal descent' (ibid.,
p.108). The dilemma of the Swat Pathan is acute:

> In the patrilineal descent system, the Pathan 'ego' is
> thus faced with a profound dilemma: the bonds between
> brothers and the bonds between fathers and sons are
> given political primacy; yet an organization based on
> these principles would unite 'ego' with his close agna-
> tic collaterals, who for reasons elaborated below are
> his prime opponents. The political dual division deve-
> lops as a direct result of the choices that individuals
> make in seeking a solution to this dilemma, and the
> political organization can thus be understood only in
> terms of the structure of the unilineal descent system
> (Barth, 1959b, p.7).

This chapter has delineated the major features of
social organization in Yusufzai Swat derived from Barth's
analysis. The central feature is of Yusufzai status expressed through almost exclusive rights to ownership of
land, endogamy and occupational hierarchy. Historical
tradition and geographical isolation reinforce the mystification of Yusufzai ascendancy. Territorial divisions
correspond with segmentary descent groups and a compulsory
interchange of land among the Yusufzai after fixed inter-
vals ensures equality. 'Wesh', or the periodic redistribution of land, is better understood conceptually as there
remains a certain measure of uncertainty regarding its im-
plementation and organization. The freezing of the 'wesh'
system would involve permanent settlement, fixed boundaries, possibility of alienation of land and a different
category of feudal landlord-peasant relationships.

Based on the struggle for land are the political alliances, networks and groups which are largely dyadic contractual and temporary. Such relationships are symmetrical, implying reciprocity. Group alliances seldom join or
reflect the larger bloc politics of the lineage system and
maintain opposition on their own levels, marked by bitter
agnatic rivalry which is exacerbated by 'wesh': 'Thus at
every periodic reallotment, the opposition of close agnatic collaterals is dramatized and made acute, while the
opposition between segments of higher levels is routinized
and involves no particular conflicts' (ibid., p.11).

4 The Swat Pathan misunderstood

چه نن سپک شی صبا ورک شی

Who today is disgraced, tomorrow will be lost

CONCEPTS, TERMS AND USAGE

Traditional functionalist schemata differentiate tribal
categories between two polar types (Fortes and Evans-
Pritchard, 1940): Group A containing organized, centralized tribal states backed by force (like the Zulu and
Ngwato) and contrasting with tribes in Group B which are
acephalous and organized along the principle of the segmentary lineage system (like the Nuer and Tallensi). The
Zulu Induna or chief was usually of royal descent, heredi-
tary and powerful in contrast to the chiefs in Group B
where the attitude to chiefship is summed up in the Tale
saying that 'chiefship belongs to all of us' (ibid., p.
256; Fortes, 1945, 1949). Between the acephaly of the
Nuer (or Tiv - Bohannan, 1955, 1957, 1968) and the mon-
archy of the Zulu (or the Nupe - Nadel, 1942) and as an
intermediary between Group A and B, Southall sees the political system of the Alur in East Africa which he calls
the 'segmentary state' (Southall, 1953).
    Barth's analysis of Swat rests on the assumption that
Yusufzai tribal society is of the acephalous, 'stateless'
Group B category (or as is shown in the next chapter of
the 'nang' Pathan type). This assumption is only partly
true. Although there is no centralized authority (until
1926) the Yusufzai social organization of Swat is in
itself a ranked and hierarchical social order based on
occupational and ethnic strata. The picture that emerges
is not of a segmentary and stateless society of the Nuer
type. Important conceptual and morphological differences

exist and a drawing up of a comparative checklist, which
ought not to be taken as a suggestion that Barth equates
the Swat Pathan to the Nuer, would bring them into relief.
For instance, a segmentary, acephalous and stateless
tribal society comprises several connected elements:

I   it contains an intrinsic philosophy of 'internal'
social cohesion reinforced and maintained by the presence
or potential of hostile 'external' agencies.

II   the tribe is culturally and racially homogeneous with
very slight and bridgeable differentiations within its
socio-political organization. Although affiliated para-
site pariah people often attach themselves alongside the
main tribe and provide a symbiotic relationship they
remain outside the lineage and phyletic boundaries.

III   the tribe reckons unilineal descent through a common
and recognized ancestor.

IV   the tribe is structured as an identifiable homologue
of its larger (and smaller) segments; what Gellner refers
to as 'monadism': primary, secondary and tertiary segmentary groups mirror each other's structures. 'The smaller
group is an embryo tribe, the tribe is the smaller group
writ large' (Gellner, 1969a, p.48).

V   the economy is mainly pastoral and primitive and functions largely on a 'reciprocal' basis. Modes of production are primitive and a response to the needs of the
immediate tribal unit.

VI   there is a patterned correspondence between territorial division and lineage segmentation and membership of
the tribes is defined in terms of filiation in this order.

VII   tendency to 'fusion' and 'fission' of segmentary
groups explains alliances and political interaction. Opposed groups on a similar level join to confront a larger
group.

VIII   the social system, defined through the segmentary
groups of the lineage charter,is wider and more dominant
than the religious and political systems which it inter-
penetrates and cuts across.

IX   and, of course, the structure prevents the growth of
a central authority of any type. 'Fusing' groups split up
into their own segmentary groups after the tribal crisis
that brought them together has been dealt with. Chiefs,
as for instance the Nuer 'leopard-skin chiefs', exist only
to mediate and consult. There is a recognized ceiling to
their authority and a conspicuous absence of 'coercive
authority' behind them.

Taking Barth's Swat model of Yusufzai tribal society,
after unambiguously excluding the Wali from it, to make a
point by point comparison with the above characteristics
major conceptual and irreconcilable differences are
observed:

I 'internal' social cohesion is maintained through the visible presence or use of coercive force. 'External' pressures only widen and alter the existing bloc alliances (Khans from Dir or Bajaur exploit internal Swat conflicts to attack or annex parts of Swat, often with the assistance of Yusufzai Khans and ostensibly to help them). Social cohesion for the non-Yusufzai carries an 'old flavour of insecurity, military occupation and temporary exploitation' (Barth, 1959a, p.68).

II an occupational hierarchy of numerous strata, almost a 'caste' system of heterogeneous ethnic and functional groups, is dominated by a feudal military aristocracy in Swat. This stratification is not entirely along ethnic lines as non-Pukhtuns may move up through acquisition of land or merit.

III although the Yusufzai Pukhtuns claim descent from a distant and near-mythical ancestor, Yusuf, the vast majority of the non-Yusufzai population including the autochthones, have no such equivalent descent pretensions or genealogical memory.

IV the endogamous caste-like strata in Swat do not exist in any wider relation to Pukhtun society in general; smaller groups mirror the fortunes of their Khans and not a wider tribal picture.

V the economy is 'redistributional' and functions around a central point which first gathers in and upwards goods and services, and then re-allocates them downwards to several points.

VI a degree of correspondence between territorial division and lineage segmentation survives as a result of 'wesh' and the periodical re-settlement assures constant shifting of the Khan within a certain territorial and lineage framework.

VII 'fusion' and 'fission' are mainly a political function of power blocs and changing strategies of personal choice. Close collateral segments confronting each other do not 'fuse' in the face of a larger challenge but continue to oppose each other within larger blocs, and illustrate a deviant case from the traditional functionalist 'fusion/fission' model (Barth, 1959b, p.19).

VIII the political system dominates all aspects of Pathan Swat society.

IX though Swat is a 'stateless society' with no central authority (except for the brief ineffectual period in the middle of the last century when the Akhund of Swat had helped elect a King), powerful Khans hold complete sway over their own territories.

Clearly, the sum-total of the Swat picture is not of an acephalous, segmentary society of the Nuer or Group B

type;   nor, in fact, is it of the Zulu or Group A type.
The conceptualization of Swat tribal organization as a
'segmentary acephalous system' (Barth, 1959a, p.134)
leaves Barth's definitions and their employment open to
comment and reexamination.

A comparison of an African tribal kingdom, like the
Shilluk, with the Walidom of Swat may help to contrast the
formal, functional and ritual aspects of the two and to
bring out the differences in socio-political organization
within which they operated and which they, in turn,
ordered:

SHILLUKDOM (1)	WALIDOM
I The King is 'divine', he is a religious figure symbolizing mystical properties, and providing a symbol of unity to the Shilluk. He is descended from generations of kings (thirty-one, starting from the common-ancestor of the tribe and their kings, Nyikang, who is the medium between God and man).	Spiritual and temporal power buttressed and supported by the army and state apparatus. No divine property attached to the Wali except as descendant of the near-mythical Akhund. The royal genealogical line is not deep (it ends with the great-grandson of the Akhund).
II The King (in his person) and the kingship (in the office) symbolize Shillukdom for both the main tribe and their client tribes. The King's frailties are believed to cause natural disasters.	The Wali does not symbolize either the Yusufzai Pukhtun or Swat. He is, however, accepted as a prominent and religious leader by the majority of both.
III The King has little control over secular matters arising from disputes over lands, crimes etc. as his main role is sacerdotal. Chiefs and heads of lineages (often one and the same thing) are not appointed by the King, although he confirms them.	The Wali, through the State bureaucracy and army, exercises complete control and appointments of any importance are made by him.
IV The kingship is circulated (although recently fixed) as is the capital.	Both Waliship, based on primogeniture, and the State capital are fixed.

From the above it is clear that the nature of the Wali's role is quite different to that of the traditional and symbolic role of the Shilluk King. The former rules a highly centralized State and backs his authority with a vast and visible 'coercive authority'. The Shilluk King, in contrast, rules his tribal society from afar and his physical presence is epiphenomenal to his spiritual and symbolic role. The latter, embodied in Nyikang and inherent in all his descendants, is of overriding tribal importance. The Wali manipulates and uses his spiritual charisma inherited from his grandfather, the Akhund, but has to fight a series of internecine dynastic battles to establish the Walidom and the State.

Certain conceptual problems, which will be discussed in the next section, arise as a result of labelling all Sayyeds, 'Mians', 'pirs' and 'faqirs' as Saints ('for simplicity in exposition I shall apply the term Saint to all persons occupying holy status, whether prominent or not' - Barth, 1959a, p.57).

Categorizing Mians and Sayyeds as 'Saints' in a Pathan society raises conceptual and heuristic problems. It is almost as misleading as categorizing all Oxbridge graduates as 'Lords' because some do become so. These stereotypes are not as fanciful as the above example might suggest: rural people on the Indian subcontinent are only now realizing that the once omnipotent 'mai-baap' ('mother-father') figures of the British Raj do not survive in the new generation of hippies and students who visit them. Mians and Sayyeds are no more Saints than Oxbridge men are Lords; both are merely candidates. But then, theoretically, every Pathan Muslim can aspire to Sainthood as can every Englishman to a title. A Saint has different and specific overriding attributes.

Similarly, a caveat is to be added when equating 'Khan' to 'chief' (ibid., p.73). Even if employed for sociological analysis this may prove confusing or misleading as this appellation is universally used by Pathans to define themselves. Non-Pathans generally use the word Khan as almost synonomous to Pathan and as an ethnic category. However, in common parlance there is a nuance to the usage which indicates a big man or petty chief of an area: 'the Khan of so and so area'.

The use of the concept of 'caste' with its ramifying social implications, in any sociological analysis of non-Hindu communities on the Indian subcontinent, requires some care, however 'structural the criteria' and whatever the distinctions from the 'Hindu philosophic scheme' (Barth, 1971). On the subcontinent it is a value-loaded concept with definite and fixed religious-cultural

connotations. (2) 'Caste' implies as its operating interconnected features:
 I   opposition of 'purity' and 'impurity' which subsume
(a) ritual categories and (b) strict observance of commen-
sal rules.
 II occupational categories and
 III endogamy maintaining and underlining hierarchical
Hindu socio-religious stratification.
    The Swat Yusufzai hierarchy, although formidably rigid
in appearance (Barth, 1959a, p.17) was always open to
social mobility through channels of marriage, money, conquest and religious reputation. Indeed, within an ideological framework of Islam which claims equality for its
believers no stratification can be permanent or rigid.
For example, the Akhund 'descended from a subject ethnic
group in Bajaur and himself a goatherd' (ibid., p.100)
married into the aristocratic Nikbi Khel section of the
Yusufzai (Caroe, 1965, pp.362-3). (3) Another observed
social mechanism for mobility is the process of 'Pathani-
zation'. An instance of this and of mass upward mobility
is that of the descendants of the carpenter group, the
Jambal Khel 'who some 200 years ago so distinguished themselves in war that they were given land and Pakhtun
status' (Barth, 1959a, p.27). Of the 476 marriages based
on statistics gathered from four villages 60 per cent were
'caste' endogamous (ibid., p.20). Kin endogamy may be
valued but statistically shows a low rate of frequency.
(4) The 60 per cent figure is not surprising when considering lack of communication and occupational status
that act as factors reinforcing endogamy in rural areas.
What is significant is that in spite of all these factors
some 40 per cent of marriages were hypo or hyper-gamous
and exogamous to 'caste'. Rural marriages, in agricultural, whether tribal or peasant, societies, in any case
usually take place within 'the kindred of cooperation'
(Mayer, 1960). A 60 per cent figure for endogamy is not
conclusively high especially keeping in mind Muslim preference for parallel cousin marriage. More convincing are
the figures for the Kurds where tribal endogamy was as
high as 80 per cent (Barth, 1953, p.68) although the
sample size of 21 was small.

SUFIS, SAINTS AND KHANS

Division of Islamic society into 'warriors' and 'priests'
or men of God is a common feature in the sociology of
Islam. The nomad and pastoral Somali are thus divided:
    In the north especially there is a very clear-cut ideal

distinction between the spiritual and secular order
which assumes concrete expression in the division which
is made between 'men of God' ('wadaad', the Somali
equivalent of the Arabic Shaikh) and 'men of the spear'
or 'warriors' ('waranleh') (Lewis, 1969, p.263).
Empirically, however, this division is rarely sustained
and its boundaries constantly crossed and recrossed:

> In reality, all men - men of God included, however re-
> luctantly - remain finally subject to the bonds of
> common dia-paying group allegiance which afford the
> only sure source of security for person and property.
> In practice therefore, while the distinction between
> the two orders is theoretically maintained and is but-
> tressed by the mystical power which is generally attri-
> buted to priests, the pastoral social system is in
> effect all-pervasive (ibid.).

Therefore for Barth to equate 'religious men' to Saints
(while discussing the role of the latter in opposition to
the Khans) has important ramifications in the Swat analysis. An understanding of the Pathan's apperception of his
religion, and his own role in it, is essential to understand the relationship between the 'Saint' and the Khan.

Sociologically, this relationship derives from two features peculiar to Pathan social organization, one with a
genealogical and the other with a geographical foundation:
I Pathans are notably unequivocal about the purity and
depth of their religious genealogy. Descent is claimed
from the putative ancestor Qais bin Rashid who was converted to Islam by the Prophet himself. The social significance of this religious belief is of utmost importance in
understanding Pathan tribal societies. Each individual
identifies with a line of unilineal descent that takes him
to the very foundation of Islam. He is aware that he
carries Islam atavistically and is no recent convert to it
as a result of conquest or commerce. The 'mullah' or
'Mian' must constantly prove his spiritual worth if he is
to achieve status or be given respect. This is borne out
by examples showing typical attitudes to 'pirs' (Barth,
1959a, p.100n). Pathan tribes are not anthropolatrous
like the Berbers of the Atlas and their Saints, for instance. Their enthusiastically orthodox Islam allows reverence to the holy but inhibits the growth of an established Saint class. The behaviour of the Saint, for example, of Tetuan (5) (Turner, 1974, p.68) would result in
the rapid death of the Saint and his partner.

The Pathan is susceptible to Islamic symbols such as
'jihad', religious wars, and quick to respond to them, but
his 'ideal-leader' combines both a spiritual and temporal
authority. He cannot compartmentalize the two

conceptually. It makes the establishment of a regular 'priest' or 'Saint' status difficult if unsupported by non-religious sanctions or constant visible proof of religiosity. The prototype of the Pathan leader is Ahmed Shah Abdali: Sufi by temperament, warrior-king by profession and Muslim by definition.

II The other important factor in understanding the inhibition to the establishment of a regular priesthood in Pathan areas, within the context of the Indian subcontinent, is the absence of large non-Muslim groups in juxtaposition or opposition to Pathan groups. The Pathan, not faced with religious threat, had no need to adopt a defensive posture against a non-Muslim presence. He, in short, needed a priest only for social 'rites de passage'.

In a society where there is no formal priesthood the lines dividing the secular and the religious are often so thin as to be indiscernible. Once the holy or religious man enters the political game he is subjected to the same rough and tumble that the other players encounter. No holds are then barred. The fate of Sayyed Ahmed Barelvi, who ruled Peshawar in 1830, and was soon deserted by his tribal followers and killed within a year, is a stereotype of Pathan tribal reaction to a continuing assumption of political power by a 'Saint'. This is also evident in the tribulations that faced the agnatic descendants of the Akhund in their attempts to establish political supremacy in Swat. In this context the illustrations given from the life of Nalkot Pacha who told Barth 'of the dilemma of choice, at critical moments in his career, between arms and the white turban, and even of the quick change from one to the other in the middle of battle' (Barth, 1959a, p.59) are quite clear. The Pacha is a Sayyed (hence Pacha) but when he enters active politics he is no longer immune to the rules of the Swat power game as applied to all its participants. The switching to arms from the white turban is not clear unless it is for the relative security of a battle head-dress; otherwise it carries little symbolic significance in war.

To place the 'Saint' and Khan on the same level of politics (ibid., p.4) distorts the political perspective of local socio-political interaction. Religious leaders, whether 'mullahs' or Saints, only emerge as natural leaders in times of great religious crises and usually against non-Islamic forces (as will be seen in chapters 6 and 7). Otherwise the 'mullah's' role is institutional, functional and humdrum. He runs the village mosque, teaches children and conducts village ritual. He may be respected but is rarely held in awe: 'One of the favourite derogatory jeers of Swat Pathans is "you wife of a mullah"' (ibid., p.47). Although placed outside the Saint category the 'mullah' may enter it:

> if a 'mullah' successfully assumes the role of a spiritual leader, making his religious and moral teaching relevant to the social problems of his day, he may come to be regarded as a Saint (usually labelled as 'faqir' in its strict meaning of a dedicated property-less man,) and his descendants will be classed as the descendants of a Saint (ibid., p.57).

The 'Mian' or (Barthian) Saint in tribal society fulfils the functional role of neutral buffer in the absence of a central adjudicating authority between 'sub-tribes in friction'. (6)   It is important to note that all religious individuals or groups are directly dependent on the good will of the tribal village council, the 'jirga',and in a socially stratified village on the Khan. It is significant that these religious people are not allowed a voice in the 'jirga'. The social development of the 'hujra' in Pukhtun society created a structural balance with the village mosque. In the Punjab, for instance, where there are no 'hujras', the mosque remains the important village socio-political focus and forum. In Pukhtun areas the 'hujra' provides the platform for political manoeuvre and tests of strength.

Chapter 7 will show the emergence of 'mullahs' (along with categories of Barthian 'Saints') as charismatic leaders, during the numerous tribal revolts in 1897 in the Frontier areas. These leaders will be seen to arise out of nowhere expressing an Islamic response to a non-Islamic threat, giving identity to a moment of social history, having 'temporarily achieved control of very large groups' (ibid., p.61), and then disappearing like bubbles. The emphasis is on the ephemeral nature of the following and the leadership.

It is difficult to conceptualize either 'mullahs' or even the local 'Mians' sustaining political authority over time unless, like the Khan, they base it on acquisition of irrigated land and incorporation into the feudal élite; 'Hence the political interests of a Saint, as well as his power to exert political influence, increase as his landed property increases. A Saint may obtain land by inheritance, gift, purchase or conquest' (ibid., p.93). This picture almost removes the thin dividing line between Barthian Saint and Barthian Khan. The words of the prominent Saint, 'I look like a simple man; I live simply - but oh! the things I do!' (ibid., p.98) could have been uttered by a Khan. Similarly, Nalkot Pacha whistling to his men to declare themselves and thereby out-manoeuvering his opponents provides an example of a quick-witted

leader. The Saint's argument is useless without his guns.
This is the crucial fact of the argument and bound to
cause confusion and be misunderstood if the concept of
Saint is used. Nalkot Pacha (Barthian Saint) appears to
be a priestly Khan, or a very laic 'Saint'. Partly because he equates the Wali to a Saint, and partly because
Pukhtun chiefs and Saints 'are active as political pretenders', Barth analyses Yusufzai politics as shifting from
Saint to Khan, and vice versa, on all levels of socio-
political interaction: 'the establishment of a state
ruled by a Saint in one part of the valley, and the expan-
sion of the formerly small Khanate of Dir, ruled by a
Pakhtun chief, into another part' (ibid., pp.134-5). The
proposition of power oscillating between Khans and Saints
over Pathan socio-political history is not a valid
hypothesis.

Professor Barth's inflation of the Saint's role and influence in Pathan society can only be traced to his using
the Akhund and the Wali as models for the Saint category.
This is obvious in his dealing both with the Akhund and
the Wali as 'Saints' rather than as extraordinary and charismatic leaders transcending religious and political
loyalties and symbolizing supra-tribal unity. The Akhund
is equated to a Saint, as the term is used in the accounts
of his career (ibid., p.60). Miangul Wadud is also so
equated: 'The Badshah of Swat, himself a Saint...' and
'The more prominent Saints are generally active in a
larger area. Thus Miangul Abdul Wahdood, later Badshah of
Swat...' (ibid., p.102).

What is unique in Pukhtun tribal history is that a religious leader established a formal and centralized State.
He did so not only backed by spiritual sanction but also
by a combination of political factors and considerable inherited material property. Both the creation of the State
of Swat and its religious origins are a unique phenomenon
in Pathan history. What deserves to be underlined is that
Miangul Wadud became Wali of Swat not because he was a religious leader but in spite of being one.

Leadership in Swat society has been divided into Khans
and Saints. Had Barth further sub-divided the category of
religious leaders into the orthodox ('mullahs', 'Sayyeds',
'Mians') and the unorthodox ('Sufis', like the Akhund) in-
stead of eliminating the latter from his analysis the problem would not have arisen; as it stands important ramifying sociological consequences are overlooked. Whereas
the orthodox 'mullah' (and also 'Barthian Saints') work
within the village social organization, and in practice
with the good will of the Khan, the Sufi works outside the
village organization and established normative patterns of

social behaviour. Sufis often chose to ignore the orthodox expressions of religion whereas the Saints interpret
them. A tripartite division of mankind was advocated by
the great eleventh-century Indian Sufi, Ali al-Hujwiri:
the worldly-'ahl-dunya' (Barthian Khans), the religious-
'ahl-din' (Barthian Saints and including 'mullahs') and
finally the 'special ones' - 'ahl-khususiyyat' (Sufis and
mystics). It is the last category that is conspicuous by
its absence in Barthian analysis.

The importance of Sufic development and interaction in
Pathan (and Islamic areas) will be discussed in later
chapters. The Sufic base to saintly power provided by the
Akhund is vital in an understanding of subsequent developments in Swat. The Akhund's male descendants formed a separate social category from those mentioned in 'Political
Leadership among Swat Pathans' (ibid., p.57) under the
general title 'Miangul': thus Miangul Abdul Wadud. This
does not, of course, imply that all the Miangul are Sufis.
The general usage of Sufi has to be guarded as this essay
does not wish to leave itself open to the charges made
against Idries Shah, a renowned Sufi writer and master
(which are similar in content to those made against
Barth's liberal use of 'Saint'): 'One of his most misleading practices is indiscriminately to label every Islamic poet, personality, religious movement, as "Sufi", a
habit that leads him, for instance, to describe Omar
Khayyam, the Yazidis, and the Isma'ilis all by the same
term' (Elwell-Sutton, 1975, p.13).

The conclusion of Turner's chapter, 'Saint and Sheikh',
in his book on 'Weber and Islam' may be quoted to sum up
this section:

In this discussion of maraboutic institutions, I have
tried to show that, given the specific sociological
nature of Islam and its cultural traditions, Islam did
not and could not have social roles corresponding to
the Christian saints, Sheikhs, yes; saints no (Turner,
1974, p.71).

'TRANSACTIONALISM' AND THE CODE OF THE PATHANS

The underlying theme of Pathan society is maintenance by
all means and at all levels of its code of life, the
'Pukhtunwali': 'The value orientations on which it (the
Pukhtun code) is based emphasize male autonomy and egali-
ty, self-expression and aggressiveness in a syndrome which
might be summarized under the concept of honour ("izzat")'
(Barth, 1969, p.120). Four typical examples of this are
given, under the title, Cases Relating to Blood Revenge,

in the Appendix to 'Political Leadership among Swat
Pathans'.

The code rests on various 'ideal-type' approximates
found in varying degrees of practice (perhaps, nearest to
pure forms in the more remote Tribal Areas for reasons
discussed in chapter 5). The code sets up ideal standards
of behaviour and acts as a constant yardstick to measure
normative or deviant behaviour. In the Tribal Areas the
code would be more visible than in a feudal situation like
Swat, none the less even the most rapacious Khan would
heed it and derive his symbols of ethnicity from it and
measure the extent of his prestige by it. If Amir Nawab
is accused of killing 'forty-one men by his own hand'
(Barth, 1959a, p.125) he not only provides an unusual example (7) of mass homicide but also runs a very poor insurance risk. Pathans measure warrior-prestige or martial
status by valour or deaths in battle and not over quarrels
for land; and for every man killed the code demands com-
pensatory 'badal' or revenge. Amir Nawab would have to be
a very powerful man or migrate to a far-away land to survive for any length of time; and in point of fact he was
killed (ibid., p.126). 'Badal', in effect, acts as deterrent to any such homicidal tendency in Pathan society.

The Pukhtun is seen as building political power through
'melmastia' (hospitality) for 'only through hospitality,
through the device of gift-giving, does he create the
wider obligations and dependence which he can then draw
upon in the form of personal political support - in the
final resort, military support' (ibid., p.12). Intended
and unintended consequences that affect social structure
may follow:

Structural change is created through the actions of individuals.... The individual continually seizes the
opportunities thus presented to him, exploits them in
his own interest, and in so doing possibly changes the
structure of society in as much as he redefines some
norm of behaviour or creates a new status (Lloyd, 1971,
p.73).

To Barth 'this striking hospitality and reckless spend-
ing only seems intelligible if we recognize that the
underlying motives are political rather than economic'
(Barth, 1959a, p.12). The Swat Pathan is thus maximizing
power:

This use of maximization as a scientific strategy involves seeking out the norms or motives (or whatever
the investigator sees as the impetus of behaviour) and
attempting to rank order them so as to see the behaviour as the (conscious or unconscious) maximization
of these things (Cancian, 1966, pp.465-70).

An explanation of the code of hospitality and honour that
Pukhtuns pride themselves on simply in terms of maximizing
political power, is difficult to accept empirically. (8)
One of the conscious or unconscious motivations and results of excessive hospitality might well be political
power and 'hujras' are no doubt one mechanism for further-
ing such ends. 'Maximizing' tendencies among the Khans
are not to be discounted: on the contrary the Pashto proverb quoted above, 'the hen is a bird belonging to him who
seizes it', corroborates Barth's vision of Swat and Swat
politics. But this is only one of the aspects of Pathan
hospitality, and one of the interpretations of its usage.
Firstly, if 'political support' alone is the reason for
hospitality then this argument cannot be sustained in explaining the 'striking hospitality' of the ordinary Pukhtun villager to any passing stranger or foreigner. This
aspect of his code has passed into the mythology of Pukhtun society and history. Secondly, the concept of
'melmastia' relates to that of 'nanawatee' or the granting
of asylum to anyone, including an enemy, who seeks it.
Barth gives an undue political emphasis by relating this
basically cultural aspect of Pathan society to the political power struggle in Swat. It is not being debated that
central village institutions, like 'hujras', are not used
for political ends but that their function and emphasis is
not entirely political. They are at least as much a cultural phenomenon as a political one.

Hospitality is part of the larger consciousness of Islamic society and is embodied in popular maxims and
Quranic verses that exhort the believers to practise it.
Examples of this are numerous and may be cited from all
over the Islamic world. (9) Barth himself observes that
among the Basseri 'hospitality is an admired social
virtue ... though economically unwise' and 'politically
unprofitable'. In fact,

> The hospitable man is admired and people speak highly
> of him whether he is present or absent. Men seek his
> company and flock to his tent, though without impor-
> tunity. By their own standards, then, most Basseri are
> miserly; and a few glaring examples are held up for
> public ridicule. Thus one of the largest herd owners
> in the group is popularly known as D.D.T. Khan because,
> they say, he is such a miser he eats his own lice
> (Barth, 1968, pp.424-5).

One should rather see 'melmastia' in terms of another
Barthian concept, that of maintenance of cultural identity
and ethnic boundaries (Barth, 1969). Hospitality whether
in the 'hujra' or outside it becomes symbolic both of the
expression of political loyalty and of ethnic identity.

For hospitality whether individually or collectively expressed, is one of the major cognitive, tangible and cohe-
rent symbols of 'Pukhtunwali' to the Pathan. A Pukhtun
does or lives the Pukhtun code which enables him to be respected in the eyes of his fellow men. Hospitality is one
source of such respect. Thus legends glorify the Pukhtun
virtues of generosity and bravery on which rest honour,
'nang'. These are the major constituent elements of
'Pukhtunwali' or the code of the Pathan and they cannot be
interpreted in terms of 'political support' alone.

The Yusufzai Khan is, therefore, aware of the nuances
of his pivotal role in interpreting 'Pukhtunwali', which
in itself distinguishes Pathan from non-Pathan behaviour.
The Khan would play Game-Theory politics to a point.
Beyond a certain stage he would come up against the severe
constraints imposed by his cultural and religious codes.

If the Barthian landlords are busy 'seizing', 'attacking', 'manipulating' and 'ousting' they still represent
only the activities of a very small percentage of the
total population (Barth, 1959a, p.44). It is difficult to
envisage the small Pathan landlord or a peasant 'attacking' and 'seizing' with impunity. Certain examples of
Pathan behaviour can be understood mainly in terms of mystical Sufic behaviour as for instance, the Akhund's grand-
daughter, who spent her entire and long life fasting and
praying in a tiny mud hut by a Swat stream, where she died
a few years ago. Her parallel cousin, the Wali, failed to
persuade her to move to the State capital at Saidu. Although the surrounding villages called her 'Bandai Bibi'
(the Lady of the village) she neither provided them with
incantatory spells and charms nor attempted to elevate her
status to sainthood. Her stark material poverty cannot be
explained away in transactionalist terms by imputing Islamic 'strategy' to her behaviour in order to 'maximize'
spirituality. This aspect of Islamic behaviour is an important dimension that Barth has chosen to ignore; the
sincerity or motives that underlie it cannot be questioned
as it is to be seen and understood through the eyes of the
actor. The imposition of the transactionalist framework,
in toto, on the Swat Pathan lays Barth's work open to
charges of a form of academic ethnocentricism as has already been suggested in the Introduction. The Norwegian
entrepreneur embodying 'initiative' and 'expansive economic policy' (Barth, 1963) is barely disguised as the Swat
Pathan. Considerations of profit, choice and strategy
chart his social behaviour while attempts to exploit and
manipulate determine his relationships. The 'Pukhtunwali', and its immediate socio-cultural constraints, and
the larger Islamic socio-religious framework are therefore
reduced to epiphenomena.

LINEAGE AND STRATIFICATION IN SWAT

Lineage provides a birthright to land among the Yusufzai
in Swat. However, with the process of density of segmentation and corresponding scarcity of land a stratification
within the Yusufzai tribe is observed, which is distinct
from the main cleavage between Pathan landowners and non-
Pathans. This section explores the consequences of the
former development. 'To the sedentary villagers, whether
tenants, craftsmen, or others, the Pakhtun represents an
unnecessary imposition ... they know the fields and the
irrigation system better than the Pakhtuns' (Barth, 1959a,
pp.68-9). This statement is not clear in explaining how
the small landowner or crofter (as the vast majority of
Pukhtuns are - ibid., p.44) remained ignorant of the irrigation systems that fed their lands after living on them
for over four hundred years. Barth employs the argument
of the 'wesh' system, whereby land is periodically changed
among landowners. But it is historically unlikely that
the majority of small (two- or four-acre) Pukhtun landowners took part in the 'wesh' resettlement and no evidence to support it.
     The lack of a quantitative comparison of Pukhtun land-
owners with the Pukhtun non-landowners is a serious omission, (10) considering that land is fundamental to maintaining positions of superiority in Swat (and to playing
games based on economic dyadic alliances and manipulations). Dr Asad makes this point with structural and conceptual implications for Barth's Swat study and particularly for developments in post-Barth Swat in the 1960s
and 1970s (Asad, 1972). Barth's references are to landowners and non-landowners, but no systematic use is made
of the distinction between the big 'landlords' and the
small 'owner farmers':
     Of all Pakhtun landowners a very small proportion holds
     most of the land. So that the majority of landowners
     in Swat are small holders, and the remainder possess
     very large estates. In other words very few Pakhtuns
     are in a position to make the traditional economic con-
     tracts with agricultural tenants and labourers (ibid.,
     p.87).
The big Khans or landowners extracted as much as four-
fifths of gross produce from tenants (Barth, 1959a, p.11).
This is a high figure by any feudal standards and if even
partly applied to the 'poorer' Khans, who often cultivate
for 'richer' Khans but are aware of common Yusufzai
descent and therefore willing to stand up for their
rights, a direct conflict course may be set. These small
Pukhtun landowners are often in the vanguard of struggles

that suggest class conflict against the bigger landowners
in the 1960s and 1970s. The small Khans or landowners
find themselves in the 'wuge sari' (hungry men) category
(ibid., p.79), who not only lose land to the big Khan but
also their Pukhtun status (ibid., p.112). Barth notices
the growth of a poor non-landowning Pukhtun class

> In fact, the evidence indicates that in the present
> century the sloughing-off process has more than offset
> the natural growth of the Pakhtun population and that
> land has been progressively concentrated in fewer lines
> and fewer hands (ibid.),

but he fails to follow it up. These poor Pukhtuns slip
into the life pattern of the non-Pukhtun villagers. The
substantial difference in incomes between the big landlord
and the average villager is brought out by Barth himself
(ibid., p.79).

For purposes of this argument it is felt that perhaps
individual consent and dyadic links have been underlined
at the cost of analysing collective exploitation and class
structure. Dr Asad's reconsideration of Barth's Swat data
challenges the equilibrium model based on a landlord-class
maintaining social order in a classical functionalist
mould

> in fact the orderly social life and potential self-
> sufficiency of the non-landlords in contrast with the
> parasitic social existence of the landlords, suggests
> something else: that the total political activity of
> the landowning chiefs is simply the historical form
> through which class domination and exploitation find
> expression not the necessary basis for social order
> (Asad, 1972, pp.91-2).

The non-landowners in an age of the mass media and a
highly politicized environment no longer remain 'merely a
kind of sea of politically unorganized peasants and
craftsmen' (Barth, 1959a, p.69). Resentment is apparent:
'Thus I have heard Swati farmers abusing their Yusufzai
overlords and cursing the incompetence of their ancestors
in the decisive battles of the sixteenth century' (ibid.,
pp.24-5).

Force provides the historical base for landownership:
'Rights to land and the status of landowner are validated
among them by traditions of conquest, and the lineage organization of the Pakhtuns is intimately linked with conquest history' (ibid., p.25). Alliances, therefore,
cannot be rigid or permanent except if mutually beneficial
or maintained by force, 'the position of a leader is thus
never secure; his following may swell or shrink almost
without warning' (ibid., p.73). So what, apart from temporary 'dyadic contracts' and 'alliances', keeps the

50,000 inhabitants of Babuzai from revolting against their
1,000 Pathan rulers or the 20,000 inhabitants of Thana
against their 500 Pathan overlords? An obvious answer is
the 'exercise of coercive authority through the use or
possibility of use of physical force'. One form of coer-
cion was provided by the 'mercenaries' (11) the Khans
employed to maintain the political system and allow them
to dominate its blocs and alliances. This cannot be a
permanent or harmonious solution to 'maintenance or establishment of social order'. The failure to develop the
conflict analysis upsets the Barthian Swat model in the
1960s and 1970s where horizontal class alignments based on
political ideology and aspirations begin to replace vertical lines of traditional alignment.

THE WARLORDS AND THE WALI

The Yusufzai warlords of Swat played a 'zero-sum' game at
a certain macro-level of Malakand politics (ibid., p.128).
The nature of their game reflected their failure to
unite, and consequently their failure to prevent the Wali
from gaining ultimate ascendancy. In fact the Khans
played a secondary but crucial role in two critical contests involving the Wali: the first was the dynastic
battles between the agnatic descendants of the Akhund,
when Khans supported first one cousin, then another (Hay,
1934). Allegiance was constantly shifted to keep the balance of power in check: 'In an attempt to check the
power of the newly appointed head of Swat, Jamroz Khan of
Babuzai and most of his allies then shifted their allegiance to Shirin Sahib, the Badshah's brother and only remaining collateral' (Barth, 1959a, p.128). The Wali
clearly saw the game the Khans were playing

> lest Amir Badshah (the Wali's cousin) be held solely
> responsible for what ensued, I would affirm that he was
> merely a tool in the hands of those unscrupulous and
> self-interested Khans of Swat who were afraid of our
> being united again and, quite possibly, hindering them
> from their cruel practices (Miangul, 1962, p.12).

The second contest involved the wars of consolidation
and annexation that the new ruler of Swat launched after
1917 (Hay, 1934). The Wali, however, was fully aware of
the nature of Swat politics and social organization, and
his capacity to exploit this knowledge led him to succeed
where others, like the Khan of Dir, had failed. His military tactics were based on the classic tradition of
'divide et impera' which found a ready expression in the
two-bloc system already in existence in most parts of

Swat. He would invade an area only after allying with the
weaker bloc and thus 'tilt' the balance in his favour.
The 'zero-sum' game ceases when participants gain power
(or value) that permanently imbalances the possibility of
success for the other side. The Wali was already making
his own rules for the game.   After emerging from the
dynastic struggles and the border battles of consolidation
he turned to confront the problem of the Swat warlords.
The fragile peace, and his short rule, could have been
upset by a simple majority of Khans in a typical 'zero-
sum' combination. The solution had to be as permanent as
congruent with Swat socio-political organization.

Firstly, the Wali approached the problem of the Khans
in neo-populist and neo-reformist terms. The Khans were
seen as 'cruel' 'tyrants' and 'despots'. The pre-1917
era, before he became Badshah of Swat, was seen as 'the
Pakhtoon Period' of the 'despotic Khans' (Miangul, 1962, p.
27):

> To quote only one instance: once in the hilly tracts
> of a despotic Khan's property a fruit, being over-ripe,
> fell from the tree. A poor peasant, who was passing
> by, committed the fatal sin of eating this fallen
> fruit, for which unpardonable audacity he was punished
> with death.... Such tyrants had made life a source of
> continual worry and unbearable misery (ibid., pp.27-8).

Secondly, he symbolized a policy that carried the majority of the non-landowners and small Khans wanting peace
and stability in Swat with him:

> Every day that passed was a new life gained, no one
> could be sure of seeing the next day. And, strange
> enough, there was moral degeneration apparent in every
> walk of life: people had grown faithless and treacher-
> ous to a degree that none were trustworthy, all were
> abject slaves of power and authority. People worship-
> ped the rising sun, regardless of the honour of the
> family and the tribe or losing or gaining good-will and
> a good name. Mammon was the deity in vogue (ibid., p.
> 28).

The Wali moved swiftly to extract the teeth of the Khans
permanently by a series of ramifying 'reforms', among
them:

I   the Swat population was completely disarmed. Simultaneously, loyalist supporters were armed (ibid., p.109).

II   roads and telephones spread out ubiquitously in an
effective network to keep him informed of any possible
revolt; a well-equipped and large army stood ready to
deal with any emergency (Barth, 1959a, pp.129-32).

III   the economic base that provided both social identity
and political power to the Khans was drastically altered:

'wesh' was abolished and the land taxes that the Khans
took from their tenants were partly diverted to the State
in the form of 'ushar'. The sources of social mobility
and economic patronage, through administrative posts, the
ruler's favours etc. were demonstrably with the State
and no longer with the Khans. The Wali thus bypassed the
Khans to reach the vast number of non-landowners in a
direct relationship (see Diagram 3). Loyal Khans were rewarded while the rebellious ones were punished:

> but with the success of the Miangul they received their
> reward. Everywhere else he had caused forts and towers
> of local headmen to be razed to the ground, and had im-
> posed his own trusted servants to manage affairs and
> enjoy the sweets of office (Stein, 1929, p.110).

As the dyadic, political contracts and alliances between
Khan-patron and tenant-client are not based on symmetrical
positions of power but are manifestly asymmetrical so in
turn, the Khans face the Wali with grossly uneven
strength. The relationship between the warlords and the
Wali is not one of equals and not symmetrical. The for-
mula of a transaction used in 'Models of Social Organization' (Barth, 1966, p.13) is expressed thus:

$$A^x \rightleftarrows_y B \quad \text{where for} \quad A, ^x \leq Y$$

$$\text{and for} \quad B, ^x \geq Y$$

However, the formulae for the transaction based on
various socio-political interactions between the Wali(W)

and the Khans (K) $(W^y \rightleftarrows_x K)$ would look like this:

for the Wali, $W, ^x \leq Y$

and for the Khan $K, ^x \leq Y$ who emerges a constant
loser in the transaction

The Khan is consistently giving more in terms of personal autonomy and power than he is getting. For surren-
der of autonomy he might be rewarded with status or wealth
by the State. This aspect of political relationships and
their omission in Barthian analysis (ibid.) has been the
subject of an illuminating recent comment (Paine, 1974, p.
7).

THE SWAT UNIVERSE AND THE SOCIO-DEMOGRAPHIC BASE

Professor Barth uses his tools of analysis on his models
in the way that a master-surgeon uses his instruments;
they cut away quantitative data, the flesh and blood of
the anthropological study, so neatly as to go almost un-
noticed. There is a notable lack of ethnographic detail
which leaves gaps in the Swat study. The central and
unique factor in land tenure, 'wesh', which explains
Yusufzai dominance and identity is illustrated by one example only, that of the 'Nikbi Khel' section (Barth,
1959a, pp.65-6; 1959b, p.8). The 'hujra', to take
another example, plays a central institutional role as the
base and index of political strength of a Khan and as an
institution that provides an integrative mechanism to
underlying social tension. Although there is an entire
section on 'the Men's House', a statistical portrayal or
analysis of the expenditure by the Khans on the 'hujras''
upkeep and the results in political loyalty over time
based on the details of a randomly selected group of
'hujras' is not attempted. Such a cost-benefit analysis
would have shown correlative directions and conclusions.
Even one detailed case-study of the fortunes of a 'hujra'
in relation to those of its owner would have been interesting, although Barth does excuse himself on this
point (Barth, 1959a, p.80). A study of the relation between tribal affluence and proliferation of 'hujras' (as
among the Yusufzai Khans in contrast to the fewer 'hujras'
in the Tribal Areas), and their effect on local political
patterns and bloc balances, would clearly demarcate the
boundaries of one category of social and economic Pathan
organization from another. Contrary to what Barth observed in the Peshawar valley, (12) the growth of general
affluence, as a result of changing agricultural cropping
patterns in favour of cash crops, has resulted in a proliferation of 'hujras'. Whereas formerly each village or
ward might have supported one 'hujra', now any Khan with
money to spare from cash crops sets one up. Such 'hujras'
are not entirely for political ends alone: visiting relatives, officials, friends and strangers break their jour-
neys and are entertained in them.
     Yet again little is perhaps made of 'ushar' and
'qalang' (the varieties of taxes and rents the landlord
took from his tenants). How were these fixed? Who
gathered them? Were they gathered in kind or cash? What
were the sanctions to ensure payment or for default? The
answers to these questions would alter with the change in
the status of the landlord from a 'rotating' to a 'permanent' (and 'post-wesh') one.

The Victorian impact on anthropology is still evident
when anthropologists add up the reciprocal services husband and wife perform for each other. Wives invariably
appear to 'provide' sexual services (Barth, 1967, p.161)
while the contribution of the husband does not appear to
qualify as a service in a positive or valued sense. In
the year of Women's Liberation this arithmetic would be
open to charges of male chauvinism. The explanation of
Pathans sleeping in men's-houses, 'its use as a dormitory
is consciously related to feelings of sexual shame at
being associated with women' and visiting 'their wives
only briefly and secretly during the night' (Barth, 1959a,
p.55) is not satisfactory nor is it observed Pathan behaviour; it has no derivative tradition from either
Pathan customary behaviour or Islamic values.

Of the seven villages that provided the statistical
data for the Swat material, five are urbanized or near
urban centres - only Nalkot and Biha, neighbouring villages, are remote and towards the north (ibid., p.15).
Statistically, it is not clear how representative these
villages are of tribal organization and how they were selected. Professor Barth's emphasis on theoretical abstraction rather than social ontology tends to leave
ethnographic gaps. For instance, demographic shifts,
population growth trends, immigration and migration, those
dynamic and influential factors affecting the shape and
structure of rural society would have been most useful in
analyses of socio-political trends after the freezing of
'wesh' and the establishment of the Swat State. It has
been documented elsewhere that there were large migrations
out of Swat in search of employment after the establishment of the State which weakened and altered traditional
social relationships (Ahmad, 1962, p.71).

In concluding this chapter it may be observed that what
seemed, at times, an exercise in hair-splitting, especially in the early sections, was considered necessary not
only to clarify concepts and terms but to explain the
bases of some of the misunderstandings that have risen regarding Pathan society. Explaining the most basic socio-
cultural codes as 'melmastia' or hospitality, in political
terms alone has been challenged as it is partly responsible for the excessively anarchic image of Pathan society
in sociological literature derived from and generally
equated to Barth's Swat models. Such material will be examined at greater length in a separate section in the last
chapter.

The argument differentiating acephalous, segmentary
societies from centralized states appears to employ a
sledgehammer to crack a nut. None the less it was felt

necessary to draw a general framework of the differentiated types of tribal organization within which to illustrate and illuminate Swat social organization. Using
terms like 'Saints' for all people of religious status is
widely misunderstood in spite of Barth's warnings to the
contrary, for example, 'mullahs' are equated with Saints
and elevated to their status (Tuden, 1966).

The exclusion of a Sufic framework of reference neg-
lects the ambience within which the Akhund lived and
emerged, and its connections with the nineteenth-century
Sufic revivalist movements in the Islamic world, which is
expanded in chapter 6. Discussion on Sufism also underlines the qualitative differences in the understanding of
Sufis and Saints in Islamic societies.

The Swat study would have benefited by inclusion of
more demographic figures generally and hard data on key
socio-political features such as 'hujras', 'wesh' and
'ushar' particularly. These data could have thrown light
on the growing stratification in Swat society resulting in
horizontal lines of political alignment that replace traditional vertical ones; a restructuring borne out by
recent trends and events in Swat. It is relevant that
earlier in the century the Wali had cast himself in the
mould of a neo-populist and neo-reformist leader. The
Khans were seen as tyrannical and despotic warlords. The
Khans could then play 'zero-sum' power games and hold the
balance among the agnatic descendants of the Akhund and
Swat's powerful neighbours in their bitter struggle for
power.

Finally, certain minor points need mention in passing,
if only because they have survived numerous prints of
'Political Leadership among Swat Pathans', and are given
in a note, p.148. (13)

Part two

5 A theory of Pathan economic structure and political organization

غرننگ او خوړ دامان تلنگ او خوړ

Honour ate up the mountains and taxes ate up the plains

'RECIPROCAL' AND 'REDISTRIBUTIVE' ECONOMIES IN TRIBAL SOCIETIES

Barth's theoretical model and its assumptions rest on land as the basis for political interaction and power and this chapter will put Swat society in a larger economic context to bring its structural features into greater relief. Although the social structure of Swat is formed by its distinct economic and ecologic base Swat society does not form a discrete socio-economic category. It forms part of wider tribal socio-economic systems differentiated and identified by answers to two key questions: the extent of irrigated land and the systems of land tenure. Most related socio-economic answers follow. It is through the economic structures and ecological constraints in Pathan society that political organization and power are to be understood. The tribal Pathan lives within three recognizable types of economy, familiar in anthropological discussion, which can be generally categorized:
I an economy based on 'reciprocity' (further subdivided into 'general', 'balanced' and 'negative reciprocity' corresponding to distance from the household) of gifts, goods and services induced by social obligation derived from kinship which produces a balance in inhibiting the growth of a person or groups of persons beyond traditionally sanctioned roles (Sahlins, 1965). The modes of production are 'domestic' and 'familial' and the economy atomized into household units. However 'familial mode of production' is not synonymous with 'familial production'

(Sahlins, 1968, p.75). Segmentary groups are presupposed
and their existence strengthened by this economy. As is
tribal democracy,

> Some tribal societies, we have seen, are ranked, but
> none is a class society. Standing against class forma-
> tion, as it stands against economic stratification, is
> the system of autonomous family production. The
> people's hold on their own means of production is fatal
> to any such design of economic power. The appropria-
> tion of critical productive means by some few is pre-
> cluded, and thereby the economic servility of the many
> others. Whatever other means tribesmen devise to ele-
> vate a man above his fellows, and they are several,
> this one, history's most compelling, is not open to
> them (ibid., p.76).

Movement is between correlative points of symmetrical
groups. Pukhtun society in the Tribal Areas operates
within a segmentary lineage system and, being patrilineal,
has developed those symptoms of authority that approximate
to Weber's patriarchal or gerontocratic forms of authority. 'Reciprocal' economies and social relationships are
a characteristic feature of the Tribal Areas.

II the second integrative economic mechanism is a 'redistributional' economy (the channelling upwards of goods
and services to socially determined allocative centres -
king, chief or priest, who then redistribute to their followers) and is found in the richer Frontier Districts of
Peshawar, Mardan and Swat, inhabited by Yusufzai tribesmen
owning large tracts of land and employing client-tenants to
help cultivate it. An asymmetrical patron-client relationship defines and binds the landlord and his tenant in
a feudal and hierarchical order. 'Hujras' become the
channel for 'melmastia' and the locational focus and index
of political strength and loyalty. Investment is thus in
followers and clients. As was seen in the last chapter,
each Khan will afford his own 'hujra' whereas in the first
category the entire village might operate one jointly; a
fact which is indicative both of economic differentials
that explain the affluence of the Khans and the different
Pathan social structure within which they operate. Post-
Wali Swat, as indeed pre-Wali Swat, fell in this category.
Goods and services (in the shape of labour and taxes) were
given to the Wali and re-channelled to the people in the
form of free schools, hospitals, etc. (cf. Diagrams in
chapter 7).

III 'market' or 'modern economy' is restricted to urban
centres like Kohat or Bannu, where money replaces other
standards of value and acts as an 'all-purpose' medium of
exchange. Trade is impersonal and profit-making. Markets

deal with customers and not kin. None the less, tribal
networks though latent or obscure, seldom die. Studies
indicate the persistence of tribal cohesiveness operating
along established tribal networks in, or juxtaposed to,
modern economic market systems (Cohen, 1972; Ahmed,
forthcoming publication).

None of the above are isolated categories; the earlier
two forms often occur together or overlap in non-market
economies. They are simply generalized and vectorial
stages of economic growth. Most societies evolve in a
manner unique to them in response to their own individual
needs in relation to external pressures.

'NANG' AND 'QALANG' AS SYMBOLS OF SOCIO-ECONOMIC
CATEGORIES

In the foregoing section Pathan tribes and areas were
generally classed into 'reciprocal' and 'redistributive'
economic categories to put the argument of their internal
socio-economic structures and boundaries within a theoretical frame. However, for taxonomical purposes Pathan
tribes are traditionally divided:
I linguistically, into those who speak hard Pukhto (like
Yusufzai and Mohmand tribes living generally north of
Peshawar) from those speaking the soft Pashto variant
(like Khattak tribes living south of Peshawar) or
II administratively, between the tribes living in the
'hills' or Tribal Areas, where the regular criminal and
judicial laws do not apply (i.e. in the six Tribal Agencies of the North-West Frontier Province and mainly along
the International border) and those in the 'plains' or
Settled Districts (in the three Administrative Divisions
of the Province). These categories may often prove arbi-
trary and empirically misleading: Khattak groups speaking
the hard Pukhto are found living in the middle of the
Yusufzai area in Mardan. As regards the second category,
the Yusufzai are found both in Tribal Areas like the Malakand Agency and Settled Districts like Mardan and Swat.
This chapter will attempt a classification of Pathan
social organization deriving from ecological and economic
factors and based on two key concepts, 'nang' and
'qalang', that influence and explain differentiated Pathan
social organization and behaviour. These are 'ideal-type'
structures based on frequency of observable behaviour and
a concept of a species type and not based on quantitative
analysis or statistical averages. Ideal-types help explain the 'ideal' while examining the 'actual' and to con-
template the 'pure forms' and not the 'average'. Like all

'ideal-type' formulations the categories suggested in this
section sometimes overlap and often borrow from each other
especially at the borders; they are not entirely discrete
nor mutually exclusive. As categories they serve to conceptualize and answer the two related questions of where
the boundaries of social organization between 'nang' and
'qalang' are drawn and how they are maintained. Together
they constitute the template that forms the social phenomena which explain Pathan behaviour and social organization to a large degree.

Tribal or 'hill' Pathans organize their socio-political
life along egalitarian lines and more in accordance with
the ideal concepts of 'Pukhtunwali' than their cousins in
the 'plains' (Barth, 1969, p.13). The important variable
generating multi-dimensional changes is located in the
difference in ecological and economic environment. Hill
Pathans organize themselves within segmentary lineage
groups corresponding to known territorial boundaries:
'The frontier tribe, whether within or beyond our border,
has almost without exception a very distinct corporate
existence, each tribe and within the tribe each clan
occupying a clearly defined tract of country' (Ibbetson,
1883, p.201). They are stateless and 'ordered anarchies'
familiar through those categorized for African tribal
societies (Middleton and Tait, 1958). Tribal battles and
raids combine with seasonal migration to maintain a rough
demographic balance between population and economic
resources.

The position and authority of the 'Malik' ('big-man' or
'petty-chief') symbolizes the socio-political structure.
The 'Malik' 'is seldom more than their leader in war and
their agent in dealings with others; he possesses influence rather than power; and the real authority rests with
the "jirgah", a democratic council composed of all the
"Maliks"'(Ibbetson, 1883, p.201). The 'Malik' of the
Mahsud tribes in Waziristan, for instance, derive authority from 'distinguishing themselves in council and war,
through wisdom and bravery' (Afridi, forthcoming publication). Deviant behaviour is confronted by tribal and customary laws based on 'Pukhtunwali' and interpreted by the
'jirga'. The 'Malik' cannot enforce decisions outside
'Pukhtunwali' for the 'maintenance or establishment of
social order within a territorial framework, by the organized exercise of coercive authority through the use, or
the possibility of use, of physical force' (Radcliffe-
Brown, in Fortes and Evans-Pritchard, 1940, p.xiv). Among
the Mahsud,
      tribal ties disallow the rule of might and the most
      powerful and affluent Malik will think twice before

imposing his will through force on the poorest or
weakest of his clansmen. The consequences of any rash
act are so severe that they have a deterrent effect
(Afridi, forthcoming publication).

Tribal life is supported by primitive modes of production and equitable forms of distribution. Equality is
thus inherent in the economic situation and acts through
circular causation with existing socio-political factors
to reinforce itself: 'Force is decentralized; legiti-
mately held in severalty, the social compact has yet to be
drawn, the state nonexistent. So peacemaking is not a
sporadic intersocietal event, it is a continuous process
within society itself' (Sahlins, 1965, p.140).

The economy is part-pastoral and part-agricultural.
Land is poor and unirrigated in the main and supports no
large towns or market places. Senior agnates often exhibit examples of segmentary 'fissures' and start their
own fort-like settlements to live within talking (or
shooting) distance of their main collateral group but as
separate economic units. Production is mainly organized
by and for families and carried on as a domestic activity.
The classic distinction between 'production for use' (i.e.
provisioning) and 'production for exchange' (i.e. profit)
here becomes apparent and relevant.

Apart from a few roads built by the British for purposes of military strategy no road networks exist. Historical caravan routes survive at the mercy of the tribal
section through which they pass. The building of roads
over the last century was a costly affair often involving
military action. The construction required new negotiations with each subsection of a tribe as it entered their
territory and military expeditions often followed breakdown of talks. The vital Kohat-Peshawar road built late
last century through Afridi territory is a famous example.

The picture that emerges is of a reciprocal and primitive economy supporting acephalous and segmentary tribal
groups that organize social life according to traditional
tribal customs and codes. No man may become excessively
powerful or excessively destitute: there is an inherent
limit to both in the tribal social structure. Beyond a
certain stage in either case the individual confronts his
immediate sub-group and the tribal norms that his situation affect.

In the absence of any other law, life revolves around
'Pukhtunwali' and its most important and dominant component element which is the concept of 'nang'. The reasons are not difficult to seek. Economic channels of mobility and power are so obviously restricted in the ecological situation in which the tribe finds itself that

'nang', as a symbol of prestige and social mobility, assumes a key aspect. 'Nang' may take various shapes approximating to the ideal concept inherent in 'Pukhtunwali'. In point of fact an entire codification of behaviour around its meaning has developed in 'nangwali' or the Code of Honour. 'Nang' thus becomes a pivotal concept and a standard of reference in understanding normative tribal behaviour and socio-political interaction. In the face of severe economic poverty, personal valour, marksmanship and skill in combat become the symbols that confer 'nang' and therefore status. For a different and older age-set wisdom and propriety achieve honour. The emphasis is on individual and personal prowess. Khushal Khan Khattak, the famous seventeenth-century poet, exemplified this type of tribal category. The word 'nang', he wrote, drove him 'mad with emotion' (Howell and Caroe, 1963). In a disparaging reference to the Yusufzai the worst expletive he could think of was 'tillers' of the land, or agriculturalists. This form of Pathan socio-political organization, itself a consequence of its economic environment, may be called the 'nang' Pathan category. In distinction to the 'ideal-type' 'nang' category, and implying a different social structure through a different economic base, is the 'qalang' category of Pathan social organization.

'Qalang' is taken to mean 'rent' or 'tax' for land usage (Barth, 1959a, p.51). It is seen as the pivotal socio-economic concept in a tribal society where large tracts of irrigated land are cultivated and 'redistributive' rather than 'reciprocal' economic interaction orders social life. Its 'giving' or 'taking' determines and differentiates subordinate from superordinate social relationships. 'Qalang' delineates the symbiotic roles of patron and client and underlines the nature of the symbiosis. It is the definitional and final act that delimits and maintains social boundaries within a stratified society. As land is the content of social interaction, 'qalang' is the form in which the latter expresses itself. The nature of 'qalang' both asks and answers the key questions in agricultural landlord-tenant relationships: who owns the land? how is land hired out? how is the rent fixed? what are the rights of the tenant? what are the sanctions for arrears or default?

It also symbolizes a stratified, hierarchical and agricultural society. It is significant that 'wesh' does not appear to have existed in the 'nang' areas as there was no need to conceptualize equality already inherent in the segmentary descent groups. On the other hand, in 'qalang' areas 'wesh' both conferred status through shares in the land based on filiation in the descent group and divided

Yusufzai from non-Yusufzai.

As social status is directly related to the economic base of the individual, social prowess becomes more a matter of mobilization of resources than one of personal talent. The difference is one between the 'warrior' (tribal) and the 'warlord' (feudal). The former participates in 'raids', the latter organizes 'battles'. Status is largely ascribed through birth and marriages are endogamous within social strata corresponding generally to occupational ones. 'Purdah' and the concept of seclusion are emphasized and begin to correspond with the status of women and their homes. 'Nangwali', as the operative element in the code is replaced by 'tarboorwali' (agnatic rivalry) based on disputes over irrigated lands and succession to property.

'Qalang' Pathan society is culturally rich and urbane. Its language is refined, its intonations orthodox and standard. Forms of address are influenced by Urdu and Persian and differentiate those of higher and lower status: 'taso' (you) for the respected and 'te' applied generally. In contrast the only form of address in the 'nang' areas is 'te' (you). From 'qalang' society come the poets and writers. The great and saintly names: Sheikh Malli, Afzal Khan, Pir Baba, Akhund Darwezah, the Akhund of Swat. Life is orthodox, formal and literate and there is a tendency towards urbanization. Mingora, Thana and Mardan are large Yusufzai towns along the main road to Swat.

The 'hill' cousins are seen in an unkindly light:
But the Pathans of our territory have been much softened by our rule and by the agricultural life of the plains, so that they look down upon the Pathans of the hills, and their proverbs have it - 'A hill man is no man', and again 'Don't class burrs as grass or a hill man as a human being'. The nearer he is to the frontier the more closely the Pathan assimilates to the original type; while on this side of the Indus, even in the riverain itself, there is little or nothing, not even language, to distinguish him from his neighbours of the same religion as himself (Ibbetson, 1883, p. 200).

It is no coincidence that whereas the 'qalang' areas have produced the established and orthodox names in Pashto literature, like Akhund Darwezah, author of the 'Makhzan-i-Afghani', one of the first extant Pashto works, the 'nang' areas have produced popular Sufic poets writing and reciting verses that reflect the informal, mystical and rural aspects of Pathan life, like Abdul Qadir Khattak, Rahman Baba, Hamid Mohmand and Khwaja Bangash. The

Roshaniya heresy in the Mughal era was supported by sections of the Mohmand and Afridi tribes falling into 'nang'
categories while the orthodox answer to the Roshaniya came
from the Akhund Darwezah and was supported by the Yusufzai. The division within Islamic societies between the
rural, informal and mystical and the urban, formal and
orthodox is examined in the next chapter but here it may
be pointed out that the 'nang' areas coincide with the
former division and the 'qalang' with the latter.

Mardan, Swat and Dir Districts, mainly inhabited by the
Yusufzai since they conquered these areas in the sixteenth
century, find themselves in the 'qalang' socio-economic
category. These lands are amongst the richest in the
Frontier Province, watered as they are by its major
rivers, the Panjkora, the Swat and in certain areas, the
Indus and the Kabul. They contain vast reserves of
forests and grow rice, wheat and more recently cash crops,
such as tobacco, in abundance.

The 'nang-qalang' division clarifies the confusion of
explaining exceptions to general inter-tribal classifica-
tions. A society may now be viewed as a form of morphological development from a particular type of economic environment. Thus the Yusufzai may fall within the 'nang'
category in parts of Bajaur and Dir, and the Mohmand in
the 'qalang' category as landlords of vast tracts in
Mardan. An example of a single tribe dramatically divided
in the 'nang-qalang' category is provided by the Mohmand.
In the Mohmand Tribal Agency in Pakistan they form an acephalous, segmentary society living within defined sub-
tribal boundaries and following the 'Pukhtunwali'. On the
other hand the Mohmand around Jelalabad, in Afghanistan,
are landlords owning vast tracts of irrigated land and organized apically into a stratified society based on
tenants, like the Tajiks, from extra-ethnic groups. The
Mohmand Khans of Lalpura before their incorporation into
the State in the last century once wielded immense feudal
power similar to that of the Yusufzai Khans of Dir and
Swat.

The 'qalang' Khans whether Yusufzai or Mohmand, are
vulnerable to the pressures that an encapsulating system
can bring to bear:

any landholding, dominant group will therefore be
forced, sooner or later, to come to terms with these
centres of power (centralized governments) or they will
be destroyed. Such landlords are trapped in a social
system where pursuit of Pathan virtues is consistently
punished, whereas compromise, submission and accommoda-
tion are rewarded. Under these circumstances, Pathan
descent may be remembered but the distinctive behaviour

associated with the identity is discontinued ... such
groups ... are the ones scathingly referred to by
Pathans as speaking but not doing Pashto (Barth, 1969,
p.129).
This exposure to central authority and the dilemma to
Pathan values it poses is not new. Since the Yusufzai migration to the Peshawar valley they have been confronted,
and eventually encapsulated, by central authority. In the
sixteenth, seventeenth and eighteenth centuries, for example, they were fully involved in the dynastic struggles
of the Mughal princes.
    Pictures confirming Yusufzai organization, in this case
in Swat, in the 'qalang' category are given by successive
writers on the Pathans. Yusufzai 'qalang' organization
presupposes ranked social groups and Elphinstone wrote
early in the nineteenth century:
    The complete property of the soil was vested in each
    clan, and the Swautees who remained were reduced to the
    condition of villains, or, as the Eusofzyes call them
    Fakeers. This is the state in which things are at this
    day (Elphinstone, 1972, II, p.14).
The Yusufzai are seen as earnest cultivators and agricul-
turists, almost in the celebrated Punjab mould, by the
British administration and too exposed to direct Government action to be the sort of threat the tribal or 'nang'
category Pathan constantly posed. They permit the encapsulation of their social structure and in turn they are
seen as representing the best of Pathanness (Caroe, 1965,
p.421):
    The Yusufzai is an agriculturist, generally a fine,
    well-limbed man, of good physique and appearance, with
    a great deal of race-pride, well-dressed and cheery,
    while his hospitality is proverbial. They have an es-
    tablished and recognised gentry, and all blue-blooded
    Yusufzai have a hereditary share in the land, their
    names appearing in the book of hereditary land-owners
    kept by the village 'patwari'. The Yusufzai plain is
    very flat, and the soil, where properly irrigated, is
    very fertile (Wylly, 1912, p.56).
In the middle of this century the picture of Yusufzai
social organization remains unaltered (Spain, 1962, p.74).
    The 'qalang' areas are today characterized by vast
tracts of irrigated (often canal) lands which provide more
than one crop. Cash crops are grown and marketed (for instance, tobacco and sugar-cane in the Mardan District).
Individual ownership of land and contact with Government
Departments result in 'progressive farming': improved
seeds, mechanization, tube-wells etc. As land has always
been a vital ramifying factor in Pathan social

organization its ownership and tenure are defined and recorded in land revenue records and field boundaries are
jealously fixed. Excess produce, augmented by the
tenant's contribution, creates the necessity and capacity
for storage facilities. Perishable grains are converted
into liquid forms of currency and this is often re-
invested to consolidate socio-political authority. The
larger encapsulating social systems merely exacerbate and
underline growing social differences: the rich send their
sons to one type of school and the poor to another, for
instance. The logical result of this social organization
is a life-style structurally and qualitatively evolving
away from that of the 'nang' areas.

Although economic and ecological environmental factors
impose restraints and reinforce sociological differences
between 'nang' and 'qalang' the division is not structurally immutable as, for example, between the African
Lele and Bushong tribes. The Lele and Bushong, as has
been studied, in spite of a common origin, related language and similar houses, crafts etc.,continue to remain
differentiated (Douglas, 1962). The Bushong, for historical and ecological reasons, are a richer and more indus-
trious tribe than the Lele. No such structural or inherent quality differentiates the 'nang' tribes from the
'qalang' ones.

Yusufzai organization in Swat, based on irrigated land
and ranked social groups, as Barth's study clearly illustrates, would fall in the 'qalang' category. Barth, in an
illustrative conversation with a Wazir Pathan from the
'nang' areas, found it difficult to convince him that
Swatis were also Pathans subscribing to the 'Pukhtunwali':

> By basic Pathan values, a Southern Pathan from the
> homogeneous, lineage-organization mountain areas, can
> only find the behaviour of Pathans in Swat so different
> from, and reprehensible in terms of, their own values
> that they declare their northern brothers 'no longer
> Pathan'. Indeed, by 'objective' criteria, their overt
> pattern of organization seems much closer to that of
> Panjabis (Barth, 1969, p.13).

This is comprehensible within the socio-economic framework
of this chapter and when Pathans of the 'nang' area confront the social organization and behaviour of the Pathans
in the 'qalang' areas. The latter, they argue, 'speak'
but do not 'do' Pashto (ibid., p.129).

The Wali himself unconsciously touched on these categories when he suggested that Swatis were different to
tribes that organize themselves around the 'nang'
concepts:

Centuries had passed since they had lost contact with

other Pathan tribes and deviated from their way of
life in all respects, so considerably that when a Shin-
wari, Bannuchi, Afridi or Khattak came to Swat he felt
himself to be among strangers. This was not surprising, for morally, socially and culturally the Swatis
were entirely unlike any of them (Miangul, 1962, p.90).
   Yet Barth's analysis treats Swat largely as if it were
in the acephalous, segmentary 'nang' tribal category.
Both categories, as has been seen, are embedded and largely predetermined by the social relations within which they
function. The 'qalang' category, however, remains more
readily adaptable in its Yusufzai Khan manifestation to
Barthian 'transactionalist analysis'. The 'nang' and
'qalang' analysis affects the Swat argument directly as it
partly explains the socio-economic preconditions for the
emergence of the Wali and the State: both would have been
a socio-political impossibility in the 'nang' Pathan
areas. The Wali's emergence was possible only in the 'qalang' areas because of the stratified and pyramidal nature
of society. Although pre-Wali Swat was a confederation of
acephalous tribes without centralized authority its village society was autocephalous with apical social structures. The stratified nature of Swat 'qalang' society enabled a homologous but vastly enlarged paternalistic State
to be imposed on it without much friction. Once the main
Khans were pacified through alliances or subdued through
force, and the number of contenders limited, the main
challenge to the Wali came from other sources as will be
examined in chapter 7.
   The 'nang-qalang' thesis does not contain a mechanism
allowing for a 'gumsa-gumlao' type of oscillation (Leach,
1954). The movement is uni-directional, from hill to
plain, from pastoral to agricultural economy; from
'tribal' social category to 'peasant-agricultural' category; (1) from concepts of 'nang' as the motivating
social factor and key symbol in understanding normative
behaviour to those of 'qalang'. Movement to 'qalang'
category is movement to either feudal landlord or tenant
status. The tribal movement is not as schematized as Ibn
Khaldun's tribal theory for it operates within tribal
boundaries and movement is of tribal segments rather than
tribes. It is difficult to envisage a reverse movement
from 'qalang' to 'nang' areas. Warlords would neither
find the economic resources to support their power nor the
social structure to maintain political hierarchy. The
categories are thus antithetical.
   Ideal - type Pathan tribal social organization corres-
ponds to ecological-geographical boundaries and it is empirically observed that groups from acephalous segmentary

tribal systems passing into irrigated plains become part
of stratified social structures interacting with other
ethnic groups, symbolized in the shift from central concepts of 'nang' to 'qalang'. However, 'nang' concepts are
not altogether ejected from Pathan 'qalang' consciousness.
They reappear in other shapes and symbolic forms, for example, the greater emphasis on individual hospitality in
the Khan's 'hujra', in the understanding of 'melmastia',
i.e. 'qalang' 'hujras' maintaining 'nang' values. 'Nangwali' is also exhibited in typically feudal chivalry in
war (Miangul, 1962, p.29). Pathan mythology and consciousness are deliberately kept visible and active by frequent reference to 'nang' values.
     The major differentiated and opposing socio-economic
attributes are listed below to illustrate the characteristics of the 'nang' and 'qalang' categories of Pathan
social organization suggested in this chapter:

	THE 'NANG' CATEGORY	THE 'QALANG' CATEGORY
I	hill areas	plain areas
II	largely unirrigated	largely irrigated
III	pastoral tribal economy	agricultural feudal economy
IV	no rents or taxes	rents and taxes
V	mainly 'achieved' status of 'elders'	mainly 'ascribed' status of Khans
VI	outside, or juxtaposed with, larger state systems; informal, illiterate, oral tradition	encapsulated within larger systems; members of Civil Service, District Boards etc. literate, orthodox, written tradition
VII	warriors participating in raids	warlords organizing battles
VIII	acephalous tribal society organized in segmentary descent groups	autocephalous village organization under Khan within larger acephalous society
IX	scarce population dispersed in 'fort-like' hamlets and nucleated settlements	dense population in large villages and tendency to urbanization
X	emphasis on 'nangwali' (Code of Honour)	emphasis on 'tarboorwali' (agnatic rivalry)

XI	'jirga' represents interests of entire tribe (the vast majority of the population)	'jirga' members from landowning Yusufzai only
XII	egalitarian social organization	hierarchical social organization based on autochthonic population

The taxonomical division of Pathan tribes presents complex problems as it involves tribal demographic shifts that express polar socio-economic organization within highly differentiated economic-ecological and political-administrative systems. An attempt has therefore been made in this section to simplify the divisions in order to create valid models which would explain subsequent and ramifying social developments. The two key symbols that explain and presuppose differentiated Pathan social organizations, 'nang' (honour, an intangible concept) and 'qalang' (rent, a material and quantifiable transaction) are not apparently congruent as they neither relate nor measure on a common yardstick. None the less, they have been selected, over other important symbols, as best helping to explain the division and types of Pathan social organization and behaviour. It is significant that Pathans themselves relate 'nang' to 'qalang' as diacritica between types of 'hill' or 'plain' social organization as in the proverb quoted at the beginning of the chapter.

The important qualifying features in understanding both the forms the symbols take, and the types of social organization they represent, are the economic-ecological and political-administrative boundaries within which Pathan tribes organize themselves. These features, in turn, define and reinforce the boundaries which maintain and perpetuate the distinctive social systems.

6 A note on Sufic orders and Islamic revivalism in the nineteenth century

نیستی پاکه بادشاهی ده ۔دولت مندے له لِزّت خبر نه دی

Poverty is a pure sovereignty and the rich man knows not
of its delights

This chapter will attempt to explain the emergence of revivalist Islamic movements in the nineteenth century in
the hinterland Muslim areas within a conceptually holist
framework. These movements have certain recognizable features as they are stimulated through interaction with
colonial, European and industrial powers. Religious and
racial (Christian and white) differences only underline
and exacerbate the nature of the encounter. The Islamic
response, still archaic and traditional, as are its symbols and weapons, is led by men of religious 'baraka'
(sociologically translated as 'charisma').

The first section of this chapter is parenthetic in
nature but provides a sociological framework for the argument developed later. However, it should be underlined
that the explanation of Sufic behaviour and apperception
is the Sufi version (1) and not necessarily a sociological
one. The discussion is therefore consciously monolithic
and undifferentiated in order to enable an understanding
of generalized Sufi ideal-types and the models that
derive from them. The reader who finds the argument excessively circuitous may go to the conclusions on p.98.

The argument will attempt to pick up the universalist
strands connecting, with mutual effect, socio-religious
normative life of geographically distant Islamic communities. The point at issue is to argue (with Swat in mind)
that an examination, however particularistic or synchronic, of an Islamic community or society in isolation
from its wider socio-religious context, is to exclude a
basic dimension of its form and thereby to omit an

important variable in its analysis.

Islamic societies are notorious in requiring a holistic framework of analysis due to their homologous structural arrangements and in the universality of their politico-religious symbolism which are maintained by contact in general with contiguous Islamic communities and persistent contact in particular with Mecca and Medina. These latter cities act both as common Islamic source-points for socio-religious activities and as disseminating points for revivalist-reformist ideas and movements. Conceptually, this locational factor gives the Islamic world a physical orientation around which to order its existence and from which to derive its spiritual inspiration. Universal and easily identified Islamic symbols are carried into and exist in the most remote Muslim societies: (2) numerous identical words and verbs, common socio-religious festivals and certain normative values. Various groups, both formal and informal, keep the channels of communication open within the Islamic world: hajjis, pilgrims, missionaries, scholars, migrants and traders. These channels sometimes block up or fall into disuse but have generally remained functional. (3) It is this channel, for example, that provided news of a Turkish victory over the Greeks in Europe in the late 1890s and stirred enthusiasm amongst the Pathans in the North-West Frontier of India against the British. Secret British Government Reports invariably begin despatches regarding tribal revolts by linking them to international events and 'foreign agents'. Conversely, Islamic defeats are reflected in the tone of the Friday sermon in the mosque where the congregation is apprised of the calamity and exhorted to reform and thereby purify itself for the 'coming crisis'. Identity with the stricken Muslim community is assumed. Such examples of information, however belated and distorted, arriving from far-away Islamic encounters to encourage and reinforce local Islamic 'jihad' or movements, are historically commonplace. (4)

The nineteenth century was one of prolonged and major crises for Islam. The crises were reflected both in external and internal Islam, the former forcing the pace of the latter. A syndrome of defeat enveloped Islamic endeavour: Islamic Empires disintegrated, Islamic armies were shattered by technically superior European forces, Islamic capitals lay in foreign hands, and the Islamic élites were dispossessed. Muslims turned inwards to confront the crises stemming from problems of identity. Once before, after the climactic sacking of Baghdad in 1258 by the Mongols, had such a universal long-lasting despair gripped Muslim consciousness and for centuries afterwards

Muslim art and literature depicted transient and despon-
dent themes (Sadiq, 1964). Then too, the urban, formal
Islamic States and their armies lay paralysed and Islamic
response came in the form of informal and personal Sufic
activity in rural areas both as escape from reality and as
a valid alternative form of worship. The Islamic world
through various periods in the nineteenth century reacted
to the European presence in certain predictable ways of
which two concern this essay. The 'modernist' (5) reaction (which eventually became the 'nationalist') accepted
the fact of subordination and resolved to accommodate
itself with the new order (Sir Sayyed Ahmed of India is
the prototype example (6)); and the 'traditional' symbolized by Sufic reaction which provided the impetus to
Sufic activity and which concerns the argument in this
section. Traditional, but at the same time reformist,
leaders selected remote, peripheral and often tribal communities to live in and through preceptorial example created Islamic confidence and revivalism. Reformists, like
Ahmad al-Sanusi and Abdul Ghaffur, the Akhund of Swat,
confined their teachings within a Sufic framework of mystical contemplation heightened through simple incanta-
tions. Their message was inner-directed and non-material
and, what is more important, non-political. However,
their preachings and popularity outstripped their core-
message and created an atmosphere of predisposability to
an Islamic revivalism which subsequently changed successfully into both millenarian activities and charismatic
leadership, as will be seen in this chapter.

GENESIS OF SUFISM

The emergence of the Akhund of Swat and the impact of his
career (and that of his agnatic progeny) on the nature of
Swat socio-political organization is not seen as an isolated historical incident, but within the framework of the
reformist-revivalist Sufic movements of the nineteenth
century interacting with the European presence. An understanding of the Akhund and the sources of his religio-
spiritual motivations entail a brief word on the nature of
Sufism and its origins in the person of the Prophet of
Islam in Arabia. (7)
     The Sufis trace their origin to the Prophet and the
Holy Quran. (8) The Prophet symbolized Sufic practices
and his personal experiences provide Sufic behaviour
precedents:
  I Sufic austerity derives from the Prophet's style of
life: he slept on the floor, mended and washed his

clothes and on his death, in 632 AD, left behind seven
'dinars' which he had willed to the poor (Esin, 1963, p.
116). The Prophet's saying 'my poverty is my pride'
(ibid., p.104) became a Sufic shibboleth. The word Sufi
itself derives from 'Suf' or wool worn constantly by the
Prophet. None the less, Sufic origin in the austere
person of the Prophet did not prevent the growth of a
whole range of exotic and syncretic Sufic forms.

II   Sufic retreat and contemplation can be traced to the
Prophet's retreats to Mount Hira (where the Quran was revealed to him).

III Sufic universality derives from examples set by the
Prophet. His saying that none could love Jesus more than
himself was well-known (ibid., p.109). (9)

IV   The Prophet insisted that Sufism must not be an ontological escape mechanism from social reality but incor-
porated within it. Sufis are consequently not restricted
within any occupational or social stratum. Many Sufi
orders like the Tijani (Cohen, 1969) or Sanusi (Evans-
Pritchard, 1949) concerned themselves with organization of
practical life; asceticism was a stimulus to eschatological problems not a substitute for it. The 'popular' image
of the semi-nude, mud-covered Sufi gyrating in perpetual
ecstatic trance is partly created by the urban and orthodox imagination based on Sufi orders such as Rumi's and
Mevlevi's (dancing 'dervishes') and partly through Sufic
association with Hindu 'sadhus' (popular Sufism in main-
land India was extensively eclectic and syncretic and
forms a unique category of its own).

Sufi socio-religious organization revolves around the
pivotal role of the Sheikh of the 'zawiya' (lodge) and is
based on dyadic relationships between him and his followers. Sufic structural organization is thus autocephalous
in nature and carries structural potential to convert flu-
ently to political or economic activity in changed circumstances. It will be seen later in this section how Sufic
orders preaching mystical contemplation and universal
peace were converted to militant political organizations
involved in extra-ethnic or extra-religious wars. Until
the colonial contact, encounter and interaction in the
nineteenth century the Sufis maintained their traditional
posture of low-key, non-political socio-religious organization (Trimingham, 1971).

To comprehend a Sufic frame of reference in Barthian
'transactionalist' terms (such as 'manipulating', 'maximizing', 'strategizing' - Barth, 1966) is to fail to understand the dominant elements in Sufi consciousness and the
cognitive values as seen through Sufi eyes; it is also to
impose a sterile sociological framework of analysis and

reference. There is a polarity of difference in the two
vocabularies and even in the definition of similar concepts. 'Maximization' to Barthian man is just that,
whereas to the Sufi the cognitive definition contains a
semantic reversal: to him 'maximization' is 'minimization' which is not the same thing as 'minimizing-loss' as
distinct from 'maximizing-gain' but a deliberate, conscious 'minimizing-gain'. For instance in the Swat situation, the Akhund repeatedly refused the kingship of Swat.
He was neither 'manipulating' nor 'strategizing', but
simply limiting an increasing involvement in extra-Sufic
activity.

The Sufi is in the world but not of it. While the
bourgeois-capitalist and the Marxist-socialist stand on
opposite ends of the politico-economic continuum and confront each other, the Sufi stands outside the relationship
forming a third mid-way and triangular point. The Sufi is
not unaware of the material world; he confronts it, com-
prehends it and then rejects it. The interaction remains
mechanistic and the world peripheral. (10) Marxist and
Barthian man (as 'maximizing entrepreneur') on the other
hand, confront the material world, comprehend it and wish
to possess it; the interaction is dialectical and the
world is central.

The world of Islam has been seen as dividing into two
contrasting and opposing socio-political categories: the
legal, rational, formal, orthodox, urban (evolving into
empires and supporting vast armies) in opposition to the
pacific, mystical, informal, unorthodox and rural. (11)
These categories are clearer as abstract constructs than
as empirically observable and discrete phenomena. (12)
Professor Gellner is the most articulate exponent of these
opposing Islamic categories (1969b). However, major exceptions and shifts within this division are empirically
observable as for instance, successful Sufic establish-
ments in modern urban environments (Gilsenan, 1973). The
opposition of the two ideal-types within Islam is a
useful heuristic tool of analysis to postulate and examine
socio-historical development, with the warning that the
categories are neither rigid nor permanent. (13)

It has been argued in the above passages that when the
encounter with nineteenth-century Europe proved disastrous
to the 'orthodox-formal' category of Islam the focus of
(unconscious) resistance and (conscious) revivalism shifted to the 'rural-informal'. (14) This shift has traditionally provided elasticity and resilience to Islamic
societies in times of crisis although it signifies more a
demographic projection of political reality than a perceptible change in theological ontology.

It is no coincidence that the 'nang' category of Pathan
tribal social organization generally coincides in its
characteristics with the rural, informal form of Islam and
the 'qalang' category with the formal and orthodox.
    The selection for comparative analysis, at this point,
of three Sufi reformist leaders in the nineteenth century
is not entirely at random as their personal history typi-
fies the shift in focus from the 'orthodox-formal' to the
'rural-informal' category which they symbolize within
their local geo-political situation. So far, thus, the
argument is concurrently methodologically holistic as it
is deterministic.

THREE CASE-STUDIES: THE SANUSI, THE MAHDI AND THE AKHUND

The fundamental aim in this section is to illustrate the
homologous and similar structural and biographical sequence of the three case-studies, in order to understand
the universal features that span two continents and diverse tribal communities, as crucial variables in the
social analysis of Muslim ethnic groups. This sequential
and biographical similarity can be largely examined in
methodologically holistic terms applicable to Islamic
societies that allow the discovery and activation of
religio-political symbols of action in each society (whether tribal, as in all three examples, agricultural-
peasant or urban). A socio-historical comparison will
illustrate this point.

Early life and Sufic Orders

Sociologically, it is of interest that none of the three
contemporaneous leaders came from the élite or feudal
social strata; they were thus 'marginal' to established
society and central political authority and not being
bound by either could reject their norms. They thus symbolized the transcendent, permanent and universal values
of Islam to their followers.
    Sayyed Mohammed bin Ali al Sanusi al Kabir was a man of
great wisdom and learning (Evans-Pritchard, 1949). Perhaps the most learned of the three leaders under discussion. He synthesized his experience and knowledge of
various Sufic orders to found his own Order, the Sanusi,
named after him. Abdul Ghaffur, the Akhund of Swat, was
of the Naqshbandi Order which lays stress on seclusion and
silent contemplation. Mohammed Ahmed, the Mahdi of Sudan,
belonged to the Samani Order (an offshoot of the Qadari
Order). These three men spent their early years in

intense piety, austerity and contemplative seclusion: al-
Sanusi at a remote oasis in the Sahara, the Akhund on the
banks of the Indus river and the Mahdi in a cave also by a
river. Each of them was attached to one or several Sufic
masters - and subsequently outshone them as their own
learning and fame grew (correspondingly equated to
'baraka' and 'charisma').

Religio-political symbolism

Though often in the eye of the storm the three leaders
were only reluctantly drawn into the political arena, and
then with varying consequences - largely dependent on the
extent of involvement with European powers. They preferred to remain king-makers rather than kings. The Mahdi
appointed Abdullah as Khalifa, while the Akhund nominated
Sayyed Akbar Shah as King of Swat. Al-Sanusi simply refused to engage in any form of political activity pre-
ferring to direct his energies in strengthening and establishing his 'lodges' as centres of learning.
    The holistic and universal symbols of Islamic tradition
were activated and reference to these symbols legitimized
the revivalist nature of their movements and confirmed
their charisma and status. The Mahdi's nominee was the
Khalifa (tracing, at least mnemonically, his descent to
the Rashidin Caliphs and Companions of the Prophet).
Sayyed Akbar Shah became 'Amir-e-Shariat' (leader of
the Faithful in the classic Islamic mould) and Swat was
declared an 'Islamic State'.
    To symbolize the establishment of the religio-political
order new townships were constructed: al-Sanusi settled
at Jagbub oasis (later to house a great Islamic University); the Akhund chose Saidu (later to be the capital of
Swat) and the Mahdi built Omdurman.
    Their charismatic appeal lay primarily with tribal and
rural populations and their following was initially and
largely among the poor. Thus the 'Sanusi Empire', the
Mahdist 'Derwish Empire' and the 'Islamic State' of Swat
became explicit symbols of two interconnected drives:
chiliastic hope on the one hand and Islamic revivalism on
the other. To the poor and dispossessed they signified
the simplicity and austerity of early Islam and not the
awesome grandeur and pomp of the imperial courts of Medieval Islam.
    It is sociologically important to note that the tribes
these leaders worked among were already Muslim: theirs
was thus a revivalist-reformist mission rather than a proselytizing one. (15) This difference becomes marked as

the movement proceeds. Revivalist-reformist symbols,
sooner or later, begin to cluster around the Islamic concept of 'jihad' to regain lost glory.

The colonial encounter

Living in remote and peripheral areas and amongst tribal
peoples the religious reformers were largely ignored by
central authorities and sometimes even accorded a certain
measure of local respect. However, in the last century,
when the central authority was organized by colonizing
Europeans (as distinct from colonizing but co-religionist
Turks, as in Cyrenaica's case) friction regarding limita-
tion of various socio-political boundaries became inevitable. It is an illustration of al-Sanusi's sincerity in
wishing to avoid contact with the Turkish administration
that he shifted his headquarters deeper into the desert.
(16) It was only when the Italians (replacing the Turks)
systematically launched a programme to destroy Sanusi
lodges in Cyrenaica that the Order mobilized and converted
its socio-religious organization into a militant and political one. Al-Sanusi himself died in 1859 and did not
live to see his organization change its objectives and
character so radically. This 'conversion' is a common
phenomenon in the late nineteenth and early twentieth century Islamic world where the 'orthodox-formal' units of
Islam capitulated or were destroyed necessitating the
struggle to be carried on by the 'rural-informal'. The
colonizing European presence is the one crucial variable
determining the conversion of peaceful religious organizations into militant 'nationalist' ones. For instance, it
was only after 1912 when Morocco was declared a French
Protectorate and military incursions were made into the
Atlas mountains that the 'igurramen', the Saints of the
Atlas, abandoned the pacificist scholarly tradition established since the fourteenth century by the founder of the
Ahansal lodge, Sidi Said Ahansal, and provided leadership
for political guerrilla bands. (17) After six centuries
of living within well-defined boundaries of piety and
peace and in harmonious opposition to the secular, temporal authority of the local chiefs they were confronted
with the colonial situation and forced into radically new
leadership roles; from Saints who spoke to their community they became leaders who spoke for their community.
    The case of the Mahdi is to be examined in the context
of a colonized Sudan and an Anglo-Egyptian presence with
its centrepoint at Khartoum. The town of Khartoum assumed
a focal position for prestige and strategy to both the

Mahdi and the Anglo-Egyptians. It thus became a symbol of
imperial honour on the one hand and local religious fer-
vour on the other and subsequently, with the names of the
main actors of the drama, among the more evocative names
of the Victorian era. A revivalist Sufic organization was
almost at birth engaged in colonial interaction and placed
in a position of confrontation. This confrontation had
distinct religious and ethnic overtones; 'jihad' against
the British Christians and political struggle against the
Egyptians. The Mahdi thus became a millenarian leader
providing evidence of his charismatic powers in repeated
success against enemy forces and promising a better life
to his followers after the establishment of his order.
Both Gordon and the Mahdi became cultural-political symbols for their people of supreme moments of heroism
against alien and great odds. The Mahdi, 'the Saviour',
to his people became the notorious 'False Prophet' to his
enemies. It had to be a fight to the finish. (18)

Swat provides an interesting example of a religious
leader who, in spite of mobilizing tribal society and involving the British Indian Army in a major campaign in
1863, emerges in colonial eyes as the best possible alternative to anarchic tribal elements. The Akhund is
accepted as a man of genuine peace who is interested in
creating an area of stability. Imperial objectives in
creating zones of stability are seen in congruence with
the Akhund's work. In this situation an interconnected
set of strategic reasons explain imperial strategy:
I The British had emerged shaken from the ferocity of
the 1857 upheavals in India and looked to 'areas of stability' and 'men of authority' who could keep them so.
II They had only recently crossed the Indus and were
still in the process of cautiously pushing towards what
was to become the International Frontier (or the Durand
Line) in 1893 dividing British India from Afghanistan.
The last thing they desired was a tribal irruption from
the north led by the Akhund who by then was an established
figure.
III The Akhund had convinced the imperial authorities
that he wished for external peace with his neighbours in
order to impose internal peace in Swat. The British administration, in turn, would rather negotiate with one
established leader than discordant and amorphous tribal
groups.

The critical variable affecting the personal success or
failure of the three leaders is the extent of local European involvement on the ground: the Mahdi and the Akhund
illustrate this. The Mahdi grew in a colonial situation
that made encounter inevitable; the Akhund, working in a

peripheral tribal area outside British boundaries, on the
other hand, was left alone as long as he made no attempt
to cross his tribal borders and into the Settled Districts
the British administered.

The 'jihads' in the colonial encounters of the nineteenth century were a last grand and futile gesture of the
'traditionalist' forces of Islam tilting against the most
powerful nations on earth. The inevitability of the out-
come merely underlines the conceptualization of the rationale contained in the 'jihad' by its participants: the
struggle is more important than victory; the principle
more important than the objective.

Sufis and States

Certain similarities are observed when analysing the political career of the agnatic progeny of the three Sufi
figures into the twentieth century. The grandsons of al-
Sanusi and the Akhund helped to create, and then ruled,
formal States supported and recognized by the British.
Their official State title displayed their sources of
religio-political authority and legitimized their secular
authority: 'Amir' Idris in Libya and the 'Wali' in Swat.
The agnatic descendants of the Mahdi also staged a come-
back and continued to play a vital role in Sudanese politics (both in Cabinet and as symbols of the Mahdist party
in the countryside).

The wheel of a family's fortune is said to turn in
three generations in sociological lore. In the three
cases under study this cycle also symbolized the crossing
of the boundary from the 'rural-informal' to the
'orthodox-formal'. What were once the symbols of religious revivalism and political resistance in the face of
the colonial presence now became, in changed circumstances, the symbols of orthodox and formal establishment.
The descendants of the old rulers faced their own people
and the new nationalist post-war sentiments that found expression in dissatisfaction with traditional orders and
the need for rapid socio-political change. As a result
King Idris and the Wali of Swat directly, and the Mahdists
indirectly, were set aside by military governments.

THE AKHUND OF SWAT

There is some genealogical uncertainty regarding the
ethnic origin of the Akhund but none concerning the social
order he came from. Early sources write: 'Born of Gujar

parents (in 1794), probably in upper Swat, Abdul Ghaffar
began life as a herd-boy' ('Peshawar Gazetteer', 1883-4,
p.221; Bellew, 1864, p.102, for a contemporary and similar
view;   Wylly, 1912, p.112). Other, more recent, sources
trace his genealogy to the Safi tribe (Hay, 1934;
Miangul, 1962, p.xli; Spain, 1962, p.68). Barth favours
the former version (Barth, 1959a, p.100). From an anthropological point of view this uncertainty is revealing as
it illustrates the priority given to ethnic rather than
social status in the framework of the Yusufzai social organization. The Gujar not only falls at the bottom of the
Swat caste schemata but is also extra-ethnic in non-Pathan
origin. Telescoping and fusion of ancestral links are
common tribal phenomena in organizing genealogical maps
(Peters, 1960). So is reorganization of genealogical
charters (Bohannan, 1952). The Akhund's descent is
graphically traced to Qais bin Rashid in the seventh century in the account of Swat by his grandson (Miangul,
1962, Appendices, p.xxii).

The Akhund's early life is structured along the classic
Sufic pattern:

> About the year 1816 he accordingly settled down, as a
> young man of barely twenty, to a life of the greatest
> austerity, at a lonely spot on the banks of the Indus,
> below the village of Beka, ten miles above Attock,
> where for twelve years he followed the Nakshbandia form
> of religious devotion - sitting silent and motionless,
> his head bowed on his chest, and his eyes fixed on the
> ground. His food was an inferior kind of millet mois-
> tened with water, and throughout his life - he died at
> the age of eighty-three, his diet was equally simple,
> milk being however, subsequently substituted for water.
> His fame as a saint dates from his sojourn at Beka, and
> even to this day, in the most distant parts of Persia,
> he is still remembered as 'the Hermit of Beka' (Wylly,
> 1912, p.112).

It is illustrative that his main intellectual stimulus
came through knowing the entire works of the great Pashto
Sufi poet, Rahman Baba, by heart (Miangul, 1962, p.lviii).

Around the age of forty (a critical age for Muslims in
Islamic tradition) he returned to Swat to preach in
earnest. Soon stories of supernatural powers and extraordinary perception were attributed to him (Barth, 1959a,
p.101). In the context of Muslim Indian Sufic tradition
exhibition of supernatural strength through 'competitive
spirituality' was a key factor in establishing the reputation and augmenting the following of the Sufi (Ahmad,
1964, p.134):

> The Akhund gained such an ascendancy over the minds of

his co-religionists that they believed all kinds of
stories about him; that he was supplied by supernatural means with the necessities of life, and that
every morning a sum of money, sufficient for his own
needs and for the entertainment of the pilgrims who
flocked to consult him, was found under his praying
carpet (Wylly, 1912, p.114).

Unlike either the Mahdi, who engaged totally in the
colonial encounter, or the Sanusi who withdrew from it,
the Akhund was personally present in only two battles, one
against the Sikhs and the other against the British. But
it appears his heart was not in it. The Imperial Gazetteer records the importance of the Akhund's role in paci-
fying Swat tribes and defusing the political situation
after the battle at the Ambela Pass in 1863:

the Akhund advised the people of Swat and Buner, and
other independent tracts, to behave towards us as good
neighbours, and if they offended the British Government, to meet such demands as it might make, and to
comply with such terms as might be imposed ('Peshawar
Gazetteer', 1883-4, p.180).

A few years earlier, in the critical days of the 1857 upheaval in the plains of India, the Akhund had also acted
as a modifying factor:

When the mutineers of the 55th Native Infantry, flying
from Mardan before Nicholson, crossed the boundary into
Swat, he caused them to be deported beyond the Indus;
and he supported our government so far as lay in his
power during the anxious days of the Mutiny (Wylly,
1912, p.115).

His presence as a leader wishing to impose some social
order upon an anarchic tribal society was therefore welcomed. Swat was notorious as a den of sedition and crime:

Plunderers and marauders, mounted and on foot, issued
from Swat, passed through Ranizai, and raided into our
territory. They kidnapped almost all classes except
Pathans; and Swat became an Alsatia where evilly-
disposed persons, criminals of all shades, and people
hostile to the British Government were readily granted
help, asylum and countenance (ibid., p.121).

The Akhund organized an informal economic network
around his pivotal person that reinforced his spiritual
authority and lent material support to his reformist
preaching. The resources and gifts of his rich followers
increased his own wealth (Miangul, 1962, p.lix) but a
great deal of this was channelled into feeding the poor:
'He established an alms-house for the poor and needy,
which also served as the public kitchen for the hundreds
of devotees who came to Saidu Sharif every day. Food for

five hundred men was cooked there daily' (ibid., p.lx).
In return, the gift-givers and followers earned a form of
socio-spiritual merit defined in this transaction and
thereby created dyadic bonds with the Akhund.

This asymmetrical material and spiritual relationship
(of gifts from the richer in exchange for spiritual merit
and to the poor) helped to shift and even alter the traditional existing dyadic alignments between patron Khans and
their clients. A new element thus entered the old alignments in drawing up two mutually exclusive circles of relationships whose successful functioning would have implications for the breakdown of traditional patron-client relationships in Swat.

In terms of political analysis, based upon social class
origin and related to Swat structural arrangements, it is
important to recall that when called upon by the united
confederation of tribes to become King of Swat the Akhund
selected Sayyed Akbar Shah (19) as his nominee rather than
a Yusufzai Khan. This act is of ramifying significance;
it legitimized the concept of a central authority, it confined the political arena to religious contestants and
limited them numerically, and by placing the crown on a
non-local, non-Yusufzai head, excluded the Khans as legi-
timate claimants for kingship. The selection of Sayyed
Akbar also reflects Pathan respect and susceptibility to
men of extraordinary religiosity and traces the links to
events and places outside local Pathan areas.

The political symbols of the State indicated a theocra-
tic order: the King was called 'Amir-e-Shariat' and the
State was to be an 'Islamic' one. However, a 'coercive
authority' was created too: 'a force of 800 mounted men,
3,000 footmen and five or six guns' (Wylly, 1912, p.125).
It would be a foolhardy Khan who would challenge the combined religious authority of the King and military authority of the State.

This incipient standing force (20) marks the foundation
of statehood. The key-word in tribal politics is 'standing force'. Where 'jihad' or tribal wars are organized in
Pathan societies on a temporary basis a regular force,
however diminutive, can be a most decisive instrument in
maintaining military initiative and political supremacy.
Of particular note is the cavalry component which in the
context of local tribal clashes may be seen as a formid-
able factor. The above figures clearly indicate some form
of elementary political establishment in Swat. Their
significance has been overlooked by Barth in his idealized
acephalous model of tribal Khans preventing the emergence
of centralized authority in Swat, and each other from
gaining political pre-eminence.

The Akhund led an uneventful life and died in 1877.
Perhaps his most fitting epitaph was written by the
British:

He lived the life of an ascetic and religious leader,
deeply venerated by the people, over whom, not only in
his own valley but throughout North-Eastern Afghanistan, he gradually acquired an unbounded influence,
which, to his credit it should be said, he used invariably for purposes that were good according to his
light;   inculcating truth, peace and morality, allaying
as far as he could the interminable feuds among the
people, and enforcing the precepts of the Muhammadan
Law as far as was compatible with ineradicable Pathan
customs ('Peshawar Gazetteer', 1883-4, p.179).

Saidu came to symbolize the town of the Akhund and contained his shrine which soon became an important focal
point for religious pilgrimages, 'The shrine of the great
Akhund of Swat at Saidu, is one of the most important in
Northern India' (ibid., p.221).   Saidu thus became the
capital of Swat and was identified both physically and
spiritually with the Akhund, a factor that was to play
heavily in favour of his agnatic descendants and their political contests with the descendants of Sayyed Akbar
Shah.   The Akhund, after his death came to be called, as
he is to this day, Saidu Baba after the town which was
given the appellation 'Sharif' (noble) to indicate its
special status.   Unlike temporal rulers such as the Khan
of Dir, the descendants of the Akhund could legitimize
their argument for political leadership with spatial reference to Saidu and its shrine.

The Akhund's life and emergence, embedded in a structurally holistic socio-religious frame, laid the base for,
and partly symbolized the sequence of, socio-political development in Swat.   A connection perhaps not apparent at
the time:

I An expanding non-Muslim (Sikh and later British) presence is partly the cause of the Akhund's emergence, and
his religious revivalist preachings an effect of it.

II The emergence of the Akhund is the first historical
event in Swat since the sixteenth century that challenges,
and then overrides, the authority of the Khans.   A skeletal spatial and conceptual framework for a Swat State is
organized and the foundations of 'Swati' ethnicity laid
by-passing the feudal Yusufzai social organization in both
cases.

III His spiritual and economic authority establish a
base for familial charisma which subsequently became an
important lever in the hands of his agnatic descent in
their struggle to establish political supremacy.

IV Swat is finally and directly involved in the larger
tribal politics of the North-West Frontier.

In concluding this chapter the implications contained
in the above arguments for the analysis of Barth's Swat
Pathans are a failure to come to terms with the other
level of Islamic consciousness and social organization
i.e. the 'rural-informal' and mystical. Thereby a crucial
aspect and dimension of Islamic rural leadership and organization is omitted. (21) As a result:

I the sociologically holistic framework that partly explains the emergence of the charismatic Akhund and the de-
rivation of a personal lifestyle traced to the Prophet of
Islam (which almost structures Sufic physical existence
and spiritual exercises) is absent. This explains the
failure to come to terms with the Sufic ambience which,
for example, explain the defining and motivating force
behind the Akhund and his descendants. The Wali is partly
to be explained by atavistic Sufic urges. After playing
the power game successfully and emerging as the ruler of a
centralized State the Wali, at the height of his career
and in full command of his facultes, abruptly retires to
a life of austerity and contemplation. His life and
character form an interesting comment on the two categories of Islamic socio-religious behaviour under discussion. It will be seen in the next chapter, when the Wali
is discussed, that the categories cannot typologize permanently or entirely.

II the social organization of the Swat Khans, though not
urbanized, is still formal, orthodox and militaristic-
aristocratic and (based as it is on 'qalang') would tend
to fall naturally into the 'orthodox-formal' rather than
'rural-informal' category. This division is significant
in an analysis of the Swat political structure for it
shifts the argument for a mystical 'saviour', defined by
his social origins, outside the 'orthodox-formal' category
and to the other one. The Akhund was not and could not
have been a 'Khan' and he therefore symbolized chiliastic
hope and articulation for the Swat majority who were the
rural dispossessed and poor.

III as mentioned earlier, Sufis fail to appear in the
general category of Swat Saints who would fit squarely in
the non-mystical, 'orthodox-formal' category. This enables some of them to live like surrogate Khans. The
greater division of Sufi and Saint (using Barth's definition of Saint as 'all persons occupying holy status, whether prominent or not' Barth, 1959a, p.57) dissolves the
weaker division between Saint and Khan. The famous examples and shrewd behaviour of 'the Saint who whistled'
(ibid., p.99) or 'the Saint who took his turban off'

(ibid., p.59) merely underline the frailty of the Barthian division between the secular (Khan) and the religious (Saint) and would have been incomprehensible and unlikely in terms of Sufic behaviour.

IV and finally, the Swat analysis appears limited both in space and time within its methodological individualist framework as it fails to take into account the redefining of the traditional dyadic patron-client, Khan-follower alignments through the interconnected dialectical events starting with the emergence of the Akhund, passing through the universal upheaval of tribal millenarian activities and ending with the establishment of Swat State. These events, in turn, are seen as the final expression of the Akhund's life-work which left behind a network of spiritual organization to be activated by agnatic descendants and charismatic leaders which will be examined in the following chapter.

Part three

7 Millennium and charisma among Pathans

پير نه الوزی خو مایدان نۓ الوزوی

Though the pir himself does not fly his disciples would
have him fly

THESIS: MILLENARIAN MOVEMENTS IN MALAKAND

Between the death of the Akhund in 1877 to the election of
his grandson as the Badshah of Swat in 1917, lie forty
years of anarchy, chaos and uncertainty. The long and
fierce struggle for power between the agnatic descendants
of Sayyed Akbar and the Akhund was reflected in the turbulence of Swat social life. The Yusufzai Khans of Dir and
Swat supported first one and then another candidate for
Swat leadership as fortunes rose and fell, often as a
direct result of external factors (Hay, 1934).
  Miangul Hannan, the elder son of the Akhund, had political ambitions
    after the death of Amir Sayyid Akbar Shah, it was he
    who approached Saidu Baba with the request that he
    should be made the Amir of Swat.... Though Miangul
    Abdul Hannan could not be the Amir, after the demise of
    Saidu Baba he lived and behaved like one. He owned
    several thorough-bred horses, maintained a regular
    Swati 'lashkar' (irregular force) and participated in
    the battles between the Nawab of Dir and the Khan of
    Bajaur from the one or the other side. He lived in
    great comfort and luxury (Miangul, 1962, p.lxiv).
However, he failed to gain power and establish a State
before his death in 1887. His younger brother was of religious bent, 'Miangul Abdul Khaliq was a devout Muslim
like his honoured father. His entire life was moulded
upon the "shariat". He spent his nights in prayers and

fasted during the day throughout the year' (ibid., p. lxviii). He, too, failed to establish a State before his death in 1892. Through the process of elimination and a singular determination on his part Miangul Wadud, son of Miangul Khaliq, the younger son of the Akhund, emerged as the single main leader in Swat at the turn of the century. In 1903 and in 1907 Miangul Wadud literally eliminated his only two agnatic cousins and sons of the Akhund's elder son (ibid., pp.9, 13) and by the age of twenty-six (in 1907) was the sole heir to the Akhund's legacy.

Between 1877 and 1917 lie the millenarian movements and tribal revolts of 1897-8 which affected traditional local structures and introduced new elements into them. They provided a shift of power and focus, however temporary, from the feudal Khan to the 'mullah', created an air of popular militancy and rebellion against authority and raised new expectancy and hopes. The Miangul, though a young man, was quick to seize the opportunities for leadership and emerged as the champion of the Swat tribes although he was initially pre-empted in this role by the Mastan Mullah (who was finally shifted from the Swat centre stage in 1908). After a short period of exile from Swat as a result of the election of Sayyed Jabbar Shah as ruler of Swat in 1915 he returned to be proclaimed 'Badshah' of Swat. This event was followed by formal re-cognition of the State in 1926 and internal and external consolidation of authority.

The closing years of the last century saw momentous happenings pregnant with immense political significance in the most northern and inaccessible reaches of the British Indian Empire at a time when a decade of food shortage was spreading famine and economic hardship all over the sub-continent. Chitral, Dir and even Mohmand were invaded and occupied by British troops. The 'purdah' of Swat was lifted. To the south of Peshawar the Kurram valley, the Samana range and Wana town were occupied. The sound of bagpipes was heard for the first time north of the Mala-kand Pass. These areas had last seen foreign troops with some of the most famous conquerors in history, Taimur, Chenghiz Khan and Alexander the Great. The Durand Line demarcated tribal boundaries and included tribal areas in the British Empire which had never known conquest and spe-cial Political Agencies were created. The nineties were an era of triumph for the Forward Policy over the Closed Border System (Bruce, 1900) and the 'scientific frontier' (from Kabul to Kandahar) was advocated. Cantonments fol-lowed troops and these in turn were followed by churches and schools and roads and bridges and, as the wheel turned full circle, soldiers again. Suddenly some of the most

remote areas of the subcontinent found themselves confronting an entirely new species of warrior, representing
an entirely alien social system. Local life was dis-
rupted, challenged or affected at all levels of human
existence. Economic and politico-religious crises coincided to threaten and disrupt normal values and
traditions.

The banners of Islam were unfurled and the word 'jihad'
appeared on the lips of men as groups of the faithful
rallied around religious leaders to prepare to throw back
the foreigner. Receptive tribesmen listened to the exhor-
tations of a new breed of leader carrying messages of
hope. Wild rumours of Turkish (Muslim) victories over
Greeks (Christian) added revivalistic fuel to the fire.
An uneasy but portentous calm hung over the mountains of
the Malakand in early 1897. (1) A report from Major
Deane, then Political Agent for the Malakand Areas, to the
Foreign Secretary, Government of India, begins: 'I have
the honour to report that persistent efforts have been and
are being made to arouse Muhammadan fanaticism in Bajaur,
Swat and Dir territory against Government' (PP Encl. 7,
dated 9 May 1897). The summer of 1897 was to be a remarkable one.

A spark was needed to start the conflagration. It came
in the form of an attack in June on the party of the Political Agent, Mr Gee, and his camp in Maizar in a remote
part of the Tochi valley, Waziristan, hundreds of miles
from the main scene of action. A fortnight later the
Malakand tribes rose and by August the Mohmand tribes
joined them. Within two weeks Afridi and Orakzai Tirah
had risen and the Khyber post fell. This chapter will
focus on the movements in Malakand to enable an understanding of the holistic framework from which the Wali of
Swat emerged; it will therefore not deal with those that
took place simultaneously in other parts of the Tribal
Areas.

What occurred then in the form of popular and mass uprisings along the Frontier can only be categorized under a
blanket term: millenarian movements. 'Millennium' here
is not defined strictly in the biblical or eschatological
sense, but loosely as meaning a spontaneous, universal and
historically short-lived, native reaction to economic or
political stimulus, expressed through the presence of
foreign troops and administrators. The reaction is led by
messianic leaders, nationalist heroes and prophets, (2)
often claiming mystical talents, promising some form of
utopia in the future or reversal to a happier order in the
past, and supported by the dispossessed and the rural.
This definition is more akin to the millenarian movements

studied by Worsley in New Guinea which contained an anti-
colonial, anti-white direction than the movements Cohn
studied of the rootless poor of western Europe in the
medieval period who were 'violent, anarchic and at times
truly revolutionary' (Cohn, 1970, p.14). The latter were
revolting within a society and as a result of rural migration to urban areas rather than against foreign
domination.

There is a significant difference in both the stimulation and objectives of the millenarian movements in the
Frontier areas and those studied in, for example, New
Guinea. Although both confront Western civilization at
the zenith of its political power the former wish to
reject the new order and revert to an older one. The historical idiomatic response through which Islamic sentiment
expresses itself in times of extreme crisis is 'jihad'.
The major stimulation is religion. Millenarian movements
create an atmosphere of predisposability to the emergence
of charisma: the relationship is dialectical and not
mechanical. In New Guinea the movements wish to absorb
the new order as symbolized by its 'cargo' and the major
stimulus is economic. The charismatic leader, in turn,
attempts to create a state which helps define the 'institutionalization of charisma'.

It is important to underline that the Frontier movements fought to re-establish the old order and reject the
new one rather than imitate or absorb the new order. The
New Guinea movements were of the latter kind in wishing to
possess the religious secrets that would provide them with
the cargo. The contents of the Frontier argument were
cultural and religious rather than economic and material.
The tribes wished to hold the social boundaries between
them and the British, whereas in New Guinea the movements
wished to alter these boundaries so as to include them.
Yali, the New Guinea millenarian leader, felt 'humiliated'
and 'ashamed' on confronting the cars, streets and
bridges, the symbols of the White Man's civilization, in
Brisbane (Lawrence, 1964, p.123). Among the Frontier
tribes there was no such cultural complex of inferiority.
The Islamic framework within which these tribes ordered
their social life gave them a cultural vitality and religious confidence. It also provided the basis for the
movements and is seen as the primary explanation of them
over 'ethnographic' 'psycho-physiological' 'Marxist' and
'Hegelian' frames of analysis (Burridge, 1969). Islamic
tribes were in fact predictably reacting to a multi-
dimensional invasion of their lands: the seeds of mil-
lenarianism were carried in the nature of the colonial interaction and situation. The ethnic-religious character

of the 1897-8 encounters is reflected in the regiments attached to the Malakand Field Force, raised in 1897 and commanded by Sir Bindon Blood, to deal with the Frontier problems: Muslim regiments were conspicuous by their absence. (3) British military authorities were obviously conscious of the religious (and ethnic) nature of the tribal uprisings and were not taking any chances.

The historical narrative of the millenarian movements in the Frontier is not of concern to this essay but the interconnected socio-political features they contained may be enumerated:

I The British penetration of hitherto untouched and sequestered areas, harbouring some of the fiercest, and enthusiastically Islamic fighting tribes of the subcontinent, was seen as a direct physical threat to moral and religious values and the immediate cause of the uprisings.

II Spontaneous and universal manifestation of support swelled tribesmen fighting numbers into war parties large enough to raid British forts. Shabkadar was raided by the Mohmand tribes, led by the Ada Mullah and the scale of the fighting may be judged by the 200-300 tribesmen who were left behind dead (4) (PP Encl. 27, dated 12 August 1897).

III The sudden proliferation of charismatic leaders along the Frontier, claiming that portents indicated that the 'appointed' time had come and salvation from the British was at hand. It is important to note that the leaders, such as Ada Mullah, Manki Mullah, Palam Mullah, and, in Swat, the Mianguls symbolized a religious or Islamic answer to the political situation and provided a religious focus for millenarian activity. They promised a land free of the infidel and a return to Islamic values (an Islamic utopia).

The Ada Mullah, perhaps the most famous of the millenarian leaders, saw the process as 'jihad' - a holy war, a fight for salvation and a return to Islam. In a letter circulated to tribal elders and 'mullahs' he explained,

The Kafirs have taken possession of all Mussalman countries and owing to the lack of spirit on the part of the people are conquering every region. They have now reached these countries of Bajaur and Swat but though these people showed want of courage in the beginning they have now realized their mistake and - attack them (the Kafirs) day and night (PP Encl. Appendix C, undated).

An extract from a communication of Ada Mullah concludes: 'Help from God (awaits us) and victory is at hand. God willing the time has come when the Kafirs (infidels) should disappear. Be not idle. What more should I insist on' (PP Encl. Annexure to Encl. 34, undated).

These leaders were not - or no longer - the ordinary
every-day village 'mullah' but were possessed men of
charisma claiming supernatural powers or having such
powers attributed to them and progressively magnified by
the faith of adherents. The ground was ripe for charisma
and heightened suggestibility made men believe in extraordinary events and leaders of immense supernatural force.
Sadullah, the Mullah Mastan (5) or as he was to be known,
the Mad Fakir of Swat, entered British despatches in the
following manner: 'About the 18th July reports were received of a Fakir who had suddenly appeared in the country
and established himself at Landakai, (6) professing that
one small pot of rice which he had with him, was sufficient to feed multitudes' (PP Encl. 28, dated 8 August
1897).
    Churchill writes in his first-hand account:
As July advanced, the bazaar at Malakand became full of
tales of the Mad Fakir. A great day for Islam was at
hand. A mighty man had arisen to lead them. The English would be swept away. By the time of the new moon,
not one would remain (Churchill, 1972, p.29).
This is the classic 'prophet' of a millenarian revolt,
he is an unknown entity with no social status or rights to
lose who turns up inexplicably and 'suddenly'. Besides
supernatural and unseen support he has magical powers too:
about the 20th and 21st the Fakir began giving out that
he had heavenly hosts with him, that his mission was to
turn the British off the Malakand and out of Peshawar,
as our rule of 60 years there was up. He claimed to
have been visited by all deceased Fakirs, who told him
the mouths of our guns and rifles would be closed and
that our bullets would be turned to water; that he had
only to throw stones into the Swat river, and each
stone he threw would have on us the effect of a gun (PP
Encl. 28, dated 8 August 1897).
The Tuka cult leader in New Guinea, Ndugumoi, claimed
prophetic, miraculous and occult powers and his spirit was
said to leave his body and move around the country
(Worsley, 1970, p.30). In Swat 'one of the superstitions
indulged in by the people regarding the Fakir was that he
could render himself invisible when he chose' (PP Encl.
28, dated 8 August 1897). As in the Cargo Cults of
Melanasia (like the Taku movement, for example) personal
property was left unattended to. It would be claimed
after the objectives at hand had been achieved: 'This
confidence was so marked that cattle and grain etc. had
all been left in the villages' (ibid.).
    To the British Administration the entire eruption of
uprisings seemed inexplicable in its suddenness, ferocity

and logic, 'The whole rising has been an astounding business and the people seem to have lost their heads and all
view of their own interests in a blind belief that we
should be turned out of the country' (ibid.).

It is of some significance to our analysis and to subsequent political developments to show the distrust and
apprehension felt among the bigger Khans to the movements.
Such upheavals contain a recognizable anarchic content and
threaten to 'disrupt' societal structures and not merely
to create 'conflict' within them. There is therefore a
real possibility and sense of change; of a new beginning
and not merely an alteration of existing arrangements. In
almost every area of revolt the Khans and privileged
groups were in secret touch with the British, fearing
political anarchy and the uncontrollable and unpredictable
religious fanaticism of the 'mullahs'. Their predictable
dilemma was either to chose the uncertain path to
'national' and religious glory or risk local opprobrium by
keeping their options open through contact with the imperial power. They chose the latter. In the event their
policies paid handsome dividends.

The Khan of Dir foiled the Palam Mullah's attempts to
disrupt the peace of Dir and to block the only and crucial
route to Chitral. The major Halimzai Khans of the Mohmand
tribe petitioned the Deputy Commissioner of Peshawar:

The (Ada) Mullah has gone to collect forces. If we do
not comply with the Mullah's orders we are denounced as
Kafirs; on the other hand, the British authorities
attack, kill and burn us. We beg to inform you that
the Mullah's lashkar is coming to Gandab. We are
obedient servants of British authorities - we furnish
this information in order that we may not be blamed
afterwards (PP Sub Encl. A to Encl. 18, dated 2 Septem-
ber 1897).

Another report discloses that

some thirty leading Mohmand Maliks of Tarakzais,
Halimzai and Pindiali sections came in to Stuart Waterfield day before yesterday asking what service they
could do at this juncture. Waterfield told them that
they had only to keep quiet and to arrest any emissa-
ries who might visit them from the Mullah of Adda (PP
Encl. 7, dated 30 July 1897).

In Swat the Akhund's agnatic progeny, the Mianguls,
with the Musa Khel Khans, were obstructing the Mastan
Mullah: 'The Mianguls have sent servants to remove the
Fakir from the country as they fear disturbance, but the
man has taken great hold of religious superstition of the
people throughout the valley and on Dir side' (PP Encl. 3,
dated 26 July 1897).

Some years later the Mullah reappears in Swat:

The Sartor Fakir ... severely beat a messenger of
Gulshahzada Miangul Wadud ... it seems possible that
more will be heard of it, because the last claim which
the Miangul's best friends make for them would be that
they have forgiving tempers (Political Department,
P.A.'s Diary, 31 May 1908, p.83).

However, the changed attitude of the British to the
Miangul and his strategy is apparent in the official note
recorded by the Political Agent:

Sartor, induced by Afghans, prepares for another raid -
on the 9th instant Gulshahzada Miangul (who of late
years has become very friendly and even received the
Political Agent as a guest in his sanctuary at Saidu)
sent word that he had heard the Fakir had reached Azzi
Khel country with his 'lashkars' and expressed his
willingness to do anything that was required in the
matter. Swat was of course instantly alive with excitement, and it seemed best to take the Khans as
frankly into our confidence as we had the Khans of Dir
(ibid., 16 May 1908, p.66).

But by this time the fury of the millenarian movements was
spent. The generalized charismatic ambience had evapora-
ted. The Mullah was out of tune with the times. A new
force in the person of Miangul Wadud was emerging in Swat.
The Mullah called off his campaign and disappeared from
the Swat stage:

The Sartor Fakir next departed Northwards, sending, as
a Parthian shot at Gulshahzada, a sealed letter to me
stating that he had been forbidden to go on by Nakash-
band Khan, and that it was for his sake and not the
Miangul's that he had given up his plans (ibid., 24 May
1908, p.66).

Subsequently, and over the next few years, it is not
difficult to construct why the British Administration
would be so readily prepared to negotiate with and support
traditionally established rulers, as in the case of the
Khan of Dir, or officially patronize emergent rulers like
the Mianguls of Swat. It was in the mutual interest of
both negotiating parties not to let such popular movements, and such revolutionary and fanatical mass leaders,
get out of hand. The 'status quo' had to be promptly restored. After the swift and numerous punitive expeditions, trials and punishments, the old order was restored.
The official Administration Report records with satisfac-
tion that by 1903,and due to the loyalty of its rulers,
Chitral, Dir and Swat were 'more or less free from the
pernicious preachings of religious agitators' (Administration Report, 1903, p.26).

Reward was not long in coming. Formal titles were conferred on the loyal rulers: the 'Mehtar' of Chitral, the
'Nawab' of Dir and the 'Nawab' of Nawagai. The former two
were also decorated with the CIE and as a final symbol of
imperial gratitude the three rulers were invited to the
grand assembly of Indian royalty that had gathered at
Delhi to attend the Coronation Darbar in 1903. Swat later
joined the Malakand States as a new State with the Wali of
Swat as its ruler. The lesson that the British had firmly
learnt from the 1857 Indian 'Mutiny' was that their interests coincided squarely with those of the ruling
houses.

The tribal movements grew passive but never quite died
out. A direct and far-reaching consequence was the creation of a separate North-West Frontier Province, under
the viceroyalty of Lord Curzon, in 1901, and the quiet
death of the 'Forward Policy' on the north-western marches
of the British Indian Empire. The movement's subsequent
history merges with the struggles of the nationalist parties to end British Rule in India and later to create an
Islamic State for the Muslims. However, for purposes of
our analysis, the only religious leader who survived the
movements intact and emerged politically victorious was
Miangul Gulshahzada, the future Wali of Swat.

ANTI-THESIS: INSTITUTIONALIZATION OF CHARISMA IN SWAT

Social pre-conditions and cultural idioms

The millenarian uprisings in the Malakand areas were led
by leaders predicating spiritual affiliation with the
Akhund: 'The Adda Mullah, the Manki Mullah and the Palam
Mullah are the principal remaining followers of the Akhund
of Swat' (PP Encl. 7, dated 9 May 1897). The legend of
the Akhund provided a general source of religious inspiration which his agnatic descendants sought to mobilize in
their claim to Swat political authority. The Mianguls had
joined the 1897 movements but, as has been seen in the
last section, kept their options open with the British.
Once the movements subsided and the 'mullahs' lost their
importance the Mianguls still remained as prominent
leaders; from these emerged the future Wali of Swat.
There is thus a certain cause and effect relationship between the millenarian movements of Malakand and the emergence of charismatic leadership in Swat.

Amorphous followings around visionary leaders promising
apocalyptic victories in a series of uprisings constituted
the thesis of the last section. The emergence of one man

who gathers around him various sections of society and, while embarked on a definite 'mission' to fulfil his 'destiny', institutionalizes charismatic leadership is the opposite and antithetical theme of this section. His emergence is partly a consequence of the thesis and partly an explanation of it. The emphasis in the analytical conceptualization of the argument shifts from the holistic frame of reference to one centring around a main actor who translates and reorders the symbols of power and authority in society into cultural idioms understood by his followers. Action and reaction, to a certain degree, become a function of the actor's stratagem; which, in turn, purports to satisfy and interpret the majoritarian needs of society. Sociologically, the actor becomes a charismatic leader - he possesses

> a certain quality of an individual personality by virtue of which he is set apart from ordinary men and treated as endowed with supernatural, superhuman, or at least specifically exceptional powers or qualities. These are not accessible to the ordinary person, but are regarded as of divine origin or as exemplary and on the basis of them the individual concerned is treated as a leader (Weber, 1947, pp.358-9).

Barth's omission from his analysis of the social and political conditions from which the Wali emerged, and of his subsequent career, as mentioned above, is similar to the omissions made by functionalist anthropologists who conceptualize isolated and static African social structures without direct reference to the office and functions of the colonial representative as agents of sociopolitical change (Fortes and Evans-Pritchard, 1940; Fortes, 1945, 1949). The omission clarifies why the Swat analysis falls into the well-known trap of equating fundamental 'contradiction' between irresolvable oppositions in society (created by the foundation of the State, and the extent of its interpenetration on all levels of Swat society in this case) for 'conflict', that involves opposition between principles of social organization (Bailey, 1960, pp.7, 239; Gluckman, 1971, pp.xxii, 109-10).

In 1947 Miangul Abdul Wadud, while on tour with Sir Olaf Caroe, then Governor of the North-West Frontier Province, stated that 'never in all history, not even in the time of Akbar or Aurangzeb, much less under the Durranis, were the Yusufzais of this country the subjects of any empire' (Caroe, 1965, p.205). This statement left unsaid the most remarkable event of Yusufzai history. The Yusufzai were now the subjects of the autarchic speaker, the Wali of Swat.

Miangul Wadud was no stranger to the concept of

established authority. Although his uncle, Miangul
Hannan, had failed to establish temporal authority over
Swat, his father, Miangul Khaliq, had succeeded in main-
taining the administrative foundations for a religious
State laid by the Akhund: (7)

> without an army or a regular force Miangul Abdul Khaliq
> succeeded in establishing an Islamic rule in Swat. He
> governed the people with the help of his followers,
> known as 'sheikhs'. These 'sheikhs' were a sort of
> police and enforced the laws and carried out the Amir's
> orders throughout the length and breadth of the State.
> Swatis entrusted him with full powers to punish them
> for their crimes in accordance with the 'shariat'
> (Miangul, 1962, pp.lxvi-lxvii).

Funds and followers go hand in hand with a charismatic
leader and are a vital index of his fortunes. There is a
circular and cumulative causation between funds, followers
and charisma. The relationship with his followers was
based on the same principles of redistributive economies
that the Akhund had established: 'The alms-house founded
by Saidu Baba was run by Miangul Abdul Khaliq on the same
grand scale as before. Food for five hundred men was
cooked there every day, often the number went up to two
thousand even' (ibid., p.lxix).

The future Wali was just over ten years old when
Miangul Abdul Khaliq died in 1892 (ibid., p.1). A fierce
internecine agnatic struggle both educated and matured him

> before I proceed to give an account of the domestic
> tussle and hostilities with my cousins I should like to
> mention that through these conflicts we received a sort
> of practical training which was very valuable in days
> to come. We shouldered responsibilities of life at a
> time when others of our age amused themselves in child-
> ish games. As a result, in this school of adversity,
> we gained experience and attained qualities and capabi-
> lities which no scholastic training or academic educa-
> tion could have imparted. While still young, we came
> to possess political understanding and organizing
> ability which later proved an asset not only in every-
> day problems but also in the establishment of the State
> and the battle of life in general. Even in childhood
> we won prominence as leaders in the field of action
> (ibid., p.3).

A sense of intense competitiveness corresponded with
belief in his religious destiny and drove him:

> I was active, hardworking and persevering, with a proud
> record of having always beaten my equals in travelling
> on foot, riding, mountain-climbing and marksmanship.
> These personal merits were desirable qualifications for

one who was ordained to be the ruler of the Pathans
some day (ibid., p.6).

The example of his father and grandfather was never far
from him:

During the four years following my father's death, I
lived in seclusion to prepare myself to be the spiritual successor of Sahib of Swat, and offered prayers
regularly.... From the time of Amir Badshah's death
when I was twenty-four till today in my seventy-seventh
year I have never missed or even delayed one prayer,
whether at home or on a journey (ibid., pp.133-4).

The deep sense of religious motivation and belief in destiny were confirmed by those who dealt with him:

He was according to his lights, a very religious man,
his prayers, his beliefs were absolutely genuine and
sincere and he was convinced in his own mind that he
was performing a great work under the eyes of and with
the approval of, the Almighty (Caroe, personal communication, 1975).

The conclusion that in power lay the key to the Swat
solution was reached early in his career, 'Swat was a
tribal territory in which power alone could command respect; self-interestedness and oppression were the law of
the land; it had never been under any firm authority
before' (Miangul, 1962, p.46).

Swat at the turn of the century passed through great
socio-political anarchy and turbulence. Swat tribes 'in
fact want a guiding hand to help them establish internal
peace which they have not enjoyed since the death of the
old Akhund of Swat' (PP Encl. 2, dated 21 July 1897). The
Miangul himself complained in a letter to the Lieutenant-
Governor of the Punjab: 'now all the people of Swat have
assumed the profession of robbery and "dakoiti" (dacoity)'
(PP Sub Encl. to Encl. 1, dated 12 June 1897). In his
autobiography he writes of the conditions prevalent in
those days and that: 'the Swatis are still an insular,
narrow-minded and uncivilized people, and it will take a
little more time to outgrow these undesirable traits'
(Miangul, 1962, pp.90-1).

Chaos and disorder reigned supreme. The leadership of
the Khans was bankrupt. All sections of society looked to
strong leadership, to a saviour: the ground was ripe for
charismatic leadership.

Miangul Wadud, facing and clearing a series of hurdles
on his way to Walidom, illustrated at each stage how the
interests of one or other section of the community, at one
or other period of Swat history, coincided with his own
interests and furthered them. From an early age he had
displayed a talent for political manoeuvre and

administrative strategy which were to characterize his extraordinary life and career. His own 'energy and saga-
city' (Stein, 1929, p.5) were vital elements in this
charismatic projection: sufficient and favourable contemporaneous accounts exist to confirm these qualities
(Caroe, 1965; Hay, 1934; Stein, 1929):

> like the Emperor Akbar a past-master in the political
> management of men, one who knew to a nicety the moment
> to seize whether in council or in battle, resolute in
> action, devout yet free of all cant, again like Akbar
> illiterate but blessed with a prodigious memory, he set
> to all around him a pattern of leadership hard to equal
> in his own country and such as the annals of any land
> would be proud to boast (Caroe, 1965, p.427).

Charisma creates following and following creates charisma.
The Miangul's successes by 1917 proved him a hero in war,
a saint in peace, a man endowed with 'supernatural',
'superhuman' and 'extraordinary powers' (Weber, 1947, p.
358). None the less, his greatest asset, and the base for
his political career, remained the charismatic reverence
inherited from his grandfather, the Akhund. This inheritance provided a sufficient backdrop to enable his political fortunes to develop and dominate events in Swat. The
Miangul manipulated the symbols that reactivated personal
networks and opened charismatic channels of communication
with his grandfather's following. Though the initial de-
posit of 'family' charisma, subject to the law of dimin-
ishing returns, was inherited at birth, each new member of
the family had to reactivate that network which would give
him easiest access to maximum authority and power. It was
an individual, not corporate family, struggle. In Miangul
Wadud's case 'inherited charisma' reinforced 'personal
charisma' but more than his agnatic ascendants he wished
to establish a formal State. After his agnatic cousins
and only brother were dead he became the sole family heir
to the vast properties and spiritual position of his
grandfather.

Rival religious challenge

The first direct and religious threat appeared in the
rather unlikely figure of Mastan Mullah, the Fakir of
Buner, who had claimed extraordinary and magical powers
and become a rallying point against the British in 1897.
The Fakir made his camp at Landakai, which must have been
uncomfortable for the Mianguls, but a more serious act was
his claim that a boy protégé in his train was heir to the
Mughal throne at Delhi. Could he not alter his direction

and make a similar claim for Swat?   However, his advancing
age was against him and the Fakir, already an old man at
the turn of the century, saw his following break up after
the failure of the movements and as a result of his in-
capacity to live up to his magical exploits and inflated
promises.   His second attempt for Swat leadership ended
abortively in 1908, partly foiled by the Miangul.

Sayyed Abdul Jabbar Shah, descended from the famous Pir
Baba of Buner and Sayyed Akbar Shah, was a more serious
threat to the Miangul and was actually appointed 'Badshah'
of the Swat confederacy of tribes by the Yusufzai Khans
from 1915-17:

> In total disregard of my wish and resolve the people of
> Swat invited Sayyid Jabbar Shah of Sitana in Hazara,
> who was in the line of Sayyid Akbar Shah, first Amir of
> Swat, to become their ruler.... Sayyid Jabbar Shah,
> acquiescing in the arrangements, arrived in Swat and
> set up his rule over the areas across the River Swat.
> The people there accepted his authority (Miangul, 1962,
> pp.33-4).

The Manguls went into temporary exile: 'So we left our
hometown and removed to our property in Dalbar, a village
in Adinzai, outside Swat, where we lived in exile for
quite some time' (ibid., p.35).   The Miangul however was
not long in returning with the aid of Dir forces.   Resum-
ing his religious mantle, and assisted by the Sandakei
Mullah, he raised a rebellion against the Sayyed by declaring him a heretic connected with the Qadiani sect
(Barth, 1959a, p.128).   This appealed to the orthodox who
rallied behind the Miangul as defender of the faith and
the Sayyed was quietly expelled from Swat.   The Miangul
was elected the new 'Badshah' of Swat.   The nature of the
contest was uneven.   The Miangul was a shrewd, dynamic
figure acutely aware of Swat political processes and the
alliances and groups that ordered them, whereas the Sayyed
was a scholarly and retiring person all too keen to quit
the contest.   The latter's headquarters in remote Sitana
kept him isolated from the hurly burly of Swat politics
and a relative stranger to its developments.

The aspect of political power derived from religious
leadership was not forgotten by the Miangul: 'his first
action on having established himself as Ruler was therefore to expel, as politically undesirable, all Saints and
mystics who did not own property' (ibid., p.102).

Dialectics of politico-symbolic factors

The Miangul surveying the field in the early twenties
assessed the political situation: 'I had to fight on the
following five fronts:
I To put down the mutinous Khans of Swat at Manja.
II To repulse the invading Kohistani 'lashkar' at
Madyan.
III To beat back the aggressive Nawab of Amb at Karakar.
IV To repulse the concentrated forces of my old and
powerful adversary, the Nawab of Dir in Adinzai.
V To outmanoeuvre the seditious activities and clandes-
tine dealing of the British Political Agent' (Miangul,
1962, p.73).
    The Nawab of Dir provided a constant and the most dan-
gerous expansionist threat to Swat leadership. . At one
stage the Khan had occupied the right bank of the Swat
river and in the time-honoured tradition of Yusufzai conquest and 'according to Pathan custom he at once established guards in the country under Akhundzadas, who habi-
tually bully and harass the people' (PP Encl. 2,
dated 21 July 1897). The proud Yusufzai Khans looking
around desperately for Swat leadership and a symbol of
supratribal unity threw in their lot with the Miangul who
led them as a political and military commander in successful and decisive battles with the Dir forces. Having consolidated his western (Dir) front the Miangul, in rapid
and successful battles, defeated his enemies to the north
and south of Swat. These military successes consolidated
and expanded his territories and they also illustrated his
relative invincibility to the Swat Khans. He was now the
unchallenged ruler of Swat.
    To further consolidate the support of loyalist Khans he
implemented numerous 'reforms' such as the abolition of
the custom of 'wesh',whereby his enemies were permanently
deprived of their lands and his allies permanently obliga-
ted. The nature of his rule, however, was personal and
informal rather than courtly or imperial. The village
peasant felt nearer to it than to the aristocratic schema
of the Khans:
    The amount of this work could be inferred merely from
    the crowds of Jirgahs (tribal councils), local Khans,
    and other individual applicants whom I saw early in the
    morning already gathered in front of the Miangul's
    terrace. It seemed a very convenient substitute for
    that 'takht' or raised seat of judgement which Indian
    as well as Central-Asian tradition necessarily associ-
    ates with the function of a ruler (Stein, 1929, p.69).
Bureaucratization was on its way with the process of the

'institutionalization of charisma' and its functions.

Colonial interaction

When discussing what the greatest achievement of his life
was the Miangul had explained
> once in the days of the British rule, the Governor of
> the Frontier Province, Sir Ralph Griffith, was in Swat
> on a visit. We were returning to Saidu Sharif from
> Buner in the same car when, in the course of a conver-
> sation he asked me the question: 'Badshah Sahib, what
> do you regard as the greatest achievement of your
> life?' promptly and without hesitation, I answered:
> 'That I have succeeded in establishing friendly rela-
> tions with the British Government, is no doubt a great
> achievement in my life' (Miangul, 1962, pp.109-10).
The British presence provided the Miangul opportunity to
display his diplomatic skill and shrewd reading of past
and future events. The lessons of the millenarian movements followed by the swift and irresistible British ad-
vance were not lost on him. He won the British over with
arguments based on the logic of mutual benefit; they
could be assured of a peaceful border and the Miangul of
non-interference in Swat's affairs. The Miangul walked a
tight-rope; his negotiations had to be conducted without
alienating his followers or compromising his role as a religious leader. The British soon saw the Swat State
become 'a haven of peace on our troubled border' (Hay,
1934, p.246). Troops and resources were diverted to other
parts of the Frontier where they were always desperately
required (in the late thirties, for instance, there were
as many troops in Waziristan as in the rest of the Indian
subcontinent).
     The Wali was left free to deal with the Swat problems.
By maintaining that '"local autonomy" as interpreted in
Swat allowed the indigenous population complete freedom to
work out their own political problems in any manner they
chose' (Barth, 1959a, p.8), Barth misreads the British administrative concept of 'local autonomy' and its implications for Swat political organization. 'Local autonomy'
was never meant literally. The Political Agent, Malakand,
(after the Agency was established in 1895), was officially
responsible to the Indian Government for the 'situation'
in Swat (apart from Malakand, Dir and Chitral). The Political Agent arranged princely 'privy purses', tribal
allowances, government agricultural loans, development
schemes etc. He was a distant but powerful force. By en-
suring 'local autonomy' or 'non-interference' in Swat, the

British became a vital factor in upsetting local political
equilibrium permanently in favour of the Wali. British
support implicitly supported and reinforced the Wali's
authority. 'Local autonomy' in this context is not of a
structural kind underwriting an acephalous stateless
tribal system but an 'autonomy' for the imperial protégé
to consolidate his power and ensure internal peace. The
Wali blocked any moves on the part of the Khans to contact
the British directly which could have exposed a flank the
latter might well have exploited. An early British report
mentions 'the Mianguls whose sole object has been to exclude the Pathan Maliks from direct contact with Government' (PP Encl. 2, dated 21 July 1897). He thus secured
his borders, and political arena, against British
interference.

The Miangul, having cleared every hurdle in his path
and consolidated every important section of the community
behind him by demonstrated and repeated success, emerged
as the main political and religious leader of the valley
restoring order and establishing law. Revolt against him
was not only a revolt against the political saviour of
Swat but the most influential living religious male agnate
of the Akhund. His 'electorate' was the poor and illiterate villager who saw in him the continuing local religious
tradition of the Akhund; a factor that balanced any group
of overly ambitious Khans. Political charisma was sanctified by religious charisma.

From millennium to Statehood

Final and formal recognition came in 1926:
    On May 3rd of the same year, Col. J.W. Keen, Acting
    Chief Commissioner of the Frontier Province, held a
    'durbar' at Saidu Sharif, in which he read out the
    letter of the Government of India proclaiming me the
    Ruler of Swat and my son, Miangul Jahan Zeb, the Heir
    Apparent (Miangul, 1962, p.94).
The establishment of the State carried within it the seeds
of 'the routinization of charisma' (Weber, 1947, p.358).
The interests of the main loyalist followers and the
Wali's immediate family coincided to bring some regularity
and legality to the problem of the successor. With the
declaration of the Waliahad, positions of authority in
ranked administrative hierarchy and social prestige were
systematically and quickly legitimized.

The aid of Figures 2-4 is enlisted to show the shift in
functional relationship between the Khan (from that of a
patron to his tenants, to a broker with the State) and the

tenant (who continues as universal client) and their relationship with the Wali, and with each other, both before
and after the establishment of the State.

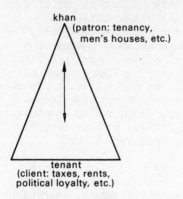

FIGURE 2   Pre-Wali Swat

Horizontal lines of socio-political alignment (between
Khans) contrast with vertical lines relating 'patron'
Khans with their 'client' tenants. Patronage is express-
ed in various forms: land tenure, membership of 'hujras',

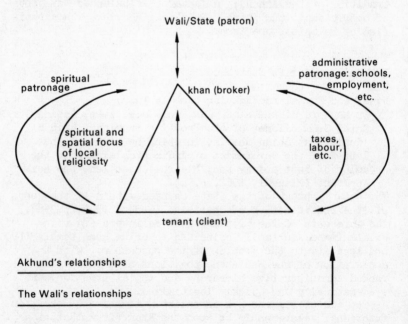

FIGURE 3   Post-Wali Swat

rates of rents etc. Clientship involves regular contractual obligations which presuppose political loyalty. With
the emergence of the Wali and the State many aspects of
the Khans' patronage are taken over by official administrative functions, for example, taxes and corvée labour.
In return, the State provides free schools, hospitals etc.
The Khan finds himself as a broker, for the peasant to the
State. The other equally strong link with the State is
spiritual as it symbolizes a spatial reference to the
Akhund for the peasantry. It is notable that the Akhund's
sphere of authority is primarily religious but the Wali
adds a new dimension to the relationship with the Khans
and, more important, directly with the tenant through the
introduction and use of all-pervasive administrative
channels (Figure 3).

Figure 4 will illustrate the post-State situation
whereby vertical lines of 'dalla' alignment convert to
vertical lines of conflict as new horizontal lines of
socio-political identity emerge cross-cutting previous
alliances and corporate groups (Asad, 1972).

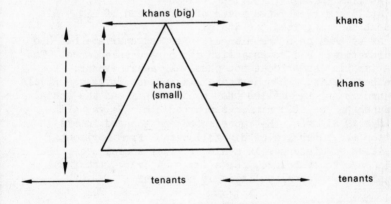

FIGURE 4 Post-State Swat

The typological sequence in the progress of charismatic
organization from a 'band' or 'audience' of followers to a

regular following to political/religious 'movement' and
finally to State/administrative 'organization' was comple-
ted during the life of Miangul Wadud. He rounded off his
career by an act which is perhaps difficult to define in
terms of material maximizing man and is yet comprehensible
in the Islamic Sufic tradition and terminology discussed
in the last chapter. His grandfather, the Akhund, had refused temporal power to the end. The Miangul established
a State and at the noonday of the State's history he ab-
dicated in 1949 (Barth, 1959a, p.129) to lead the monastic
life of a religious recluse by fasting, praying and
contemplation,

> Two life-long ambitions of mine remained to be fulfil-
> led. I had always cherished the desire of acquiring
> knowledge, especially to acquaint myself thoroughly
> with the Holy Quran and the 'Sunnah'. Secondly, I
> wished to work for spiritual and moral amelioration of
> the Swatis and, travelling with a group of enlightened
> and sophisticated scholars from village to village, en-
> deavour to mould their actions and character according
> to Islamic precepts so that they might become true
> Muslims (Miangul, 1962, pp.129-30).

He still had twenty-two years of life ahead of him. His
eldest son inherited the State.

As we have seen the Miangul inherited charisma but had
to reactivate and re-establish it to gain ascendance. The
charismatic leader does not passively await events. He
creates events. To understand his success it is essential
to understand the milieu that produced him and the social
groups who resisted him or supported him. He was all
things to all men. He represented and focused in his
person the interests of his followers. From horizontal
politics of dissensus in a hierarchical social order the
Wali came to symbolize, for a large majority, the focal
point for a general politics of consensus.

SYNTHESIS: THE STATE OF SWAT

The central thesis of popular millenarian activities in
the Malakand partly explained the milieu, and partly provided a base, for the antithesis in the form of the emergence of a charismatic leader and institutionalization of
authority. It also explained the logic of the socio-
political developments which provided a unique synthesis
in the State of Swat. The holistic framework, applied to
the analysis of the millenarian movements, was largely
abandoned for an individualist one to explain the emergence of the Wali of Swat and with the establishment of a

formal centralized and bureaucratized State the analysis
shifts away from an understanding of charisma to explaining the processes of 'institutionalization' of charisma.
Unfortunately the undefined boundaries between 'personal
charisma' and 'institutional charisma' and the transition
between them have not been sufficiently dealt with in
Weber's analysis of charismatic authority. The argument
again shifts to a holistic frame of sociological reference: the State through its symbols of authority now per-
vades social life at all levels of Swat society and social
relations are, in turn, and in varying degree, an interaction with its ubiquitous agents.

Barth's analysis of the development of the State and
its all-embracing impact on the Swat social structure is
as marginal and brief as his account of the rise of the
Wali. He almost dismisses the most significant political
development in Swat history (and an important one in
Pathan society) by an explanation resting on 'some technological innovations, mainly the telephone' (8) (Barth,
1959a, p.135). This renders unsatisfactory Barth's account of political developments in Malakand from the turn
of the century, encompassing as they do the two major and
interconnected events discussed above. The implication
for his Game-Theory model is evident. Recalcitrant Khans
find it increasingly difficult to 'manoeuvre' and 'manipulate' in a game that does not pretend to have either fixed
rules or impartial umpire; they and their plans become a
function of the State's over-all strategy and not a function, as in the past, of 'maximizing' individual
ambitions.

Individuals are no longer entirely free 'to plan and
make choices in terms of private advantage and a personal
political career' (ibid., p.2). 'Group commitments' can
no longer 'be assumed and shed at will' nor 'self-
interest' alone 'dictate action' (ibid.). 'Seizing' land
or 'attacking' and 'ousting' rivals involves confrontation
with the laws of the State and its ever-present forms of
'coercive authority'. 'Maximizing' man was up against the
strait-jacket structural framework of a highly centralized
State; 'manoeuvre' and 'strategy' could only operate
within radically changed tactics and networks.

The three traditional sources of the feudal power base
of Swat were affected by the State, irreparably emasculat-
ing the Khan and thereby altering the nature of the network of dyadic social relationships that he created around
him (both with client peasants and other Khans). Social
structure on all levels was thus altered and social relationships redefined:

I 'Wesh' was frozen and therefore, by confirming the

possession of land held at that moment in time, the State
left the Khan in a vulnerable position as he could no
longer claim land as his lineage right based on belonging
to a segmentary Pukhtun group. The unit of land he owned
was his in perpetuity and therefore his main economic base
but if the State took it on some pretext, he could do
little about it. Under the previous 'wesh' system the
entire tribe would be affected and react jointly to the
challenge. Freezing of rights in landed property struck
at the roots of Yusufzai Pukhtun mystification regarding
inherent rights to the land. The formal ending of this
custom meant a loss of symbolic status and implied rejection of the Yusufzai myth.

II   Just as land was the source of economic power and
social prestige to the Khan, his weapons were the means to
translate this power to political action. The Wali attempted what no ruler of Pathans had ever done: (9) he
disarmed his subjects:

> The time at last came, when an order restricting the
> possession and use of fire-arms could be safely en-
> forced.... My friends were the first to do so, closely
> followed by others, till all present disarmed them-
> selves there and then; the rest of the public did
> likewise; and before long the rather tricky task of
> disarming the people had been completed successfully
> (Miangul, 1962, p.109).

Simultaneously, 'loyalists' and 'supporters' were issued
arms in each village to discourage revolt or to contain it
until official forces acted. The socio-political significance of this act cannot be overemphasized in Pathan
society. Pathans believe in the right to carry arms from
childhood and even the administration of the Settled Districts of the Frontier Province found it exceedingly difficult to restrict their use and transportation.

III   The traditional tax on grain and agricultural pro-
ducts was partly diverted from the Khan to the State in
the form of 'ushar' and indicated to the peasantry that
the State had succeeded and substituted the Khan as a sort
of universal landlord and patron. The change in the revenue collection underlined the altered status of the peasant; from a vassal tied to a particular Khan through
dyadic links he became a citizen of a State where, theoretically at least, all were equal in the eyes of the law.
In turn the State provided free schools, medical dispensa-
ries etc. Thus the Khan's 'redistributive' economic
system (gathering of goods and services upwards to a central point and then a downwards redistribution of resources to numerous points) was reflected structurally in the
homologous nature of the State.

IV The military and temporal authority of the feudal
warlord was replaced by the patriarchal and moral authority of the State. The latter was legitimized both in temporal and spiritual terms. A revolt against the State was
a revolt against the Islamic Pathan State of the House of
the Akhund of Swat. Saidu symbolized the temporal capital
of the State and the Akhund's shrine in it a spiritual
focus. A new social and religious order was emphasized.
The establishment of this new order was symbolized in the
formal recognition of the Wali's eldest son as the
Waliahad, the heir-apparent. A dynasty was established.
    The role of the State itself was seen as partly
reformist:

    Womenfolk were restored to their rightful place in
    society, and were given the rights and privileges ex-
    pounded in the 'shariat'. Gambling and other objec-
    tional modes of entertainment were legally banned. In
    short, I spared no effort in weeding out all moral and
    social evils (ibid., p.115).

And

    no sooner was a territory annexed to the State than I
    appointed learned Molvis to instruct the people in Is-
    lamic theology and to teach them to read and write.
    Stress on religious instruction was necessary then, for
    the Swatis had little knowledge of the religion they
    practise (ibid., p.116).

Pashto became the official lingua franca representing
the folk language rather than the traditional subcontinental court languages such as Persian or Urdu, often only
spoken by the rural élites:

    On coming into authority, I declared Pashto to be the
    official language of the State and adopted the Urdu
    script as the style of writing.... Both officials and
    the public were directed to employ simple, everyday
    language in all their writings, and express themselves
    briefly and to the point; especially avoiding lengthy
    salutations and adulatory phrases (ibid., p.117).

'Swati' ethnicity was created and further reinforced in
the border wars of conquest and consolidation that the
Wali embarked upon immediately after establishing centralized authority in Swat. Territory was annexed as a
result of battles with the Nawab of Dir, the Nawab of Amb
and the Kohistanis in the north. These military encounters served two connected purposes: while ostensibly providing new conquests they also offered a valid justifica-
tion to crush rebellious Khans. Ethnically, they created
geographical boundaries of 'Swatiness' and therefore
helped define it in spatial rather than phyletic terms.
    It is worth noting that though the facts and figures

pertaining to the authority of Swat State, given in 'Political Leadership among Swat Pathans', add up to an arithmetical total of awesome proportions they are relegated in the analysis to an auxiliary position. The sum-total of the arithmetic reveals a form of Oriental Despotism (Wittfogel, 1957) and not a variety of those African tribal societies, organized into states around a central authority, like the Zulu (Fortes and Evans-Pritchard, 1940). Power is absolute; the individual is reduced to a function and extension of the State's will. The State as the final expression of the ruler is omnipresent and omnipotent. This is all the more remarkable in a Pathan society that bases its social organization and cultural ethos on democratic concepts of individuality:

> The Pathans, who reside in the tribal territory on our border, are essentially a democratic race, and though from time to time a Khan or Mullah has arisen amongst them who has acquired such influence that he has come to be regarded locally more or less as a king, it is doubtful whether any individual has ever before succeeded in establishing over any part of their country such absolute power as that now enjoyed by the Ruler of Swat, Miangul Gulshahzada Sir Abdul Wadud, KBE (Hay, 1934, p.236).

However, a comparison with other forms of Oriental Despotism must be qualified by the nature of the ruler and the ruled. The Swat court never attained the formality and inaccessibility of imperial Mughal or Saffawid dynasties. The Wali was highly mobile, accessible and visible.

The features whereby Wittfogel defines the mathematics of Oriental Despotism are basically in terms of a highly centralized political system organized around, and as a function of, vast irrigation schemes that require mass corvée labour (for flood protection etc.) drawn from a subject peasantry and directed by a powerful bureaucracy; exalted rulers with unlimited authority rule this pyramidal organization. If the structural concept could be borrowed without its concomitant and grandiose superlatives then an examination of the Swat State could be seen as a template for a miniature hydraulic State or Oriental Despotism.

Swat is demographically dense and thereby satisfies an essential characteristic of an Oriental Despotic State. For a purely agricultural and herding population 'settlement is extremely dense; it can be roughly estimated at eight hundred persons per square mile of productive land' (Barth, 1959a, p.6). Complex and extensive irrigation systems are maintained, 'water is drawn from the main Swat river and from its smaller tributaries by a complex system

of channels, which irrigate a large part of the valley
bottom' (ibid.). This justifies the growth of bureaucracy
based on careful recording of land units and land is
periodically assessed by the Revenue officers of the administration and two-thirteenths of all agricultural produce taken as tax (ibid., p.130).

The Wali embodies unlimited supreme authority: 'The
Ruler claims absolute power, and conceives of his administration as "a family concern" in which duties and respon-
sibilities are informally delegated, at his pleasure, to
trusted individuals' (ibid., p.129). The Wali is the
State ('charisma' in the process of its 'institutionalization'): 'All persons employed by the State of Swat are
the "servants" of the Ruler ("da Badshah naukaran")'
(ibid., p.48).

A network of communication meets in the person of the
Wali

He is, furthermore, in constant telephonic communication with administrators in the districts. One of the
first acts of the Badshah after his election as Ruler
was the construction of (1,500 miles of) telephone
lines from the capital to the main local centres. The
radial pattern of construction offered the further advantage that while he had direct communication with
every place, persons in the different centres could not
communicate with each other without his knowledge.
Roads (375 miles) have also been constructed to give
direct access to all areas (ibid., p.131).

His policy is therefore reflected in all State decisions:
Information and appeals travel upwards in this hierarchy, while instruction and decisions are passed down-
ward and implemented by it. The personnel of this organization are civil servants, many of them of Saint
caste; they are frequently transferred and rarely permitted to serve in their native area (ibid., p.129).

The army numbering about ten thousand
which can be mobilized only from the centre, consti-
tutes the final sanction against leaders. Moreover the
Ruler maintains a rough balance between the blocs by
supporting now one and now the other. The powers of
the Khans are offset also by those of the appointed administrators, such as the 'Tahsildars' - who are transferred frequently to prevent collusion with local
leaders. Their local powers of subversion are further
limited by their dependence on the local police officers - independently appointed by the Ruler - for
actual force (ibid., p.131).

The police supplement the strength of the army: 'the
police forces permanently on duty, which are distributed

between eighty fortresses in different parts of the State, have a strength of two thousand' (ibid., p.130).

Every manipulable device heightens and strengthens the central authority of the ruler. Power in such cases can only be assessed in total sums; so can individual terror or impotence. In the classical tradition of the Oriental Despots the main deputies are extra-ethnic who owe total loyalty to the ruler and remain politically emasculated: of Chitrali descent (Hazrat Ali Khan, the Wazir-i-Azam or Chief Minister, and his brother, the Sipah-Salar or Commander-in-Chief) or Punjabi (the Chief Secretary and the Chief Medical Officer).

It is difficult to envisage how in this monolithic State structure the Khan and his alliances have, except the most marginal, room for manoeuvre at any level of social action. Alliances and blocs formed around political functions cannot exist in a centralized system like the one just described. Even the local power of the Khan is now balanced by the Tehsildar, the Police and the Army. Barth gives an example of Khans stepping out of (State) line:

> an appeal a few years ago by a number of landowners was punished by severe beating with the rifle-butts of the Ruler's bodyguard, and thus cost most of the pleaders their front teeth - enough to make them feel they had got off easy without encouraging them to try again.

But though the local Khan thus wields autonomous power within his own area, he is in no position to challenge the Ruler's wider authority (ibid., p.132).

The State as described above is conceptually antonymous to an acephalous tribal society within which powerful warlords may play power games. Yet Barth maintains that 'the description of the bloc organization thus remains valid and accurate within the area of Swat State as well as outside its boundaries' (ibid.) - as if the State and its all-pervasive agencies simply do not exist or affect the social structure in Swat. In spite of the structural web that the State has spun around him, requiring holist analysis, Barth's Swat Pathan is still seen in individualist terms and his socio-political milieu continues to be equated to that of 'transactionalist' Western man: 'the political life of Swat resembles that of Western societies' (ibid., p.2).

In 1969 the Government of Pakistan merged the State of Swat within its administrative structure. Swat became a District and the Wali, stripped of all administrative authority, was replaced by a Deputy Commissioner. The inherent ambiguity in accepting the Wali as a spiritual, informal leader and the emergence of a centralized State

with increasingly impersonal power was never really resolved. Although in 1969 there was considerable, often
latent, political opposition to the Wali in Swat, his son
and heir was returned in the National Assembly elections,
based on adult universal suffrage, the next year. This
illustrates that loyalty to the Wali, and his family, was
based on more factors than just State patronage and authority. The last traces of familial charisma were barely,
but still, visible.

8 Models and method in anthropology

THE KHAN'S EYE-VIEW OF THE WORLD

The Introduction suggested that Barth's analysis of Swat
society was 'synecdochic' in nature i.e. it saw the world
through the eyês of the Khan and that view was taken as
representative of what is apperceived by Swat society as a
whole. The main sources of information, and certainly
those providing the material for the four chapters that
analyse Swat political organization and social action
(Barth, 1959a, chapters 5, 7, 8 and 9), appear to be the
big Khans such as Nalkot Pacha, Khan Bahadur Sahib and Taj
Mahomed Khan (Figure 7, p.103). Paragraphs describing in-
formants in these chapters might well begin: 'Malak Baba
of Maruf Khel and the chief of Juna khel' (ibid., p.113),
or 'There were four Khans: Mohammed Awzel Khan, Taj
Mohammed Khan, Amir Khan and Biha Malak' (ibid., p.71).
Some of these Khans (or as in the case of Nalkot Pacha,
'Saints') were personal acquaintances of Barth during his
field-work and presumably his 'respondents'. Thus 'the
Nalkot Pacha, my sometime host' (ibid., p.99), and 'one of
my acquaintances among the more prominent chiefs had an
approximate income of 50,000 Pakistan rupees (then about
£5,000) from the sale of grain' (ibid., p.79).
    Examples exhibiting the social prejudices of the Khan,
which confirm the theme of this section, appear frequently
in 'Political Leadership among Swat Pathans', for instance, the reference to the 'wife of a mullah' (ibid.,
p.47). The 'Mians' are seen as miserly and mean (ibid.,
p.101). Concubinage, an institution based on wealth and
feudal power, and unknown in the tribal or 'nang' areas,
is observed (although this is empirically difficult to
verify): 'Chiefs may employ them as servants on more exclusive occasions in their men's houses, to add spice to
the life of distinguished visitors, though their sexual

services are apparently usually monopolized by their
owners' (ibid., p.50).

An inevitable Khan's eye-view of politics enters
Barth's analysis of Swat society, which partly explains
the 'minimization' of the impact of the Wali on Swat society and the exaggeration of the role of the Khans. The
Swat thesis is structured around the Khan, his genealogical charters, his avunculate and agnatic rivalries, his
institutions and his alliances which explain his participation in and the political extrapolation of the Swat
Game-Theory.

Barth's is thus more a 'macro' than a 'micro' view of
social relations and political processes. His is not the
usual anthropological 'village study'. And because of its
macro construction and diachronic theoretical assumptions
and treatment it sees the wood clearly but often at the
cost of neglecting the trees. At times the theory appears
to be outpacing the ethnography and therefore retains the
quality of an abstraction lacking ontological contact with
the object under study (which is the polychromic socio-
political process in motion and over time in Swat society). Because of this macro view-point, and the inbuilt
equilibrium of the model, the Swat study appears to concentrate on the maintenance and circulation of élites in a
fashion almost reminiscent of Pareto (1965). The Yusufzai
Khan élite is seen as perpetuating itself in power over an
autochthonic majority up to this century as feudal lords.
Because Barth's study focuses on this élite rather than
the entire society and is more an 'élite' study than a
'total' one it leads to major socio-political trends being
overlooked, for example, the underlying class tension and
conflict situation. 'The peasant view of the bad life'
(Bailey, 1971) is conspicuously absent in the analysis.
Talal Asad, never having visited Swat, and basing his critique on Barth's data alone, puts his finger accurately on
the interaction among Swat hierarchies, drawn along horizontal class lines, and anticipates the armed confrontation that was to develop in Swat: 'I have been arguing,
against Barth, that horizontal cleavages into asymmetric
classes are more important than vertical ones into homologous blocs. The tenant's class interests are always opposed to those of his landlord' (Asad, 1972, p.85).

Professor Barth was based in the capital town of Swat,
Saidu, and it might be reasonable to assume that his in-
formants in Saidu were more urbane and educated than those
living in remote villages (of the seven villages on which
he based his data only two were 'remote'; the others were
either towns or within the radius of towns). The fact
that he did not live in one of the villages ensured the

exclusion of data based on first-hand empirically observed
social behaviour of the entire village and consequently
the representation of majority non-Khan categories and
groups. A similar suggestion was made regarding Professor
Barth's field-work situation among the Basseri where he
spent his three months in the chiefly Darbar camp (Tapper,
1971, p.132).

DYNAMICS OF SOCIAL CHANGE IN SWAT

The impact of post-colonial 'national' independence cannot
be over-emphasized in its pervasive and universal influence on tribal or marginal societies and crystallization
of new political directions and social configurations.
Today, the component elements of social change involve
(i) the politics of the universal vote, (ii) undisguised,
often Western, symbols of material values and (iii) a universal desire for social mobility and rejection of castes
and social hierarchies. These factors may have been somewhat underplayed by anthropologists looking for factors of
continuity and 'equilibrium' within social structures.
The anthropological quest for an 'ethnographic present'
may result in either a dated or a distorted picture. The
vote, the radio and the bus can change a society, however
remote and tribal, almost beyond recognition. Those anthropologists who revisit their initial areas of field-
work study find substantial signs of change. Professor
Firth found this in Tikopia (Firth, 1959) which he visited
in 1952 after his field-work in 1929, and Professor Mayer
when he revisited Fiji after twenty years in 1971 (Mayer,
1971).
    Professor Barth also saw visible changes in Swat during
his visit in 1960 (Barth, 1966). What is important to
note is that unlike Firth and Mayer visiting after two or
three decades Professor Barth was visiting Swat only six
years after his field-work. Some of the institutions on
which his cherished analytic concepts were based, like the
'men's houses', had radically altered in function. Yet
nothing of socio-political significance occurred between
1954 and 1960 to escalate observable change unless one
were to argue that the processes of change were already in
visible motion in 1954 but Professor Barth had either
overlooked them or ignored them in order to build models:
    A brief revisit to Swat in 1960 revealed a predominant
    change in the main valley, with men's houses serving
    mainly as places for the demonstration of wealth to-
    wards co-members of the wealthy élite and clientship
    disappearing as a vital relationship (ibid., p.17).

The 'hujra' had become a club for equals emphasizing horizontal lines of social equality rather than a political
focus connecting the Khan to his clients.

Looking back, Barth even recognizes trends he saw in
1954 but did not incorporate in his study (so as not to
disturb the construction of his 'models'):   'The use of
force was controlled and punished with increasing rigour
by the ruler, so the effectiveness of a large following
for expansive and even defensive purposes was declining'
(ibid., p.16).   In 'Political Leadership among Swat
Pathans' Barth had argued that the centralized State
system was 'merely superimposed' on the acephalous, segmentary system, but Barth's observations in 1960 surely
describe the ruler as an all-powerful oriental potentate
as defined in chapter 7 of this book and not one who would
allow himself to be checked and balanced by powerful Khans
in a constant 'zero-sum' game.

Sociologically, feudal landlords divert their energies
to accumulating wealth as the new symbol of prestige when
their estates are 'encapsulated' by national or centralized politics.   The 'political lord' becomes an 'economic
master'.   This explains the sterility in continuing traditional politics for the Khan after the establishment of
the State.   His alternative is to make money.   Barth recognizes this in 1960

> a few chiefs started acting in deviation from the old
> pattern as early as the late nineteen-thirties;   they
> gained greatly in wealth but lost their political fol-
> lowing by discontinuing their men's house feasting;
> they lost their autonomy through having to rely on the
> ruler and his power for the protection of their estate
> (ibid.).

In turn, when the Government of Pakistan absorbed the
State of Swat the Wali's family turned to economic enter-
prise for the outlet of their energies.   Like the princes
of Bali they changed from 'political princelets' into
'economic lordlings' (Geertz, 1963).

Swat, twenty years after Professor Barth did his field-
work, but mainly after his 1960 visit, has undergone deep
structural social changes as a result of three major and
interconnected developments: (a) the removal of the Wali
as the ruler in 1969;   (b) the absorption of the State
into the administrative structure of Pakistan;   and (c)
the 1970 universal election (adult franchise was brought
to Swat within a year of its loss of status as a State).
These changes have created new rapidly shifting alliances,
the breakdown of established social networks and phyletic
boundaries, and a dramatic reversal of roles as, for instance, in the 1970 election when the Khans were backing

non-Pukhtun candidates for Assembly seats. There is much
more mobility between Swat and the rest of the country and
the processes of 'encapsulation' and integration have
begun. The famous 'purdah' of Swat has finally been removed. Powerful Khans stripped of mystagogy can no longer
play power games based on local politics alone: national alignments, economics and education are now factors of
importance.

THE RELEVANCE OF MODELS IN ANTHROPOLOGY

One of the penalties of fame for a classic work, such as
Barth's, is that it becomes a standard reference for the
people under study. Unfortunately, partly understanding
the ethnographic application of Barth's theoretical models
or using, or often simply picking tendentious models from,
Barth the most unlikely homologues and analogies to Pathan
society have also resulted. Barth's Swat Pathan has
become the Pathan, or more specifically, Barth's eye-view
of the Khans of Swat has become the general image of
Pathan society. The particular has become the general.
This section will give some examples of how the understanding of Pathan society has been affected in varying
degrees by Barth's study of the Swat Pathans. These examples will also show the widespread popularity and influence of Barthian models.
    Talal Asad argues that Barth views Swat Pathan society
through Hobbesian eyes: 'The similarity of this view of
Swat Pathans with the Hobbesian vision of human nature and
political society is striking and significant' (Asad,
1972, p.80). Professor Bailey goes one step further.
Swat Pathan society is not only Hobbesian in nature, nasty,
brutish and short, but is generally representative of
entire Pathan society (cf. section on 'Pakhtouns in conflict'in chapter 6, Bailey, 1970). Stimulated by a tele-
vision programme, he sees Pathan bloc and alliance structures as homologous to the 'cosa nostra' ('our thing' or
'our affair') criminal organization in the USA: 'The
people of Swat and the criminals of the American "cosa
nostra" arranged their violent successions in broadly the
same fashion' (ibid., p.viii). It appears there is little
substantial progress or difference in the stereotype of
'the wild Pathans' (ibid., p.ix) that featured in the
swashbuckling turn of the century novels about the North-
West Frontier of India and those studied in the social
sciences. This leads to a general reflection on the
nature of anthropology and the study of primitive people:
    Social anthropology, it seems, picks on the exotic and

the eccentric and the deviant and the aberrant: it
cannot deal with the normal and the usual. The subject
is as one particularly obtuse critic said, merely bar-
barology: and my implied excitement at discovering the
Pathans behaved like the 'cosa nostra' gangsters would
have confirmed him in this view (ibid., p.viii).

Bailey would even employ value judgments, unusual for
contemporary anthropologists, such as the adjective 'wild'
when referring to 'the Pathans'(ibid., p.ix). Unusual examples, among them a highly suspect one, (1) of a 'successful Pakhtoun politician with over two hundred murders to
his credit' (ibid., p.91), are cited to support this.

Professor Bailey sums up Pathan society: 'There are
some straightforward cultures like the Pathans, the gangsters and racketeers of the American cities, or some
totalitarian nations of our own day, where the job can be
simply carried out by murder' (ibid., p.79).

Concepts and figures that explain Swat structure and
society are developed into caricatures: 'the Pathan Saint
who whistled' (ibid., p.64) or 'the cunning saint' ('I
look like a simple man; I live simply - but oh! the
things I do!' - ibid., p.141). The ambiguity in Barth's
general application of the word Saint to all 'religious'
men and its consequences in explaining Swat social interaction (opposed in a discussion in chapter 4 for this very
reason) are apparent in Bailey's comprehension of socio-
political organization in Swat. To Bailey Nalkot Pacha
(the 'Saint' who whistled - Barth, 1959a, p.99) is a Saint
with a capital 'S' which the latter never was. Nalkot
Pacha was a powerful landlord from north Swat

Thus the Nalkot Pacha, as well as being the headman of
his own village, owns plots of land in various others,
and so has a personal hold over some villagers in the
men's houses of most of the neighbouring chiefs, while
he himself is removed from the direct control of any
one chief (ibid., p.96).

By pushing him into 'Saint' category his behaviour and
consequently the Saint-Khan analysis and balance, become
skewed. Similarly, the Wali is equated to Saint 'The man
who emerged as ruler of the Swat valley was a Saint'
(Bailey, 1970, p.141). In 'Conceptual systems in the
study of politics' Professor Bailey attempts to develop
the thesis that a Saint's stature diminishes as his land
holdings increase (the Saint is defined as a gloss for
'pir', 'baba', 'sayyed', and 'mian') and offers a graphic
illustration:

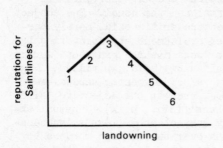

Point 6 on the graph illustrates the 'theoretical position of a Saint who has disqualified himself from saintliness by becoming a large landowner' (Bailey, 1972, p.32). This statement, supported by the graphic illustration, clearly express both Bailey's empirical and theoretical misunderstanding of Barth's thesis. For example, one of the crucial factors in the Wali's struggle for power was his great landed property and he had, as Bailey himself observes, not 'disqualified himself from saintliness'. As mentioned above, Bailey's other Saint, Nalkot Pacha, also owned large tracts of land (Barth, 1959a, p.96). Barth is unambiguous on the point of the increase in a Saint's power and political influence with the increase of his property (ibid., p.93). The misunderstanding springs from the development of the concept of Saint. Bailey is unthinkingly imposing a Western and Christian connotation of the term, (2) 'When Western anthropologists talk about Islamic Saints, they use the term as a shorthand for a diversity of social roles' (Turner, 1974, p.61).

As Barth's model gains in anthropological popularity and currency its finer points get lost in its more general structure. The 'mullahs', for instance, are equated to Saints, something Barth had assiduously avoided (Barth, 1959a, p.57), as it raises serious conceptual problems in the analysis of Islamic societies. While stating that Khans provide one segment of leadership for political power in Swat it has been analysed that 'the second segment of leadership is composed of the saints, "fakirs" or "mullahs" (dedicated and propertyless men)' (Tuden, 1966, p.280). In the same work it is also suggested that, like Bailey's Saint, the 'mullah's' religious status declines with an increase in material possessions, which prevents him from participating in the pursuit of land and power: 'Because of their religious position the mullahs cannot employ the violent techniques of land seizure practised by the Khans' (ibid.).

The influence and popularity of Barth's study is

evident in its wide usage for cross-cultural analysis, as
for example in Professor Haimendorf's work (Fürer-
Haimendorf, 1969). The Swat study is referred to in an
account titled 'Pir and Murshid: an aspect of religious
leadership in West Pakistan' by Professor Mayer (1967).
Dr Parkin draws a comparison of Swat Pathans with the
Giriama in East Africa. However, he is critical of
Barth's analysis of Swat in terms of political power based
on transactional relationships alone. Other factors, such
as economic and religious ones, play a crucial role in explaining social interaction and behaviour as Dr Parkin de-
velops in his Giriama study (1972). He finds that Barth's
'Swat chiefs seem preoccupied with acquiring political
support at all costs.... However much land they have, in
the end, Swat chiefs have nothing in which to invest their
wealth except political support' (Parkin, 1972, p.78).
   To Professor Gluckman, Barth's 'Political Leadership
among Swat Pathans' becomes 'an analysis of the two-party
system' in a discussion of Anuak headmen and factions in
villages (Gluckman, 1971, p.166). The noted Indologist,
Professor Dumont, sees Swat society as divided into groups
'linked together by something equivalent to a jajmani
system, they are ranked by status, and a high proportion
of marriages are endogamous. The influence of the Hindu
model is obvious, and the lowest castes are considered
impure (barber, washerman, etc)' (Dumont, 1972, pp.254-5).
The discussion on endogamy and stratification early on in
this book attempts to show how the concepts of 'purity'
and 'caste' are not satisfactory ones in the Swat situation and that social divisions are based on ownership of
land corresponding to membership in genealogical charters
and consequently, Pukhtun political status.
   Professor Mair pins the Swat study to a particular
'ethnographic present' with a confidence even Barth does
not exhibit: the study 'describes the essence of Swat
politics as they were observed in 1954' (Mair, 1972, p.
135) in an otherwise useful summary of the Swat analysis.
   Barth's influence is not restricted to the social
sciences alone. Berry, for instance, in his legal monograph called 'Aspects of the Frontier Crimes Regulation in
Pakistan' warns the reader of two important caveats, that
(a) 'no field research was undertaken' (Berry, 1966, p.
viii) and that (b) 'there is a deviation in Swat from the
normal Pathan social structure' (ibid., p.12). None the
less the book leans heavily on Barth's anthropological
material and quotes extensively from it. He might have
added another caveat for the student of law: that the
Frontier Crimes Regulation did not apply to Swat. Berry
also, and inevitably, falls into the familiar pitfall

created by Barth's use of Saints that has claimed others
and betters. He sees Swat as a unique Pathan society because of its proliferation of Saints and their political
power (ibid., p.36). Even the 'Encyclopaedia Britannica'
includes Barth's Swat study in the limited bibliography
for its section on India-Pakistan (1967, p.158).

Descriptions of 'wild Pathans', 'savages' and 'bar-
barians' would have been understandable in the writing of
imperial administrators whose job was to maintain Pax Britannica over the most troubled frontier in the British
Empire or in those of popular novelists like John Masters,
but in the writings of social scientists they appear unusual and incomprehensible. Compared to some anthropologists imperial administrators have been kinder to the
Pathans and their society. (3) Herbert Edwardes, a famous
name on the Frontier, in the last century wrote of Pathan
'jirgas':

> The 'Mullicks' talked Pushtoo. The deliberate way in
> which each delivered his opinion, the expressive ges-
> tures with which they enforced it, and the courteous
> silence observed by all the rest while one was speak-
> ing, was a model for any deliberative assembly
> (Edwardes, 1846-9, vol.v, p.43 quoted in Caroe, 1965,
> p.455).

This impression is confirmed by an ex-Governor of the
North-West Frontier Province: 'It is true that the
"jirga" tradition is all in favour of order at time of
council, and "jirgas" can often give points to any parlia-
ment in matters of usage and decorum' (ibid., p.402). To
a contemporary American writer a Pathan assembly 'is probably the closest thing to Athenian democracy that has
existed since the original' (Spain, 1963, p.69).

Methodological individualists hope to understand social
action through ego: 'To understand a man who is acting
socially (rather than simply behaving) we need to grasp
the intentions of his actions' (Turner, 1974, p.70).
Turner's thesis in 'Weber and Islam' is that 'Although
Weber accepted these procedures as a necessary part of any
sociological inquiry, he often ignored them in his own research' (ibid., p.71). It appears that Weber was not the
only one guilty of ignoring the actor's definition of the
situation and concepts. A certain ethnocentric stance is
discerned in many of the examples given above regarding
the Swat Pathans which touches a wider general criticism:

> The irreducibility of cultures leads to a questioning
> of the cultural background of the anthropologist and to
> the introduction of the notion of 'cultural relativ-
> ism': one's vision of the other culture is in part de-
> termined by one's own culture and can be seen in

ethnocentrically formulated projects (Bonte, 1974, p. 54).

Barth's Swat Pathan has become the Pathan. A theoretical model has been accepted and substituted for ethnographic reality. Swat, a 'unique' (4) Pathan situation has become representative of Pathan society at large. The aberrant or deviant has become the standard and the normal.

CONCLUSION

The Swat study is a strong demonstration for methodological individualist analysis; but not an entirely successful one. One of the aims of this essay has been to show that the Swat Pathan is not entirely in a position where 'group commitments may be assumed and shed at will' and 'self-interest may dictate action which does not bring advantage to the group' (Barth, 1959a, p.2). It has been argued that on the contrary, he is born into an interconnected number of social matrices that may continue to determine or limit his 'choices' and 'strategies'. Neither the single application of individualist analysis nor an entirely holist one is advocated in this essay. For instance, the concept of charisma is not found 'sociologically sterile'. In the Swat context it is of particular interest as it exhibits itself both in various stages of development in one person and in its applicability in response to particular social situations. The contrast in the example of Miangul Hannan, the son of the Akhund, and Miangul Wadud, is worth recalling: in spite of a considerable spiritual and material legacy and repeated attempts the former made little headway in consolidating the authority of his father into a formal political organization.

The analysis of mystical Sufic behaviour and its impact on the Akhund and his society is understood within a general methodological holist framework. A note on Sufism has been found necessary; the note does not concern itself with metaphysical or eschatological Sufic problems but how their cognition of these problems affect their social behaviour and, as a direct result, the social behaviour and organization of their followers. Therefore the ethnic origin, social background and Sufic practice of the Akhund is not an academic matter only.

This essay also offers a straight sociological reinterpretation of socio-historical developments in Swat that helps explain social structure and behaviour. Historical events, like anthropological societal sequences, require

dates to remove ambiguity and provide useful diacritical
boundaries. This has been attempted and helps to view
Barth's material in better relief. A Weberian and vectorial quality is observed in the development of types of
authority: from the paternal, traditional authority of
the Yusufzai Khans to that of the charismatic Miangul
Abdul Wadud and finally to the highly centralized State of
Swat. Alongside this linear political progression the definition of Swat ethnicity becomes relevant: a 'Swati'
consciousness replacing a Yusufzai Pukhtun one defined by
new political boundaries and changed socio-political circumstances. The elastic geographical boundaries of the
Yusufzai tribe are now firmly replaced by the known and
defined political boundaries of the State. The symbolism
of Yusufzai origin, which was so effective in articulating
a great deal of the organizational functions of this interest group, is replaced by the symbols of the new State
and its ruler.

Granted that Barth's society and his theoretical analysis of it are not static in the classic structuralist-
functionalist tradition, their inherent 'equilibrium
models' still deny them evolutionary, sequential or structural change. Each Khan as 'a central island of authority' (ibid., p.91), symbiotically surrounded by a cluster
of client groups, and interlocked in functional reciprocal
dependence expresses a somewhat unreal social picture.
Motion through conflict is circulatory among the Khans but
is sterile of new social developments; the analysis is
like a static and well-regulated machine that could function ad infinitum if undisturbed. The 'static' elements
in Swat ethnography and the 'dynamic' elements in Barth's
theory do not relate fully and remain on different levels
of analysis. This is precisely why the Swat 'model' does
not account for the Wali whose emergence disrupts and re-
structures the old equations with ramifying consequences
on all levels of Swat society. Barth largely ignores the
intrusion of the Wali, as his emergence cannot be compre-
hended entirely in the 'model'. He explains the Wali and
the organization of the State as merely superimposed on
the acephalous tribal system, 'presupposing rather than attempting to replace it' (ibid., p.132).

This essay has attempted, if the term is understood
correctly, a 'dynamic' approach in studying the socio-
political factors lying outside synchronic situations and
static social relationships. It has attempted to relate
the milieu that allowed the growth of the Miangul to his
unchallenged ruler status within a tribal situation, and
the creation of the State with those social forces opposing both the former and the latter; and on the other

hand, those forces converging through mutual interest to elevate the Miangul to the Walidom, and thereby encouraging the subsequent morphological reordering of Swat society. The sequence is complex and polychrome but has a pattern and a cause-effect relationship: it is the development of a typological sequence starting from the generalized spiritual authority of the Akhund to the millenarian mass movements which act as catalyst in static feudal and tribal societies and ending in the institutionalization of charisma symbolized in the establishment of a State. The unfolding of the socio-historical sequence also brings into relief one of the contentions of this essay that Swat man is not simply 'political man'; he is also 'economic' and 'religious man'. The attempt to include the latter leaves Barth's study open to criticism of a form of academic ethnocentricity, reductionism and synecdochic approach already referred to in the introductory chapter.

Formerly, the Pathans, probably the largest tribal grouping in the world, did not even feature on anthropological global tribal maps (Gluckman, 1971; Sahlins, 1968, p.4). It is a tribute to Professor Barth that he has put them firmly on the map of the social sciences. Apart from creating brilliant theoretical models which enable an understanding of Pathan social organization in general, Professor Barth's Swat study provides the heuristic conditions that lay the academic foundations for further sociological work. It is a lasting and rich ethnographic contribution to the limited number of serious books on the North-West Frontier Province.

Notes

CHAPTER 1   INTRODUCTION

1 The future of social anthropology: disintegration or
   metamorphosis? (Needham, 1970) and Crisis of British
   anthropology (Banaji, 1970).
2 Which partly explains the steady growth in academic
   influence and general popularity of the subject: 'In
   Great Britain alone there are at least 97 people who
   hold University teaching posts specifically as social
   anthropologists, 26 of them are Professors. There are
   numerous others who masquerade under the label of
   "sociologist"' (Leach, 1974, p.6).
3 The iconoclasts, in turn, face new idol-breakers:
   The combination of these factors determines what I
   have called the crisis of modern anthropology and
   adds new dimensions to the problem of the critique
   of anthropology. Today this critique is at the
   centre of an extensive theoretical, ideological and
   political debate which began, especially in France,
   in the sixties. The scale and the sharpness of
   this debate are related to the central positions of
   anthropology in the construction of a general
   theory of human societies and to the ideological
   functions it fulfils. The critique of anthropology
   in fact directly exposes the central ideological
   and metaphysical presuppositions at the foundation
   of a new materialist and dialectic conception.
   Every success achieved in this arena is of major
   importance; it is therefore important to denounce
   revived forms of criticism, which I have already
   labelled as the 'Rightist Critique' of anthropology
   (Bonte, 1974, p.60).
4 These positions can be strongly stated and defended:
   I feel uneasy when faced with any analysis which

does not allow man a central role as an entrepreneur. In Britain Raymond Firth has been the pro-
ponent of this view and I acknowledge the influence
of his writings and those of Fredrik Barth (Bailey,
1970, p.18).

5   Actually the substitution of the reality-principle
for the pleasure-principle denotes no dethronement
of the pleasure-principle, but only a safeguarding
of it. A momentary pleasure, uncertain in its results, is given up, but only in order to gain in
the new way an assured pleasure coming later
(Freud, 1925, p.18).

6 Pathan is the popular name for Pukhtuns; they refer
to themselves as Pukhtun. This essay will use Pathan
generally and Pukhtun specifically with reference to
the Swat Yusufzai dominant tribal groups, while following the convention established by Professor Barth
of using Pathan and Pukhtun interchangeably.

7   The analysis of boundary-maintaining processes in
different parts of the Pathan areas, which will be
made below, requires an understanding of three such
institutions which dominate three major domains of
activity: 'Melmastia' - 'hospitality', and the
honourable uses of material goods, 'jirga' - coun-
cils, and the honourable pursuit of public affairs,
and 'purdah' - seclusion, and the honourable organization of domestic life (Barth, 1969, p.120).

Such Codes are characteristic of tribal Muslim groups;
the Bedouin have a Code identical to Pukhtunwali:

By 'nuruwwa' the Arab means all those virtues
which, founded in the tradition of his people, constitute the fame of an individual or the tribe to
which he belongs; the observance of those duties
which are connected with family ties, the relationship of protection and hospitality and the fulfil-
ment of the great law of blood revenge (Turner,
1974, p.30).

8 Sahlins in his study, 'Tribesmen' (1968, p.5), takes a
Hobbesian view of his subject:

In its broadest terms the contrast between tribe
and civilization is between War and Peace....
Lacking these institutional means and guarantees,
tribesmen live in a condition of War, and War
limits the scale, complexity, and all round rich-
ness of their culture, and accounts for some of
their more 'curious' customs.

This would appear strange judgment to a 'tribesman'
pronounced by a 'civilization' standing for 'peace'
which has recently involved mankind in two global wars

lasting for years and costing millions of lives.

9 The great Pashto poet, Khushal Khan Khattak (1613-89),
   recalls in a poem that seven ruling Indian dynasties
   were Pathan.

10 A parallel situation is described for another Muslim
    tribal people, the Berbers of the Atlas mountains:
    'Here, it is perfectly clear why the geographical
    boundary between plain and mountain, was also, for
    so long, a political boundary between the "land of
    government" and the "land of dissidence". Prior to
    modern times, there is no record of an army of the
    central state successfully penetrating these gorges,
    though some did try' (Gellner, 1969a, p.31).

11 'Settled' is a relative term: during British rule
    Peshawar, the main District of the Frontier Province,
    usually recorded as many annual murders as the Punjab
    Province which in turn equalled those for the rest of
    the Indian subcontinent (Coen, 1971, p.202).

12 Some of the extra-ethnic leaders who appear in this
    essay have received a similar treatment: thus the
    'Mad Mullah' of Swat and the 'False Prophet' of Sudan.
    The Akhund is immortalized in the English language
    through Lear's famous poem, 'Akond of Swat', with the
    refrain that asks:
        Who or why, or which or what
        is the Akond of Swat?

13 Malakand Division today comprises the former princely
    states of Dir, Chitral and Swat, and takes its name
    from the Malakand Agency which was formed in 1895.

CHAPTER 2   THE SWAT PATHANS AND THE THEORY OF GAMES

1 All Pashto proverbs in the text and their translations
   are from Ahmed, 1975.

2 A two 'bloc' system is mentioned in 'Political Leadership among Swat Pathans' (pp.4, 134) but why there are
   two and how they are restricted to two only is not examined. In fact, were there only two 'dallas'? Dr
   Ahmad, who was doing his field-work contemporaneously
   to Professor Barth, observed that 'even during the
   time Dr Barth was in Swat the centuries old two-
   "dalla" society had four "dallas"' (Ahmad, 1962, p.
   71).

3 M.T. Ahmad in the Introduction to his 'Social Organization of Yusufzai Swat', while commenting on Barth's
   book, expresses his views on this point: 'in other
   words, what existed before 1925 when there was no central political authority in the State has been

confused with what exists today' (ibid.).

4 'The Story of Swat', by Miangul Abdul Wadud (1962), is mentioned as an undated and 'undistributed translation of an Urdu account' titled 'History of Swat' in the 1965 edition of 'Political Leadership among Swat Pathans'. The work suffers from minor historical inaccuracies and poor editing, and its chief value lies in the fact that it is the only written account purporting to tell the story of Swat by its founder.

5 Rebellious Khans are promptly and permanently exiled 'south' of the Malakand Pass and out of Swat. There is a colony of Swat Khans still living south of the Malakand Pass testifying to this fact. The all powerful 'deputy' of the Miangul was thus abruptly banished (Barth, 1959a, p.129).

6 The Pathan would make a rebellious subject under centralized authority. He has 'a reputation for willingness to defend his honour and interests, for violence and impetuousness, for bravery and valour' (ibid., p. 85).

7 Lord Curzon, the Viceroy of India, who created the NWFP in 1901, observed 'no man who has read a page of Indian history will prophesy about the Frontier' (1916, p.43).

8 References to Parliamentary Papers (1898) are based on 'Military Operations on the N.W. Frontiers of India', vol.2, printed for Her Majesty's Stationery Office 1898, but will be abbreviated to 'PP Encl.' and the date in the text.

CHAPTER 3 THE SWAT PATHAN UNDERSTOOD

1 The Yusufzai in the rural areas still retain this memory by referring to themselves as Afghan, which is used interchangeably with Pathan.

2 The Yusufzai, far from their mountain homes, in Rampur, India, retained this consciousness of military aristocracy:

> Pushtoo is the principal language, and one sees in the square before the 'Nabob's' palace, fair, strong, and handsome young men, sitting or lounging on beds, with that air of idleness and independence which distinguishes the Eusofzyes - All admit that the Rohillas are the bravest soldiers we have ever contended with in India (Elphinstone, 1972, II, p. 36).

3 The Fakeers are much more numerous than the Eusofzyes. The greatest part of them are Swautees, who

remained in their country after it was conquered, a considerable number of Deggauns, some Hindkees, (who have been driven by famine to emigrate from the Punjab) a few Cashmeeres and Hindoos (classes which are led into all countries by the desire of gain) and some members of Afghaun tribes (who have migrated into the Eusofzye country in circumstances which have degraded them to the rank of Fakeers), or the rest of that body. Most of the Fakeers work in husbandry, and many feed herds of buffaloes on the mountains (ibid., p.27).

4 From the Pashto verb, 'weshal', 'to distribute'.

5 The lands of the Naikpeekhail are divided into two parts, equal in extent, but, of course, not exactly equal in fertility; the Oolooss is also divided into two parts, which draw lots every ten years for the choice of land. If the lot falls on the half which is already possessed of the best share it retains its possession; but if it falls on the other half, an immediate exchange takes place, the two half Ooloosses meet every ten years to draw lots (ibid., p.15).

6 The godfather-godson relationship symbolizes the patron-client relationship in Sicily; the contract is formal, solemn and moral. The patron is a 'santo' or saint substitute (Boissevain, 1966). No such formality or morality marks patron-client relations in Swat society. Barth's Khan is neither a formal nor a moral superordinate and his status and authority are based on possessions of land and a certain mystification about its ownership and his rights to it.

7 Of the societies on the Indian subcontinent Rajput society has many parallels with the Pathan one (Hitchcock, 1958). For an interesting socio-political comparison of Pathans and Rajputs see Caroe, 1965, pp. 85-8, who draws in his arguments from H.W. Bellew and Vincent Smith.

CHAPTER 4 THE SWAT PATHAN MISUNDERSTOOD

1 Evans-Pritchard (1962), Gluckman (1971).

2 Professor Dumont is led to comment on this point, 'in the case in question, Barth, curiously enough, was led to exaggerate the similarity with Hindu India on certain points' (Dumont, 1972, p.256).

3 Miangul Jahanzeb, the great-grandson of the Akhund, contradicts this by stating that the Akhund's wife was a Mian from Spal Bandai, near Saidu, and not a

Yusufzai Pathan. This does not affect the point at
issue which is the relationship between social status,
hypergamy and hypogamy.

4 C. McPastner (1972) for similar trends in Baluchistan
tribal endogamy.

5   Sexual intercourse with a saintly person is considered beneficial. Chenier speaks of a saint in
Tetuan who seized a young woman and had commerce
with her in the midst of the street; 'her companions, who surrounded her, uttered exclamations
of joy, felicitated her good fortune, and the husband himself received complimentary visits on this
occasion' (Westermarck, 1968, p.34, quoted in
Turner, 1974, p.68).

6 'Where, as among the Cyrenaica Bedouin (Evans-
Pritchard, 1949), descent groups have fixed territories, there is a natural tendency for opposed
groups, on re-establishing peace, to locate the grants
to Saints along the border between them' (Barth,
1959a, p.93).

7 It was not possible to locate the source or authenti-
city of such examples in recent history in spite of
extensive questioning in Swat. Miangul Jahan Zeb's reaction and incredulity were typical: 'simply impossible' he said.

8 This attribute of Pathan social behaviour is recorded
on first British contact with the Pathans at the turn
of the last century:
One of the most remarkable characteristics of the
Afghauns, is their hospitality. The practice of
this virtue is so much a national point of honour,
that their reproach to an inhospitable man, is that
he has no Pooshtoonwullee (nothing of the customs
of the Afghauns). All persons indiscriminately are
entitled to profit by this practice (Elphinstone,
1972, I, p.295).

9 Mrs Ali writes of Indian, non-Pathan, Muslims in the
last century,
You perceive a system of charitable feeling is in-
culcated by the laws of Mahumud; and in every-day
practice it is found to be the prominent feature in
their general habits. It is common with the
meanest of people to offer a share of their food to
any one calling upon them at mealtime. I have seen
this amiable trait of character in all classes of
the people (Ali, 1973, p.257).

10 Figure 6 (Barth, 1959a, p.41) based on data from four
villages pertains to 'marriage frequencies' and sub-
divides Pukhtun 'chiefs' from 'other' Pukhtuns but

this still does not reveal data or proportion of non-landowning to landowning Pukhtuns.

11 M.T. Ahmad writes of 'ting sarays' or 'mercenaries' the Khan used as 'muscle' to intimidate tenants (Ahmad, 1962, p.28).

12 'At the same time, the introduction of an effective monetary economy made possible the conversion of perishable wealth into cash. The result of these inter-connected changes was the disappearance from Peshawar District of the men's house' (Barth, 1959a, p.80).

13 (a) 'Brakha-khor' as category of tenant who 'eats the share' is mistranslated as 'sister-of-the-plot' (ibid., p.44). (b) Miangul Wadud admits to killing both his agnatic cousins, Sayyid Badshah and his brother Amir Badshah, personally (Miangul, 1962, pp.9, 13), whereas Barth writes that 'in 1903, Amir Badshah, killed his brother' (Barth, 1959a, p.128). (c) The index to 'Political Leadership among Swat Pathans' would benefit if important words such as 'wesh', 'zberge' and 'ushar' were included, as the use of those like 'daftar' indicate that Pashto words are not excluded in favour of their English equivalents. (d) The Wali of Swat is referred to as His Royal Highness (ibid., Preface). In fact the ruler of Swat was only given the title of 'Wali' in 1926 by the British; the Pakistan Government added 'His Highness' subsequently. This is an important distinction when the rulers of over 560 Indian Princely States vied for such symbols of status and the corresponding privileges they conferred. (e) The use of two different spellings, Wahdood and Wahdud, for the Wali's name could have been resolved by the selection of one. The Wali himself used Wadud (Miangul, 1962) which is nearer the Arabic name, one of the ninety-nine names of God, than Wahdood. (f) The caste list includes 'landap' (cotton-carder), 'qasai' (butcher) and, at the end, 'kashkol' (Barth, 1959a, p.17). In Swat, as indeed in other Yusufzai areas, these names are 'nandap', 'qasab' and 'kachkol'.

CHAPTER 5 A THEORY OF PATHAN ECONOMIC STRUCTURE AND POLITICAL ORGANIZATION

1 'The general type so defined would include the following: (a) The peasant family farm as the basic unit of multi-dimensional social-organization. (b) Land husbandry as the main means of livelihood directly

providing the major part of the consumption needs.
(c) Specific traditional culture related to the way of
life of small communities. (d) The underdog position
- the domination of peasantry by outsiders' (Shanin,
1971, p.14-15).

CHAPTER 6 A NOTE ON SUFIC ORDERS AND ISLAMIC REVIVALISM
IN THE NINETEENTH CENTURY

1 To begin this argument it is useful to accept the
   Sufi's own cognitive definition of socio-religious
   reality. A comment by an anthropologist on problems
   of religious definition would be helpful: 'The most
   obvious basis for religious behaviour is the one which
   any religious actor tells us about when we ask him -
   and, unlike some anthropologists, I believe him'
   (Spiro, 1973, p.112).
2 Professor Gellner writes of the Berber tribesmen of
   the Atlas mountains, 'Tribes of siba-land are, indeed,
   politically independent. But they are not culturally
   independent. They are in this case embedded in the
   wider civilisation of Islam. In large measure they
   share the religion, concepts, symbols of the whole of
   the Muslim world' (Gellner, 1969a, p.2) and of the
   Berber 'he is, firmly and in a manner pregnant with
   consequences for his life, a Muslim - irrespective of
   whether he is specially pious or well-informed in
   matters of religion' (ibid., p.15).
3 Paradoxically, the closure of these channels of communication is threatened in the post-colonial era by
   the growth of modern nationalist Muslim States putting
   up border barriers that require documents and permits
   for ingress and egress. Another level of pan-Islamic
   communication has opened through the mass media of
   radio and newspapers but this is largely politically
   slanted, secular and nationalist as distinct from the
   traditional, religious, pan-Islamic content of past
   communication.
4 A dramatic, if somewhat rare, example is the communication from Shah Waliullah seeking assistance to check
   the liquidation of Muslim power in India to Ahmad Shah
   Abdali, the King of Afghanistan, which is said to have
   resulted in the battle of Panipat in 1761 and the
   final defeat of the Hindu Maratha and Jat confederacy
   (Ahmad, 1964, p.209). Similarly, one of the answers
   to Pathan lack of response to the 1857 'Indian Mutiny'
   is that it was seen primarily as a distant, localized
   and non-Muslim rebellion. The effete and impotent

Mughal Emperor, confined to Delhi, did not symbolize Islamic rule. Except for some excitement caused by the revolt of the 55 Native Infantry and its passage to Swat and eventual destruction in the Kaghan valley, the trans-Indus areas passed without a murmur in 1857.

5 Most modern nationalist Muslim intellectuals, with the maximum impact on their societies, passed through a 'Sufic phase' at one stage of their lives: Mohammad Abduh and Hassan al Banna (in Egypt), Mohammed Iqbal (in India-Pakistan) and Zia Gokalp (in Turkey) (Smith, 1957, p.56).

6 Many 'modernists', like Sir Sayyed, arguing that Islam in its primitive form is compatible with rational existence derived their inspiration from the Wahabis. The Wahabis, in the eighteenth and nineteenth century provided an intense stimulus to Islamic activity based on rational reform within Islam. They were deliberately opposed to 'baraka' exploiters and Sufi orders as having compromised the purity of Islam. They shocked the Islamic world by destroying tombs of Saints and especially that of Imam Husain ibn Ali (the grandson of the Prophet) at Karbala in 1802. Wahabi thinking laid down the template for what eventually became 'modernist' Islam.

7 The reference to Arabia is not wholly improbable. The Wali of Swat drew up a picture of pre-Wali Swat and compared it to pre-Islam Arabia:

It would not be wrong to compare the Swat of a few years before and after 1915, to Arabia prior to the advent of Islam - both were as ignorant and licentious. The powerful and the rich were cruel and immoral: the poor and the down-trodden were weak and uninformed (Miangul, 1962, p.58).

8 'Even if Islam had been miraculously shut off from contacts with foreign religions and philosophies, some form of mysticism would have arisen within it, for the seeds were already there' (Nicholson, 1914, pp.19-20).

9 This universalistic philosophy is condensed in the famous Sufic precept of 'sulh-i-kul' or 'peace with all'. The great thirteenth-century Andalusian Sufi, Ibn al-Arabi, summed it thus: 'Love is the creed I hold - whether the Kabah, the Torah or the Cloister.' Centuries ago there were bands of passivists facing social and political persecution - and often death - by their co-religionists for declaring that they believed in 'love not war'.

10 'Fana' or 'annihilation' is the bedrock concept of Sufi thinking and practice: 'annihilation' of self, of desire, of ambition etc. Proximity to the Supreme

Being is seen as inversely proportionate to involvement with material possessions and their symbols and
with total 'fana' a total state of identification is
aimed at.

11   Talal Asad's powerful 'crie de coeur' (1973) against
Orientalists and social scientists studying Islamic
societies in the traditional nineteenth-century Victorian mould brings to bear on this division of Islam.
Orientalists and Western journalists (Asad is moved to
remark bitterly that there is often little difference
in the two) usually confront and grapple with the
militaristic, urban, orthodox form of Islam - and
react to it with predictable hostility. The pacific
and mystical category of Islam is lost in its esoteric
and often disguised forms and therefore more difficult
to locate or comprehend for Western man.

12   These categories derive sociologically from Ibn
Khaldun's circular theory of tribal élites: tribes
possessing 'asabyah', or social cohesion, invade civi-
lized urban centres, assimilate, and over three generations are, in turn, subject to tribal invasion by
tribes that are more vigorous. Tribes, at the moment
of conquest, begin the process of losing their most
vital qualifying social factor. The seeds of destruction are carried in the situation of triumph.

13   The frailty of these categories, divided by Professor
Gellner (1969b) into those containing a 'syndrome of
characteristics' P (puritanical, egalitarian, non-
mystical, formal) in opposition to those with a 'syndrome of characteristics' C (hierarchical, mystical,
informal) is exhibited when typologizing in such obvious examples as those mentioned in note 5, p.150.

14   For the sake of brevity these labels will be employed.

15   For methods and examples of Sufic proselytizing see
the collection of essays in Lewis (1969) for Africa,
and Ahmad (1964) for India.

16   Like his contemporary, Ahmad at-Tijani (1737-1815),
the founder of the great West African order that bears
his name, who also had to shift deeper into the desert
to avoid trouble with the Turkish administration.

17   The Saints had attempted early in the eighteenth century to provide political leadership but got their
fingers badly burnt. Their leader was captured and
executed and thereafter they stayed in the mountains.

18   Holt (1958a and b) for a historical survey of this
period, Churchill (1972) for a contemporary view and
Saburi Biobaku and Muhammad Al-Hajj in Lewis (1969)
for a modern nationalist one.

19   Sayyed Akbar came from the Sayyed family of Sitana and

was a descendant of Pir Baba, the famous Saint, buried
in Buner, Swat. Sitana for decades provided a sanctuary for the 'Mujahidin' (called Hindustani Rebels by
the British). Sayyed Akbar was no Sufi recluse, on
the contrary, he was an active political leader and a
prominent follower of Sayyed Ahmed Barelvi in his
'jihad' against the Sikhs.

20 If this standing force is abstracted as a percentage
of the total Swat population then of less than 100,000
(Wylly, 1912, p.108) the figures assume significance.
A regular military force representing over 4 per cent
of a total population is vast by any standards: it
would mean an army of over two million for Britain and
one of almost twenty-five million for India.

21 Which is not to say that Barth is unaware of the presence of Sufic organization in Islamic tribal
societies. See for instance his Kurd study (Barth,
1953).

CHAPTER 7 MILLENNIUM AND CHARISMA AMONG PATHANS

1 The mood over the Frontier was captured by the account
of Sir Winston Churchill, an eye-witness of the 1897
Frontier campaigns:
> A vast, but silent agitation was begun. Messengers
> passed to and fro among the tribes. Whispers of
> war, a holy war, were breathed to a race intensely
> passionate and fanatical. The tribes were taught
> to expect prodigious events. A great day for their
> race and faith was at hand (Churchill, 1972, p.27).

2 A prophet is he or she who organizes the new assumptions and articulates them; who is listened to
and found acceptable; whose revelation is accorded
authority for however brief a period. But a prophet cannot identify himself in terms of the community as it is: he identifies himself in an image
of what might or should be (Burridge, 1969, p.14).

3 Apart from regular British Regiments there were the
35th and 45th Sikhs, 38th Dogras, 10th and 11th Bengal
Lancers, No. 5 Company Madras Sappers and Miners, No.
3 Company Bombay Sappers and Miners (Wylly, 1912, pp.
137-9).

4 Among the British expeditions in 1897-8 the biggest
was led by Sir W. Lockhart to Afridi Tirah and had
some 60,000 troops (Elliot, 1968, p.199): this reflects the size of the operations as much as the dif-
ficulty of the terrain and campaigning.

5 'Mast' derives from a form of ecstasy or trance-like

state. The Mullah was also called 'sartor baba'.
'Sartor' literally meaning 'black head' and implying
one who is either too poor, too demented or too ecstatic to cover his head.

6 The main border town of Swat on the Malakand road and
known as 'the Gate of Swat'.

7 A contemporary account explains the authority of the
Akhund: 'He also now issues circular edicts regarding
religious ceremonies and secular observances. These
are acted on and considered as binding as the
"shariat", which, indeed, they are considered to be by
his followers' (Bellew, 1864, p.107).

8 Swatis themselves offer a similar simplistic
explanation:

> The entrance to Swat State, a picture-book fort
> with four square towers stands beside the rushing
> waters of the river. We stopped for tea in the
> police station placed in the base of one of the
> towers. An elderly sub-inspector with waxed
> handle-bar moustache worthy of a British sergeant-
> major presided over the tea-pot. The few hundred
> words of English he had at his disposal, as well as
> his hearty, no-nonsense manner and bulging muscles,
> would also have become his British counterpart. He
> pointed at an antique telephone hanging on the
> wall, 'with those our Miangul conquered this
> state,' he announced. 'He built forts like this
> everywhere. He put telephones in them. Every time
> those beggars in the hills made trouble, we would
> call him up and tell him. Then he would send more
> men or come himself. We tell his son the Wali
> Sahib, who is now our king, everything too. You
> watch'(Spain, 1962, pp.66-7).

9 The problems facing Amir Abdur Rahman, 'the Iron Amir
of Afghanistan', in his attempts to centralize political authority and to effectively incorporate and en-
capsulate Pathan tribes into the State structure are
documented in his autobiography and reflect the difficulties inherent in such a situation (Abdur Rahman,
1900; Fraser-Tytler, 1950; Gregorian, 1969; Kakar,
1968).

CHAPTER 8   MODELS AND METHOD IN ANTHROPOLOGY

1 See n.7, chapter 4.
2 'What counts as a saint in the Christian tradition is
any canonized, dead, orthodox Christian, regarded as
an inhabitant of heaven. All of this contrasts

sharply with so-called Islamic saintship' (Turner, 1974, p.60). In concluding the chapter, Saint and Sheikh, in his book on 'Weber and Islam' Turner writes: 'Similarly, Weber informed us that Islam "was diverted completely from any really methodological control of life by the advent of the cult of saints, and finally by magic". One answer to this assertion would be that Islam could not be diverted by something it never possessed' (ibid., p.71).

3 For highly readable and general accounts of administration in the Frontier Province by administrators see Woodruff, 1953-4, and Coen, 1971.

4 Spain begins the section entitled 'Swat, a unique State', with 'Before we leave the tribal area, it is desirable to look briefly at its most unusual phenomenon, Swat State' (Spain, 1963, p.223).

References

'Administration Report of the NWFP from 9th November 1901 to 31st March 1903', Government Press (NWFP), Peshawar 1903.

AFRIDI, O. (1976), 'Mahsud Monograph' (forthcoming publication).

AHMAD, A. (1964), 'Islamic Culture in the Indian Environment', Oxford University Press.

AHMAD, M.T. (1962), 'Social Organization of Yusufzai Swat: a study in social change', Punjab University Press.

AHMED, A.G. (1973), Some remarks from the Third World on anthropology and colonialism: the Sudan, in 'Anthropology and the Colonial Encounter', ed. T. Asad, Ithaca Press, London.

AHMED, A.S. (1974), 'Mansehra: a journey', Ferozsons, Pakistan.

AHMED, A.S. (1975), 'Mataloona: Pukhto Proverbs', Oxford University Press, Karachi.

AHMED, A.S. (1976), 'Tribal Strategies and the Organization of International Trading Networks: an analysis of the Bara market' (forthcoming publication).

ALAVI, H. (1973), Peasant classes and primordial loyalties, 'Journal of Peasant Studies', vol.1, no.1, October.

ALI, MRS M.H. (1832), Observations on the Mussulmans of India: descriptions of their manners, customs, habits and religious opinion, vols 1 and 2, Idarah-i-Adabiyat-i, Delhi, reprinted 1973.

ASAD, T. (1972), Market model, class structure and consent: a reconsideration of Swat political organization, 'Man', vol.7, no.1, March.

ASAD, T. (1973), Introduction and Two European images of non-European rule in 'Anthropology and the Colonial Encounter', Ithaca Press, London.

BADEN-POWELL, B.H. (1896), 'The Indian Village Community', Longmans, Green, London.

BAHA, L. (1968), The administration of the NWFP 1901-1919, SOAS (History), Ph.D. thesis.

BAILEY, F.G. (1960), 'Tribe, Caste and Nation', Manchester University Press.

BAILEY, F.G. (1961), 'Tribe' and 'Caste' in India, 'Contributions to Indian Sociology', October.

BAILEY, F.G. (1970), 'Stratagems and Spoils', Basil Blackwell, Oxford.

BAILEY, F.G. (1971), The peasant view of the bad life, in 'Peasant Societies', ed. T. Shanin, Penguin Books, Harmondsworth.

BAILEY, F.G. (1972), Conceptual systems in the study of politics, in 'Rural Politics and Social Change in the Middle East', ed. R. Antoun and I. Harik, Indiana University Press.

BANAJI, J. (1970), Crisis of British anthropology, 'New Left Review', no.64, pp.71-85.

BARNES, J.A. (1954), Class and committees in a Norwegian island parish, 'Human Relations', vol.7, pp.39-58.

BARNES, J.A. (1966), Comment, 'Current Anthropology', vol. 7, no.5, December.

BARNES, J.A. (1969), Networks and political process, in 'Social Networks in Urban Situations', ed. J.C. Mitchell, Manchester University Press.

BARTH, F. (1953), Principles of social organization in Southern Kurdistan, Universitets Etnografiske Museum Bulletin no.7, Oslo.

BARTH, F. (1956), 'Indus and Swat Kohistan', Studies honouring the centennial of Universitets Etnografiske Museum, vol.2, Oslo.

BARTH, F. (1959a), 'Political Leadership among Swat Pathans', LSE Monograph, Athlone Press, London.

BARTH, F. (1959b), Segmentary opposition and the theory of games: a study of Pathan organization, 'Journal of the Royal Anthropological Institute', 89, pt 1.

BARTH, F. (1961), 'Nomads of South Persia', Allen & Unwin (for Oslo University Press), London.

BARTH, F. (ed.) (1963), 'The Role of the Entrepreneur in Social Change in Northern Norway', Scandinavian University Books, first published Arbook for Universitet in Bergen Humanistick series.

BARTH, F. (1966), Models of social organization, occasional paper no.23, Royal Anthropological Institute.

BARTH, F. (1967), Exchange spheres in Darfur, in 'Themes in Economic Anthropology', ed. R. Firth, ASA Monograph 6, Tavistock Publications, London.

BARTH, F. (1968), Capital, investment and the social structure of a pastoral nomad group in South Persia, in

'Economic Anthropology: Readings in Theory and Analysis', ed. E.E. LeClair and H.K. Schneider, Holt, Rinehart & Winston, USA.

BARTH, F. (1969), Introduction and Pathan identity and its maintenance, in 'Ethnic Groups and Boundaries: the social organization of culture difference', Allen & Unwin, London.

BARTH, F. (1971), The system of social stratification in Swat, North Pakistan, in 'Aspects of Caste in South India, Ceylon and North-West Pakistan', ed. E.R. Leach, Cambridge University Press.

BARTH, F. (1975), 'Ritual and Knowledge among the Baktaman of New Guinea', Yale University Press, New Haven.

BELLEW, H.W. (1864), 'A General Report on the Yusufzai', Government Press, Lahore.

BENDIX, R. (1960), 'Max Weber', Heinemann, London.

BERRY, W. (1966), Aspects of the Frontier Crimes Regulation in Pakistan, Monograph 3, Duke University.

BLOCH, M. (1961), 'Feudal Society', Routledge & Kegan Paul, London.

BOHANNAN, L. (1952), A genealogical charter, 'Africa', vol.22.

BOHANNAN, P. (1955), Some principles of exchange and investment among the Tiv, 'American Anthropologist', vol.57, pp.60-9.

BOHANNAN, P. (1957), 'Justice and Judgement among the Tiv', Oxford University Press, New York.

BOHANNAN, P. and BOHANNAN, L. (1968), 'Tiv Economy', Northwestern University Press, Evanston.

BOISSEVAIN, J. (1966), Patronage in Sicily, 'Man', NS, vol.1, pp.18-33.

BOISSEVAIN, J. (1968), The place of non-groups in the social sciences, 'Man', NS, vol.14, no.4, December.

BOISSEVAIN, J. (1971), Second thoughts on quasi-groups, 'Man', NS, vol.6, pp.468-72.

BOISSEVAIN, J. (1974), 'Friends of Friends: networks, manipulators and coalitions', Basil Blackwell, Oxford.

BONTE, P. (1974), From ethnology to anthropology: on critical approaches in the human sciences, 'Critique of Anthropology', no.2, Autumn.

BOTT, E. (1957), 'Family and Social Network', Tavistock Publications, London.

BOTTOMORE, T.B. and MAXIMILIEN, R. (eds) (1956), 'Karl Marx: selected writings in sociology and social philosophy', C.A. Watts, London.

BRUCE, R.I., C.I.E. (1900), 'The Forward Policy and its Results', Longmans, Green, London.

BURLING, R. (1962), Maximization theories and the study of economic anthropology, 'American Anthropologist', vol.64, pp.802-21.

BURRIDGE, K. (1969), 'New Heaven, New Earth: a study of millenarian activities', Basil Blackwell, Oxford.

CANCIAN, F. (1966), Maximization as norm, strategy and theory: a comment on programmatic statements in economic anthropology, 'American Anthropologist', vol.68, pp.465-70, April.

CAROE, O. and HOWELL, E. (1963), 'The Poems of Khushal Khan Khattak', Pashto Academy, University of Peshawar.

CAROE, O. (1965), 'The Pathans', Macmillan, London.

CHURCHILL, W.S. (1972), The Malakand Field Force, in 'Frontiers and Wars', Penguin Books, Harmondsworth. (First published 1898.)

COEN, T.C. (1971), 'The Indian Political Service', Chatto & Windus, London.

COHEN, A. (1969), 'Custom and Politics in Urban Africa', Routledge & Kegan Paul, London.

COHEN, A. (1972), Cultural strategies in the organization of trading diasporas, in 'The Development of Trade and Markets in West Africa', ed. C. Meillasoux, Oxford University Press.

COHEN, A. (1974a), 'Two-Dimensional Man: an essay on the anthropology of power and symbolism in complex societies', Routledge & Kegan Paul, London.

COHEN, A. (ed.) (1974b), 'Urban Ethnicity', ASA Monograph no.12, Tavistock Publications, London.

COHEN, P.S. (1968), 'Modern Social Theory', Heinemann Educational, London.

COHN, N. (1970), 'The Pursuit of the Millennium: revolutionary millenarians and mystical anarchists of the Middle Ages', Paladin, London.

COULSON, N.J. (1971), 'Succession in the Muslim Family', Cambridge University Press.

CURZON, G.N. (1916), 'Speeches as Viceroy and Governor General of India', John Murray, London.

DALTON, G. (1967), 'Tribal and Peasant Economies: Readings in Economic Anthropology', Natural History Press, New York.

DALTON, G. (ed.) (1971), 'Economic Development and Social Change', Natural History Press, New York.

DOUGLAS, M. (1962), The Lele-resistance to change in 'Markets in Africa', ed. P. Bohannan and G. Dalton, Northwestern University Press, Evanston.

DOUGLAS, M. (1968), The social control of cognition: some factors in joke perception, 'Man' (New Series) 3, pp. 361-76.

DUMONT, L. (1972), 'Homo Hierarchicus: the caste system and its implications', Paladin, London.

DURKHEIM, E. (1962), 'The Rules of Sociological Method', Chicago University Press.

DURKHEIM, E. (1963), 'Suicide', Routledge & Kegan Paul, London.

DURKHEIM, E. (1964), 'The Elementary Forms of Religious Life', Allen & Unwin, London.

EDWARDES, H. (1846-9), in 'Lahore Political Diaries', vol. 5, Punjab Printing Press, Lahore.

ELLIOTT, J.G. (1968), 'The Frontier 1839-1947: the story of the North-West Frontier of India', Cassell, London.

ELPHINSTONE, M. (1972), 'An Account of the Kingdom of Caubul', vols 1 and 2, Oxford University Press, Karachi.

ELWELL-SUTTON, L.P. (1975), Sufism and Pseudo-Sufism, 'Encounter', vol.44, no.5, May.

'Encyclopaedia Britannica' (1967), vol.12, William Benton, USA.

EPSTEIN, T.S. (1967), The data of economics in anthropological analysis, in 'The Craft of Social Anthropology', ed. A.L. Epstein, Tavistock Publications, London.

EPSTEIN, T.S. (1973), 'South India: Yesterday, Today and Tomorrow', Macmillan, London.

ESIN, E. (1963), 'Mecca the Blessed, Madinah the Radiant', Elek Books, London.

EVANS-PRITCHARD, E.E. (1940), 'The Nuer: the description of the modes of livelihood and political institutions of a Nilotic people', Clarendon Press, Oxford.

EVANS-PRITCHARD, E.E. (1949), 'The Sanusi of Cyrenaica', Oxford University Press.

EVANS-PRITCHARD, E.E. (1962), The Divine Kingship of the Shilluk of the Nilotic Sudan, in 'Essays in Social Anthropology', Faber & Faber, London.

FERRIER, J.P. (1858), 'History of the Afghans', John Murray, London.

FIRTH, R. (1959), 'Social Change in Tikopia', Humanities Press, New York.

FIRTH, R. (1967), 'Themes in Economic Anthropology', ASA no.6 of same title, Tavistock Publications, London.

FORTES, M. (1945), 'The Dynamics of Clanship among the Tallensi', Oxford University Press.

FORTES, M. (1949), 'The Web of Kinship among the Tallensi', Oxford University Press.

FORTES, M. and EVANS-PRITCHARD, E.E. (eds) (1940), 'African Political Systems', Oxford University Press.

FRASER-TYTLER, W.K. (1950), 'Afghanistan', Oxford University Press.

FREEDMAN, R. (1961), 'Marx on Economics', Penguin Books, Harmondsworth.

FREUD, S. (1925), Formulations regarding the two principles in mental functioning, 'Collected Papers', vol.4, pp.13-21.

FÜRER-HAIMENDORF, C. VON (1939), 'The Naked Nagas', Methuen, London.

FÜRER-HAIMENDORF, C. VON (1962), 'The Apa Tanis and the
Neighbours', Free Press, New York.
FÜRER-HAIMENDORF, C. VON (1969), 'Morals and Merit: a
study of values and social controls in South Asian
societies', Weidenfeld & Nicolson, London.
GEERTZ, C. (1963), 'Peddlers and Princes: social change
and economic modernization in two Indonesian towns', Uni-
versity of Chicago Press.
GELLNER, E. (1969a), 'Saints of the Atlas', Weidenfeld &
Nicolson, London.
GELLNER, E. (1969b), A pendulum swing theory of Islam, in
'Sociology of Religion', ed. R. Robertson, Penguin Books,
Harmondsworth.
GERTH, H.H. and MILLS, C.W. (trs and eds) (1948),
'From Max Weber: essays in sociology', Routledge & Kegan
Paul, London.
GILSENAN, M. (1973), 'Saint and Sufi in Modern Egypt',
Oxford University Press.
GLUCKMAN, M. (1971), 'Politics, Law and Ritual in Tribal
Society', Basil Blackwell, Oxford.
GODELIER, M. (1968), 'Rationaliste et irrationaliste en
economie', François Maspero, Paris.
GOODY, J. (1971), Feudalism in Africa, in 'Economic De-
velopment and Social Change', ed. G. Dalton, American
Museum Sourcebooks, Natural History Press, New York.
GREGORIAN, V. (1969), 'The Emergence of Modern Afghani-
stan', Stanford University Press.
HAY, W.R. (1934), The Yusufzai State of Swat, 'Geographi-
cal Journal', vol.84, no.3.
HITCHCOCK, J.T. (1958), The idea of the martial Rajput,
'Journal of American Folklore', July-September.
HOLT, P.M. (1958a), 'The Mahdist State in the Sudan 1881-
1898', Clarendon Press, Oxford.
HOLT, P.M. (1958b), The Sudanese Mahdia and the outside
world, 'Bulletin of School of Oriental and African
Studies', vol.21, pp.276-90.
HOWELL, E. and CAROE, O. (1963), 'The Poems of Khushal
Khan Khattak', Pashto Academy, University of Peshawar.
HUNTER, G. and BOTTRALL, A. (eds) (1974), 'Serving the
Small Farmer', Croom Helm, London.
IBBETSON, D.C.J. (1883), 'Outlines of Panjab Ethnography,
being extracts from the Panjab Census Report of 1881
treating of Religion, Language and Caste', Government
Printing, Calcutta.
'Imperial Gazetteer of India', Provincial Series, NWFP,
Calcutta, 1908.
KAKAR, M.H. (1968), The consolidation of the central
authority in Afghanistan under Amir Abdal-Rahman 1880-
1896, SOAS (History), M.Ph. thesis.

LAWRENCE, P. (1964), 'Road Belong Cargo: a study of the cargo movement in the Southern Madang District, New Guinea', Manchester University Press.

LEACH, E.R. (1940), 'Social and Economic Organization of the Rowanduz Kurds', LSE, London.

LEACH, E.R. (1954), Political Systems of Highland Burma: a study of Kachin social structure, LSE Monograph 44, University of London.

LEACH, E.R. (1974), Presidential Address to the Royal Anthropological Institute, 'RAIN', no.4, September-October.

LE CLAIR, E.E. and SCHNEIDER, HAROLD K. (eds) (1968), 'Economic Anthropology: readings in theory and analysis', Holt, Rinehart & Winston.

LEWIS, I.M. (1969), Conformity and contrast in Somali Islam, in 'Islam in Tropical Africa', Oxford University Press.

LLOYD, P.C. (1971), 'Classes, Crises and Coups', Paladin, London.

MCLELLAN, D. (1975), 'Marx', Fontana/Collins.

MACRAE, D.G. (1974), 'Weber', Fontana/Collins, London.

MAIR, L. (1972), 'An Introduction to Social Anthropology', Clarendon Press, Oxford.

MALINOWSKI, B. (1922), 'Argonauts of the Western Pacific', Routledge, London.

MALINOWSKI, B. (1944), 'A Scientific Theory of Culture', Oxford University Press.

MARX, K. (1964), 'Pre-Capitalist Economic Formations', Lawrence & Wishart, London.

MAUSS, M. (1954), 'The Gift: forms and functions of exchange in archaic societies', Free Press, Chicago.

MAYER, A.C. (1960), 'Caste and Kinship in Central India', Routledge & Kegan Paul, London.

MAYER, A.C. (1966), The significance of quasi-groups in the study of complex societies, in 'The Social Anthropology of Complex Societies', ed. M.P. Banton, Tavistock Publications, London.

MAYER, A.C. (1967), Pir and Murshid: an aspect of religious leadership in West Pakistan, 'Middle Eastern Studies', vol.3, no.2, January.

MAYER, A.C. (1971), 'Peasants in the Pacific: a study of Fiji Indian rural society', Routledge & Kegan Paul, London.

MEILLASOUX, C. (1964), 'Anthropologie economique des Gouro de Cote d'Ivoire', Mouton, Paris.

MEILLASOUX, C. (1972), From reproduction to production: a Marxist approach to economic anthropology, 'Economic Sociology', vol.1, pp.93-105.

MERK, W.R.H. (1898), 'Report on the Mohmands', Punjab Government Press, Lahore.

MIANGUL, A.W. (1962), 'The Story of Swat', Ferozsons, Pakistan.

MIDDLETON, J. and TAIT, D. (eds) (1958), 'Tribes without Rulers', Routledge & Kegan Paul, London.

MORGENSTIERNE, GEORG (1927), An etymological vocabulary of Pashto, 'Det Norske Videnskaps - Akademi i Oslo II'. Hist-Filos, Kl. no.3.

MYRDAL, G. (1967), 'Asian drama', vols 1, 2 and 3, Pantheon.

MYRDAL, G. (1970), 'The Challenge of World Poverty', Penguin Books, Harmondsworth.

NADEL, S.F. (1942), 'A Black Byzantium: the kingdom of the Nupe of Nigeria', Oxford University Press.

NEEDHAM, R. (1970), The future of social anthropology: disintegration or metamorphosis?, in 'Anniversary Contributions to Anthropology: twelve essays', Leiden.

NEUMANN, JOHN VON and MORGENSTERN, OSKAR (1947), 'Theory of Games and Economic Behaviour', Princeton.

NICHOLAS, R.W. (1965), Factions: a comparative analysis, in M. Banton (ed.), 'Political Systems and the Distribution of Power', ASA Monograph no.2, Tavistock Publications, London.

NICHOLSON, R.A. (1914), 'The Mystics of Islam', Bell, London.

OXAAL, I., BARNETT, T. and BOOTH, D. (eds) (1975), 'Beyond the Sociology of Development', Routledge & Kegan Paul, London.

PAINE, R. (1974), Second thoughts about Barth's models, 'RAI', Occasional Paper no.32.

PARETO, V. (ed.) J. Lopreato (1965), 'Vilfredo Pareto: Selections from his Treatise', Crowell Collier, New York.

PARKIN, D.J. (1972), 'Palms, Wine and Witnesses', Chandler.

PARLIAMENTARY PAPERS (1898), 'Military Operations on the North-West Frontiers of India', vol.2. Papers regarding British relations with the neighbouring tribes of the North-West Frontier of India and the military operations undertaken against them during the year 1897-1898, HMSO.

PASTNER, C.MC. (1972), A social structural and historical analysis of honour, shame and purdah, 'Anthropological Quarterly', vol.45, no.4, October.

PASTNER, S. and PASTNER, C.MC. (1972), Agriculture, kinship and politics in Southern Baluchistan, 'Man', vol.7, no.1, March.

PEHRSON, R.N. (1966), 'The Social Organization of the Marri Baluch. Compiled and analyzed from his notes by Fredrik Barth', Viking Fund Publications in Anthropology, no.43, Chicago.

PESHAWAR DISTRICT, 'Gazetteer', Punjab Government,
Calcutta, 1883-4.
PETERS, E. (1960), The proliferation of segments in the
lineage of the Bedouin of Cyrenaica, 'Journal of the Royal
Anthropological Institute', vol.90, pp.26-53.
'Political and Secret Department', North-West Frontier:
Mohmand Affairs, 1903, India Office, no.1552, PT 1 and 2.
RAHMAN, A. (ed.) Mir Munshi S.M. Khan- (1900), 'The Life
of Abdur Rahman, Amir of Afghanistan', 2 vols, John
Murray, London.
REY, P.P. (1975), The lineage mode of production,
'Critique of Anthropology', no.3, Spring.
SADIQ, M. (1964), 'A History of Urdu Literature', Oxford
University Press.
SAHLINS, M.D. (1965), On the sociology of primitive ex-
change, in 'The Relevance of Models for Social Anthropo-
logy', ASA no.1, Tavistock Publications, London.
SAHLINS, M.D. (1968), 'Tribesmen', Prentice-Hall, Univer-
sity of Michigan.
SHANIN, T. (1971), Introduction, 'Peasants and Peasant
Societies', Penguin Modern Sociology Readings, Penguin
Books, Harmondsworth.
SMITH, W.C. (1957), 'Islam in Modern History', Princeton.
SOUTHALL, A.W. (1953), 'Alur Society', W. Heffer,
Cambridge.
SPAIN, J.W. (1962), 'The Way of the Pathans', Robert Hale,
London.
SPAIN, J.W. (1963), 'The Pathan Borderland', Mouton, The
Hague.
SPIRO, M.E. (1973), Religion: problems of definition and
explanation, in 'Anthropological Approaches to the Study
of Religion', ed. M. Banton, Tavistock Publications,
London.
SRINIVAS, M.N. (1952), 'Religion and Society among the
Coorgs of South India', Clarendon Press, Oxford.
SRINIVAS, M.N. (1974), Review of T.S. Epstein's South
India: yesterday, today and tomorrow, 'South Asian
Review', vol.7, no.3, April.
STEIN, SIR A. (1929), 'On Alexander's Track to the Indus:
personal narrative of explorations to the North-West Fron-
tier of India', Macmillan, London.
STONE, J.R. (1948), The theory of games, 'Econ. Journal',
58.
TAPPER, R. (1971), The Shahsavan of Azarbaijan: a study
of political and economic change in a Middle Eastern
tribal society, Ph.D. thesis, University of London (SOAS).
TERRAY, E. (1972), Marxism and primitive societies: two
studies, 'Monthly Review Press', New York.
TERRAY, E. (1975), Technology, tradition and the state,

'Critique of Anthropology', no.3, Spring.
THOMAS, B. (1929), Among some unknown tribes of South Arabia, 'Journal of the Royal Anthropological Institute', 59, pp.97-111.
TRIMINGHAM, J.S. (1971), 'The Sufi Orders in Islam', Oxford University Press.
TUDEN, A. (1966), Leadership and decision-making process among the Ila and the Swat Pathans, in 'Political Anthropology', ed. M.J. Swartz, V.W. Turner and A. Tuden, Aldine, Chicago.
TURNER, B.S. (1974), 'Weber and Islam: a critical study', Routledge & Kegan Paul, London.
WEBER, MAX (1947), 'The Theory of Social and Economic Organization', Free Press, Chicago.
WEBER, MAX (1962), 'The Protestant Ethic and the Spirit of Capitalism', Allen & Unwin, London.
WEBER, MAX (1965), 'The Sociology of Religion', Methuen, London.
WEBER, MAX (1968), 'The Religion of India', Free Press, New York.
WITTFOGEL, K. (1957), 'Oriental Despotism: a comparative study of total power', Yale University Press.
WOODRUFF, PHILIP (1953-4), 'The Men Who Ruled India', vol. 1, 'The Founders', vol.2, 'The Guardians', Jonathan Cape, London.
WORSLEY, P.M. (1966), The end of anthropology?, paper for 6th World Congress of Sociology, mimeo.
WORSLEY, P.M. (1970), 'The Trumpet Shall Sound: a study of cargo cults in Melanasia', Paladin, London.
WYLLY, H.C. (1912), 'From the Black Mountain to Waziristan', Macmillan, London.

Index

Routledge Social Science Series

Routledge & Kegan Paul   London and Boston

68–74 Carter Lane   London EC4V 5EL
9 Park Street   Boston   Mass 02108

Contents

*Authors wishing to submit manuscripts for any series in
this catalogue should send them to the Social Science Editor,
Routledge & Kegan Paul Ltd, 68–74 Carter Lane,
London EC4V 5EL*

●*Books so marked are available in paperback
All books are in Metric Demy 8vo format (216 × 138mm approx.)*

International Library of Sociology

General Editor John Rex

GENERAL SOCIOLOGY

Barnsley, J. H. The Social Reality of Ethics. *464 pp.*
Belshaw, Cyril. The Conditions of Social Performance. *An Exploratory Theory. 144 pp.*
Brown, Robert. Explanation in Social Science. *208 pp.*
● Rules and Laws in Sociology. *192 pp.*
Bruford, W. H. Chekhov and His Russia. *A Sociological Study. 244 pp.*
Cain, Maureen E. Society and the Policeman's Role. *326 pp.*
●**Fletcher, Colin.** Beneath the Surface. *An Account of Three Styles of Sociological Research. 221 pp.*
Gibson, Quentin. The Logic of Social Enquiry. *240 pp.*
Glucksmann, M. Structuralist Analysis in Contemporary Social Thought. *212 pp.*
Gurvitch, Georges. Sociology of Law. *Preface by Roscoe Pound. 264 pp.*
Hodge, H. A. Wilhelm Dilthey. *An Introduction. 184 pp.*
Homans, George C. Sentiments and Activities. *336 pp.*
Johnson, Harry M. Sociology: *a Systematic Introduction. Foreword by Robert K. Merton. 710 pp.*
●**Keat, Russell,** and **Urry, John.** Social Theory as Science. *278 pp.*
Mannheim, Karl. Essays on Sociology and Social Psychology. *Edited by Paul Kecskemeti. With Editorial Note by Adolph Lowe. 344 pp.*
  Systematic Sociology: *An Introduction to the Study of Society. Edited by J. S. Erös and Professor W. A. C. Stewart. 220 pp.*
Martindale, Don. The Nature and Types of Sociological Theory. *292 pp.*
●**Maus, Heinz.** A Short History of Sociology. *234 pp.*
Mey, Harald. Field-Theory. *A Study of its Application in the Social Sciences. 352 pp.*
Myrdal, Gunnar. Value in Social Theory: *A Collection of Essays on Methodology. Edited by Paul Streeten. 332 pp.*
Ogburn, William F., and **Nimkoff, Meyer F.** A Handbook of Sociology. *Preface by Karl Mannheim. 656 pp. 46 figures. 35 tables.*
Parsons, Talcott, and **Smelser, Neil J.** Economy and Society: *A Study in the Integration of Economic and Social Theory. 362 pp.*
Podgórecki, Adam. Practical Social Sciences. *About 200 pp.*
●**Rex, John.** Key Problems of Sociological Theory. *220 pp.*
  Discovering Sociology. *278 pp.*
  Sociology and the Demystification of the Modern World. *282 pp.*
●**Rex, John** (Ed.) Approaches to Sociology. *Contributions by Peter Abell, Frank Bechhofer, Basil Bernstein, Ronald Fletcher, David Frisby, Miriam Glucksmann, Peter Lassman, Herminio Martins, John Rex, Roland Robertson, John Westergaard and Jock Young. 302 pp.*
Rigby, A. Alternative Realities. *352 pp.*

Roche, M. Phenomenology, Language and the Social Sciences. *374 pp.*
Sahay, A. Sociological Analysis. *220 pp.*
Strasser, Hermann. The Normative Structure of Sociology. *Conservative and Emancipatory Themes in Social Thought. About 340 pp.*
Urry, John. Reference Groups and the Theory of Revolution. *244 pp.*
Weinberg, E. Development of Sociology in the Soviet Union. *173 pp.*

FOREIGN CLASSICS OF SOCIOLOGY

●**Durkheim, Emile.** Suicide. *A Study in Sociology. Edited and with an Introduction by George Simpson. 404 pp.*
　　Professional Ethics and Civic Morals. *Translated by Cornelia Brookfield. 288 pp.*
●**Gerth, H. H.,** and **Mills, C. Wright.** From Max Weber: *Essays in Sociology. 502 pp.*
●**Tönnies, Ferdinand.** Community and Association. (*Gemeinschaft und Gesellschaft.*) *Translated and Supplemented by Charles P. Loomis. Foreword by Pitirim A. Sorokin. 334 pp.*

SOCIAL STRUCTURE

Andreski, Stanislav. Military Organization and Society. *Foreword by Professor A. R. Radcliffe-Brown. 226 pp. 1 folder.*
Coontz, Sydney H. Population Theories and the Economic Interpretation. *202 pp.*
Coser, Lewis. The Functions of Social Conflict. *204 pp.*
Dickie-Clark, H. F. Marginal Situation: *A Sociological Study of a Coloured Group. 240 pp. 11 tables.*
Glaser, Barney, and **Strauss, Anselm L.** Status Passage. *A Formal Theory. 208 pp.*
Glass, D. V. (Ed.) Social Mobility in Britain. *Contributions by J. Berent, T. Bottomore, R. C. Chambers, J. Floud, D. V. Glass, J. R. Hall, H. T. Himmelweit, R. K. Kelsall, F. M. Martin, C. A. Moser, R. Mukherjee, and W. Ziegel. 420 pp.*
Jones, Garth N. Planned Organizational Change: *An Exploratory Study Using an Empirical Approach. 268 pp.*
Kelsall, R. K. Higher Civil Servants in Britain: *From 1870 to the Present Day. 268 pp. 31 tables.*
König, René. The Community. *232 pp. Illustrated.*
●**Lawton, Denis.** Social Class, Language and Education. *192 pp.*
McLeish, John. The Theory of Social Change: *Four Views Considered. 128 pp.*
Marsh, David C. The Changing Social Structure of England and Wales, 1871-1961. *288 pp.*
●**Mouzelis, Nicos.** Organization and Bureaucracy. *An Analysis of Modern Theories. 240 pp.*
Mulkay, M. J. Functionalism, Exchange and Theoretical Strategy. *272 pp.*
Ossowski, Stanislaw. Class Structure in the Social Consciousness. *210 pp.*
●**Podgórecki, Adam.** Law and Society. *302 pp.*

SOCIOLOGY AND POLITICS

Acton, T. A. Gypsy Politics and Social Change. *316 pp.*

Clegg, Stuart. Power, Rule and Domination. *A Critical and Empirical Understanding of Power in Sociological Theory and Organisational Life. About 300 pp.*

Hechter, Michael. Internal Colonialism. *The Celtic Fringe in British National Development, 1536–1966. 361 pp.*

Hertz, Frederick. Nationality in History and Politics: *A Psychology and Sociology of National Sentiment and Nationalism. 432 pp.*

Kornhauser, William. The Politics of Mass Society. *272 pp. 20 tables.*

●**Kroes, R.** Soldiers and Students. *A Study of Right- and Left-wing Students. 174 pp.*

Laidler, Harry W. History of Socialism. *Social-Economic Movements: An Historical and Comparative Survey of Socialism, Communism, Co-operation, Utopianism; and other Systems of Reform and Reconstruction. 992 pp.*

Lasswell, H. D. Analysis of Political Behaviour. *324 pp.*

Mannheim, Karl. Freedom, Power and Democratic Planning. *Edited by Hans Gerth and Ernest K. Bramstedt. 424 pp.*

Mansur, Fatma. Process of Independence. *Foreword by A. H. Hanson. 208 pp.*

Martin, David A. Pacifism: *an Historical and Sociological Study. 262 pp.*

Myrdal, Gunnar. The Political Element in the Development of Economic Theory. *Translated from the German by Paul Streeten. 282 pp.*

Wootton, Graham. Workers, Unions and the State. *188 pp.*

FOREIGN AFFAIRS: THEIR SOCIAL, POLITICAL AND ECONOMIC FOUNDATIONS

Mayer, J. P. Political Thought in France from the Revolution to the Fifth Republic. *164 pp.*

CRIMINOLOGY

Ancel, Marc. Social Defence: *A Modern Approach to Criminal Problems. Foreword by Leon Radzinowicz. 240 pp.*

Cain, Maureen E. Society and the Policeman's Role. *326 pp.*

Cloward, Richard A., and **Ohlin, Lloyd E.** Delinquency and Opportunity: *A Theory of Delinquent Gangs. 248 pp.*

Downes, David M. The Delinquent Solution. *A Study in Subcultural Theory. 296 pp.*

Dunlop, A. B., and **McCabe, S.** Young Men in Detention Centres. *192 pp.*

Friedlander, Kate. The Psycho-Analytical Approach to Juvenile Delinquency: *Theory, Case Studies, Treatment. 320 pp.*

Glueck, Sheldon, and **Eleanor.** Family Environment and Delinquency. *With the statistical assistance of Rose W. Kneznek. 340 pp.*

Lopez-Rey, Manuel. Crime. *An Analytical Appraisal. 288 pp.*

Mannheim, Hermann. Comparative Criminology: *a Text Book. Two volumes. 442 pp. and 380 pp.*

5

Morris, Terence. The Criminal Area: *A Study in Social Ecology. Foreword by Hermann Mannheim. 232 pp. 25 tables. 4 maps.*

Rock, Paul. Making People Pay. *338 pp.*

●**Taylor, Ian, Walton, Paul,** and **Young, Jock.** The New Criminology. *For a Social Theory of Deviance. 325 pp.*

●**Taylor, Ian, Walton, Paul,** and **Young, Jock** (Eds). Critical Criminology. *268 pp.*

SOCIAL PSYCHOLOGY

Bagley, Christopher. The Social Psychology of the Epileptic Child. *320 pp.*

Barbu, Zevedei. Problems of Historical Psychology. *248 pp.*

Blackburn, Julian. Psychology and the Social Pattern. *184 pp.*

●**Brittan, Arthur.** Meanings and Situations. *224 pp.*

Carroll, J. Break-Out from the Crystal Palace. *200 pp.*

●**Fleming, C. M.** Adolescence: Its Social Psychology. *With an Introduction to recent findings from the fields of Anthropology, Physiology, Medicine, Psychometrics and Sociometry. 288 pp.*

● The Social Psychology of Education: *An Introduction and Guide to Its Study. 136 pp.*

●**Homans, George C.** The Human Group. *Foreword by Bernard DeVoto. Introduction by Robert K. Merton. 526 pp.*

● Social Behaviour: *its Elementary Forms. 416 pp.*

●**Klein, Josephine.** The Study of Groups. *226 pp. 31 figures. 5 tables.*

Linton, Ralph. The Cultural Background of Personality. *132 pp.*

●**Mayo, Elton.** The Social Problems of an Industrial Civilization. *With an appendix on the Political Problem. 180 pp.*

Ottaway, A. K. C. Learning Through Group Experience. *176 pp.*

Plummer, Ken. Sexual Stigma. *An Interactionist Account. 254 pp.*

Ridder, J. C. de. The Personality of the Urban African in South Africa. *A Thermatic Apperception Test Study. 196 pp. 12 plates.*

●**Rose, Arnold M.** (Ed.) Human Behaviour and Social Processes: *an Interactionist Approach. Contributions by Arnold M. Rose, Ralph H. Turner, Anselm Strauss, Everett C. Hughes, E. Franklin Frazier, Howard S. Becker, et al. 696 pp.*

Smelser, Neil J. Theory of Collective Behaviour. *448 pp.*

Stephenson, Geoffrey M. The Development of Conscience. *128 pp.*

Young, Kimball. Handbook of Social Psychology. *658 pp. 16 figures. 10 tables.*

SOCIOLOGY OF THE FAMILY

Banks, J. A. Prosperity and Parenthood: *A Study of Family Planning among The Victorian Middle Classes. 262 pp.*

Bell, Colin R. Middle Class Families: *Social and Geographical Mobility. 224 pp.*

Burton, Lindy. Vulnerable Children. *272 pp.*

Gavron, Hannah. The Captive Wife: *Conflicts of Household Mothers. 190 pp.*

SOCIOLOGY OF INDUSTRY AND DISTRIBUTION

Anderson, Nels. Work and Leisure. *280 pp.*

● **Blau, Peter M.,** and **Scott, W. Richard.** Formal Organizations: *a Comparative approach. Introduction and Additional Bibliography by J. H. Smith. 326 pp.*

Dunkerley, David. The Foreman. *Aspects of Task and Structure. 192 pp.*

Eldridge, J. E. T. Industrial Disputes. *Essays in the Sociology of Industrial Relations. 288 pp.*

Hetzler, Stanley. Applied Measures for Promoting Technological Growth. *352 pp.*

Technological Growth and Social Change. *Achieving Modernization. 269 pp.*

Hollowell, Peter G. The Lorry Driver. *272 pp.*

Jefferys, Margot, *with the assistance of Winifred Moss.* Mobility in the Labour Market: *Employment Changes in Battersea and Dagenham. Preface by Barbara Wootton. 186 pp. 51 tables.*

Millerson, Geoffrey. The Qualifying Associations: *a Study in Professionalization. 320 pp.*

● **Oxaal, I., Barnett, T.,** and **Booth, D.** (Eds). Beyond the Sociology of Development. *Economy and Society in Latin America and Africa. 295 pp.*

Smelser, Neil J. Social Change in the Industrial Revolution: *An Application of Theory to the Lancashire Cotton Industry, 1770–1840. 468 pp. 12 figures. 14 tables.*

Williams, Gertrude. Recruitment to Skilled Trades. *240 pp.*

Young, A. F. Industrial Injuries Insurance: *an Examination of British Policy. 192 pp.*

DOCUMENTARY

Schlesinger, Rudolf (Ed.) Changing Attitudes in Soviet Russia.

2. The Nationalities Problem and Soviet Administration. *Selected Readings on the Development of Soviet Nationalities Policies. Introduced by the editor. Translated by W. W. Gottlieb. 324 pp.*

ANTHROPOLOGY

Ammar, Hamed. Growing up in an Egyptian Village: *Silwa, Province of Aswan. 336 pp.*

Brandel-Syrier, Mia. Reeftown Elite. *A Study of Social Mobility in a Modern African Community on the Reef. 376 pp.*

Crook, David, and **Isabel.** Revolution in a Chinese Village: *Ten Mile Inn. 230 pp. 8 plates. 1 map.*

Dickie-Clark, H. F. The Marginal Situation. *A Sociological Study of a Coloured Group. 236 pp.*

Dube, S. C. Indian Village. *Foreword by Morris Edward Opler. 276 pp. 4 plates.*

11

India's Changing Villages: *Human Factors in Community Development. 260 pp. 8 plates. 1 map.*

Firth, Raymond. Malay Fishermen. *Their Peasant Economy. 420 pp. 17 pp. plates.*

Firth, R., Hubert, J., and **Forge, A.** Families and their Relatives. *Kinship in a Middle-Class Sector of London: An Anthropological Study. 456 pp.*

Gulliver, P. H. Social Control in an African Society: a Study of the Arusha, Agricultural Masai of Northern Tanganyika. *320 pp. 8 plates. 10 figures.*

Family Herds. *288 pp.*

Ishwaran, K. Shivapur. *A South Indian Village. 216 pp.*

Tradition and Economy in Village India: *An Interactionist Approach. Foreword by Conrad Arensburg. 176 pp.*

Jarvie, Ian C. The Revolution in Anthropology. *268 pp.*

Little, Kenneth L. Mende of Sierra Leone. *308 pp. and folder.*

Negroes in Britain. *With a New Introduction and Contemporary Study by Leonard Bloom. 320 pp.*

Lowie, Robert H. Social Organization. *494 pp.*

Peasants in the Pacific. *A Study of Fiji Indian Rural Society. 248 pp.*

Smith, Raymond T. The Negro Family in British Guiana: *Family Structure and Social Status in the Villages. With a Foreword by Meyer Fortes. 314 pp. 8 plates. 1 figure. 4 maps.*

SOCIOLOGY AND PHILOSOPHY

Barnsley, John H. The Social Reality of Ethics. *A Comparative Analysis of Moral Codes. 448 pp.*

Diesing, Paul. Patterns of Discovery in the Social Sciences. *362 pp.*

●**Douglas, Jack D.** (Ed.) Understanding Everyday Life. *Toward the Reconstruction of Sociological Knowledge. Contributions by Alan F. Blum. Aaron W. Cicourel, Norman K. Denzin, Jack D. Douglas, John Heeren, Peter McHugh, Peter K. Manning, Melvin Power, Matthew Speier, Roy Turner, D. Lawrence Wieder, Thomas P. Wilson and Don H. Zimmerman. 370 pp.*

Jarvie, Ian C. Concepts and Society. *216 pp.*

●**Pelz, Werner.** The Scope of Understanding in Sociology. *Towards a more radical reorientation in the social humanistic sciences. 283 pp.*

Roche, Maurice. Phenomenology, Language and the Social Sciences. *371 pp.*

Sahay, Arun. Sociological Analysis. *212 pp.*

Sklair, Leslie. The Sociology of Progress. *320 pp.*

International Library of Anthropology

General Editor Adam Kuper

Brown, Paula. The Chimbu. *A Study of Change in the New Guinea Highlands. 151 pp.*

Hamnett, Ian. Chieftainship and Legitimacy. *An Anthropological Study of Executive Law in Lesotho. 163 pp.*

Hanson, F. Allan. Meaning in Culture. *127 pp.*

Lloyd, P. C. Power and Independence. *Urban Africans' Perception of Social Inequality. 264 pp.*

Pettigrew, Joyce. Robber Noblemen. *A Study of the Political System of the Sikh Jats. 284 pp.*

Street, Brian V. The Savage in Literature. *Representations of 'Primitive' Society in English Fiction, 1858–1920. 207 pp.*

Van Den Berghe, Pierre L. Power and Privilege at an African University. *278 pp.*

International Library of Social Policy

General Editor Kathleen Jones

Bayley, M. Mental Handicap and Community Care. *426 pp.*

Butler, J. R. Family Doctors and Public Policy. *208 pp.*

Davies, Martin. Prisoners of Society. *Attitudes and Aftercare. 204 pp.*

Holman, Robert. Trading in Children. *A Study of Private Fostering. 355 pp.*

Jones, Kathleen. History of the Mental Health Service. *428 pp.*
   Opening the Door. *A Study of New Policies for the Mentally Handicapped. 260 pp.*

Thomas, J. E. The English Prison Officer since 1850: *A Study in Conflict. 258 pp.*

Walton, R. G. Women in Social Work. *303 pp.*

Woodward, J. To Do the Sick No Harm. *A Study of the British Voluntary Hospital System to 1875. 221 pp.*

International Library of Welfare and Philosophy

General Editors Noel Timms and David Watson

● **Plant, Raymond.** Community and Ideology. *104 pp.*

Primary Socialization, Language and Education

General Editor Basil Bernstein

Bernstein, Basil. Class, Codes and Control. *3 volumes.*
   1. *Theoretical Studies Towards a Sociology of Language. 254 pp.*
   2. *Applied Studies Towards a Sociology of Language. 377 pp.*
   3. *Towards a Theory of Educational Transmission. 167 pp.*

Brandis, W., and **Bernstein, B.** Selection and Control. *176 pp.*

Brandis, Walter, and **Henderson, Dorothy.** Social Class, Language and Communication. *288 pp.*

Cook-Gumperz, Jenny. Social Control and Socialization. *A Study of Class Differences in the Language of Maternal Control. 290 pp.*

● **Gahagan, D. M.,** and **G. A.** Talk Reform. *Exploration in Language for Infant School Children. 160 pp.*

Robinson, W. P., and **Rackstraw, Susan D. A.** A Question of Answers. *2 volumes. 192 pp. and 180 pp.*

Turner, Geoffrey J., and **Mohan, Bernard A.** A Linguistic Description and Computer Programme for Children's Speech. *208 pp.*

Reports of the Institute of Community Studies

Cartwright, Ann. Human Relations and Hospital Care. *272 pp.*

● Parents and Family Planning Services. *306 pp.*

Patients and their Doctors. *A Study of General Practice. 304 pp.*

Dench, Geoff. Maltese in London. *A Case-study in the Erosion of Ethnic Consciousness. 302 pp.*

● **Jackson, Brian.** Streaming: *an Education System in Miniature. 168 pp.*

Jackson, Brian, and **Marsden, Dennis.** Education and the Working Class: *Some General Themes raised by a Study of 88 Working-class Children in a Northern Industrial City. 268 pp. 2 folders.*

Marris, Peter. The Experience of Higher Education. *232 pp. 27 tables.*

Loss and Change. *192 pp.*

Marris, Peter, and **Rein, Martin.** Dilemmas of Social Reform. *Poverty and Community Action in the United States. 256 pp.*

Marris, Peter, and **Somerset, Anthony.** African Businessmen. *A Study of Entrepreneurship and Development in Kenya. 256 pp.*

Mills, Richard. Young Outsiders: *a Study in Alternative Communities. 216 pp.*

Runciman, W. G. Relative Deprivation and Social Justice. *A Study of Attitudes to Social Inequality in Twentieth-Century England. 352 pp.*

Willmott, Peter. Adolescent Boys in East London. *230 pp.*

Willmott, Peter, and **Young, Michael.** Family and Class in a London Suburb. *202 pp. 47 tables.*

Young, Michael. Innovation and Research in Education. *192 pp.*

● **Young, Michael,** and **McGeeney, Patrick.** Learning Begins at Home. *A Study of a Junior School and its Parents. 128 pp.*

Young, Michael, and **Willmott, Peter.** Family and Kinship in East London. *Foreword by Richard M. Titmuss. 252 pp. 39 tables.*

The Symmetrical Family. *410 pp.*

Reports of the Institute for Social Studies in Medical Care

Cartwright, Ann, Hockey, Lisbeth, and **Anderson, John L.** Life Before Death. *310 pp.*

Dunnell, Karen, and **Cartwright, Ann.** Medicine Takers, Prescribers and Hoarders. *190 pp.*

George, Victor, and **Wilding, Paul.** Motherless Families. *248 pp.*
Klein, Josephine. Samples from English Cultures.
 1. Three Preliminary Studies and Aspects of Adult Life in England. *447 pp.*
 2. Child-Rearing Practices and Index. *247 pp.*
Klein, Viola. Britain's Married Women Workers. *180 pp.*
 The Feminine Character. *History of an Ideology. 244 pp.*
McWhinnie, Alexina M. Adopted Children. *How They Grow Up. 304 pp.*
● **Morgan, D. H. J.** Social Theory and the Family. *About 320 pp.*
● **Myrdal, Alva,** and **Klein, Viola.** Women's Two Roles: *Home and Work.* *238 pp. 27 tables.*
Parsons, Talcott, and **Bales, Robert F.** Family: Socialization and Interaction Process. *In collaboration with James Olds, Morris Zelditch and Philip E. Slater. 456 pp. 50 figures and tables.*

SOCIAL SERVICES

Bastide, Roger. The Sociology of Mental Disorder. *Translated from the French by Jean McNeil. 260 pp.*
Carlebach, Julius. Caring For Children in Trouble. *266 pp.*
George, Victor. Foster Care. *Theory and Practice. 234 pp.*
 Social Security: *Beveridge and After. 258 pp.*
George, V., and **Wilding, P.** Motherless Families. *248 pp.*
● **Goetschius, George W.** Working with Community Groups. *256 pp.*
Goetschius, George W., and **Tash, Joan.** Working with Unattached Youth. *416 pp.*
Hall, M. P., and **Howes, I. V.** The Church in Social Work. *A Study of Moral Welfare Work undertaken by the Church of England. 320 pp.*
Heywood, Jean S. Children in Care: *the Development of the Service for the Deprived Child. 264 pp.*
Hoenig, J., and **Hamilton, Marian W.** The De-Segregation of the Mentally Ill. *284 pp.*
Jones, Kathleen. Mental Health and Social Policy, 1845-1959. *264 pp.*
King, Roy D., Raynes, Norma V., and **Tizard, Jack.** Patterns of Residential Care. *356 pp.*
Leigh, John. Young People and Leisure. *256 pp.*
● **Mays, John.** (Ed.) Penelope Hall's Social Services of England and Wales. *About 324 pp.*
Morris, Mary. Voluntary Work and the Welfare State. *300 pp.*
Morris, Pauline. Put Away: *A Sociological Study of Institutions for the Mentally Retarded. 364 pp.*
Nokes, P. L. The Professional Task in Welfare Practice. *152 pp.*
Timms, Noel. Psychiatric Social Work in Great Britain (1939-1962). *280 pp.*
● Social Casework: *Principles and Practice. 256 pp.*
Young, A. F. Social Services in British Industry. *272 pp.*
Young, A. F., and **Ashton, E. T.** British Social Work in the Nineteenth Century. *288 pp.*

SOCIOLOGY OF EDUCATION

Banks, Olive. Parity and Prestige in English Secondary Education: a Study in Educational Sociology. *272 pp.*

Bentwich, Joseph. Education in Israel. *224 pp. 8 pp. plates.*

● **Blyth, W. A. L.** English Primary Education. *A Sociological Description.*
   1. Schools. *232 pp.*
   2. Background. *168 pp.*

Collier, K. G. The Social Purposes of Education: *Personal and Social Values in Education. 268 pp.*

Dale, R. R., and Griffith, S. Down Stream: *Failure in the Grammar School. 108 pp.*

Dore, R. P. Education in Tokugawa Japan. *356 pp. 9 pp. plates.*

Evans, K. M. Sociometry and Education. *158 pp.*

● **Ford, Julienne.** Social Class and the Comprehensive School. *192 pp.*

Foster, P. J. Education and Social Change in Ghana. *336 pp. 3 maps.*

Fraser, W. R. Education and Society in Modern France. *150 pp.*

Grace, Gerald R. Role Conflict and the Teacher. *150 pp.*

Hans, Nicholas. New Trends in Education in the Eighteenth Century. *278 pp. 19 tables.*

●   Comparative Education: *A Study of Educational Factors and Traditions. 360 pp.*

● **Hargreaves, David.** Interpersonal Relations and Education. *432 pp.*

●   Social Relations in a Secondary School. *240 pp.*

Holmes, Brian. Problems in Education. *A Comparative Approach. 336 pp.*

King, Ronald. Values and Involvement in a Grammar School. *164 pp.*
   School Organization and Pupil Involvement. *A Study of Secondary Schools.*

● **Mannheim, Karl, and Stewart, W. A. C.** An Introduction to the Sociology of Education. *206 pp.*

Morris, Raymond N. The Sixth Form and College Entrance. *231 pp.*

● **Musgrove, F.** Youth and the Social Order. *176 pp.*

● **Ottaway, A. K. C.** Education and Society: An Introduction to the Sociology of Education. *With an Introduction by W. O. Lester Smith. 212 pp.*

Peers, Robert. Adult Education: *A Comparative Study. 398 pp.*

Pritchard, D. G. Education and the Handicapped: *1760 to 1960. 258 pp.*

Richardson, Helen. Adolescent Girls in Approved Schools. *308 pp.*

Stratta, Erica. The Education of Borstal Boys. *A Study of their Educational Experiences prior to, and during, Borstal Training. 256 pp.*

Taylor, P. H., Reid, W. A., and Holley, B. J. The English Sixth Form. *A Case Study in Curriculum Research. 200 pp.*

SOCIOLOGY OF CULTURE

Eppel, E. M., and M. Adolescents and Morality: *A Study of some Moral Values and Dilemmas of Working Adolescents in the Context of a changing Climate of Opinion. Foreword by W. J. H. Sprott. 268 pp. 39 tables.*

● **Fromm, Erich.** The Fear of Freedom. *286 pp.*
● The Sane Society. *400 pp.*
Mannheim, Karl. Essays on the Sociology of Culture. *Edited by Ernst Mannheim in co-operation with Paul Kecskemeti. Editorial Note by Adolph Lowe. 280 pp.*
Weber, Alfred. Farewell to European History: *or The Conquest of Nihilism. Translated from the German by R. F. C. Hull. 224 pp.*

SOCIOLOGY OF RELIGION

Argyle, Michael and **Beit-Hallahmi, Benjamin.** The Social Psychology of Religion. *About 256 pp.*
Nelson, G. K. Spiritualism and Society. *313 pp.*
Stark, Werner. The Sociology of Religion. *A Study of Christendom.*
  Volume I. *Established Religion. 248 pp.*
  Volume II. *Sectarian Religion. 368 pp.*
  Volume III. *The Universal Church. 464 pp.*
  Volume IV. *Types of Religious Man. 352 pp.*
  Volume V. *Types of Religious Culture. 464 pp.*
Turner, B. S. Weber and Islam. *216 pp.*
Watt, W. Montgomery. Islam and the Integration of Society. *320 pp.*

SOCIOLOGY OF ART AND LITERATURE

Jarvie, Ian C. Towards a Sociology of the Cinema. *A Comparative Essay on the Structure and Functioning of a Major Entertainment Industry. 405 pp.*
Rust, Frances S. Dance in Society. *An Analysis of the Relationships between the Social Dance and Society in England from the Middle Ages to the Present Day. 256 pp. 8 pp. of plates.*
Schücking, L. L. The Sociology of Literary Taste. *112 pp.*
Wolff, Janet. Hermeneutic Philosophy and the Sociology of Art. *150 pp.*

SOCIOLOGY OF KNOWLEDGE

Diesing, P. Patterns of Discovery in the Social Sciences. *262 pp.*
● **Douglas, J. D.** (Ed.) Understanding Everyday Life. *370 pp.*
● **Hamilton, P.** Knowledge and Social Structure. *174 pp.*
Jarvie, I. C. Concepts and Society. *232 pp.*
Mannheim, Karl. Essays on the Sociology of Knowledge. *Edited by Paul Kecskemeti. Editorial Note by Adolph Lowe. 353 pp.*
Remmling, Gunter W. The Sociology of Karl Mannheim. *With a Bibliographical Guide to the Sociology of Knowledge, Ideological Analysis, and Social Planning. 255 pp.*

Remmling, Gunter W. (Ed.) Towards the Sociology of Knowledge. *Origin and Development of a Sociological Thought Style. 463 pp.*

Stark, Werner. The Sociology of Knowledge: *An Essay in Aid of a Deeper Understanding of the History of Ideas. 384 pp.*

URBAN SOCIOLOGY

Ashworth, William. The Genesis of Modern British Town Planning: *A Study in Economic and Social History of the Nineteenth and Twentieth Centuries. 288 pp.*

Cullingworth, J. B. Housing Needs and Planning Policy: *A Restatement of the Problems of Housing Need and 'Overspill' in England and Wales. 232 pp. 44 tables. 8 maps.*

Dickinson, Robert E. City and Region: *A Geographical Interpretation 608 pp. 125 figures.*

The West European City: *A Geographical Interpretation. 600 pp. 129 maps. 29 plates.*

● The City Region in Western Europe. *320 pp. Maps.*

Humphreys, Alexander J. New Dubliners: *Urbanization and the Irish Family. Foreword by George C. Homans. 304 pp.*

Jackson, Brian. Working Class Community: *Some General Notions raised by a Series of Studies in Northern England. 192 pp.*

Jennings, Hilda. Societies in the Making: *a Study of Development and Re-development within a County Borough. Foreword by D. A. Clark. 286 pp.*

●**Mann, P. H.** An Approach to Urban Sociology. *240 pp.*

Morris, R. N., and **Mogey, J.** The Sociology of Housing. *Studies at Berinsfield. 232 pp. 4 pp. plates.*

Rosser, C., and **Harris, C.** The Family and Social Change. *A Study of Family and Kinship in a South Wales Town. 352 pp. 8 maps.*

●**Stacey, Margaret, Batsone, Eric, Bell, Colin,** and **Thurcott, Anne.** Power, Persistence and Change. *A Second Study of Banbury. 196 pp.*

RURAL SOCIOLOGY

Chambers, R. J. H. Settlement Schemes in Tropical Africa: *A Selective Study. 268 pp.*

Haswell, M. R. The Economics of Development in Village India. *120 pp.*

Littlejohn, James. Westrigg: *the Sociology of a Cheviot Parish. 172 pp. 5 figures.*

Mayer, Adrian C. Peasants in the Pacific. *A Study of Fiji Indian Rural Society. 248 pp. 20 plates.*

Williams, W. M. The Sociology of an English Village: *Gosforth. 272 pp. 12 figures. 13 tables.*

Medicine, Illness and Society

General Editor   W. M. Williams

Robinson, David. The Process of Becoming Ill. *142 pp.*
Stacey, Margaret, *et al.* Hospitals, Children and Their Families. *The Report of a Pilot Study. 202 pp.*
Stimson, G. V., and **Webb, B.** Going to See the Doctor. *The Consultation Process in General Practice. 155 pp.*

Monographs in Social Theory

General Editor   Arthur Brittan

●**Barnes, B.** Scientific Knowledge and Sociological Theory. *192 pp.*
Bauman, Zygmunt. Culture as Praxis. *204 pp.*
●**Dixon, Keith.** Sociological Theory. *Pretence and Possibility. 142 pp.*
Meltzer, B. N., Petras, J. W., and **Reynolds, L. T.** Symbolic Interactionism. *Genesis, Varieties and Criticisms. 144 pp.*
●**Smith, Anthony D.** The Concept of Social Change. *A Critique of the Functionalist Theory of Social Change. 208 pp.*

Routledge Social Science Journals

The British Journal of Sociology. *Managing Editor – Angus Stewart; Associate Editor – Michael Hill. Vol. 1, No. 1 – March 1950 and Quarterly. Roy. 8vo. All back issues available. An international journal publishing original papers in the field of sociology and related areas.*
Community Work. *Edited by David Jones and Marjorie Mayo. 1973. Published annually.*
Economy and Society. *Vol. 1, No. 1. February 1972 and Quarterly. Metric Roy. 8vo. A journal for all social scientists covering sociology, philosophy, anthropology, economics and history. Back numbers available.*
Religion. Journal of Religion and Religions. *Chairman of Editorial Board, Ninian Smart. Vol. 1, No. 1, Spring 1971. A journal with an interdisciplinary approach to the study of the phenomena of religion.*
Year Book of Social Policy in Britain, The. *Edited by Kathleen Jones. 1971. Published annually.*

Printed in Great Britain by Unwin Brothers Limited
The Gresham Press Old Woking Surrey
A member of the Staples Printing Group   June 1975